MARTIN LUTHER KING, JR.

Also by C. Eric Lincoln

The Black Muslims in America

My Face Is Black

Sounds of the Struggle: Persons and Perspectives in Civil Rights

The Negro Pilgrimage in America

A Pictorial History of the Negro in America (Editor
with Langston Hughes and Milton Meltzer)

Is Anybody Listening to Black America?
(Editor)

The Blackamerican

Martin Luther King, Jr.

A PROFILE

EDITED BY

C. ERIC LINCOLN

AMERICAN PROFILES

General Editor: Aïda DiPace Donald

American Century Series
ⓦ HILL AND WANG : NEW YORK

4 5 6 7 8 9 10 11 12 13 14 15

Contents

* To avoid repetition of the name Martin Luther King, Jr., I have supplied new titles for all selections in this book [ed.].

Introduction

When the full story of Martin Luther King, Jr., is written, it will be in the form of a commentary on a culture rather than the biography of an individual; for the enduring significance of Martin Luther King has far less to do with the life of an individual than with the times and the circumstances against which that life was played out. Martin Luther King is the tragic hero by whose lumen the profile of Western culture, *American style,* was projected on the conscience of the nation for one brief moment of history. The significance of King is measured not so much by the nature of his accomplishments or the realization of his dreams as by the power of the paradox he created for America by being who he was and doing what he did. Martin Luther King was never on trial at all. America was on trial—self-consciously on trial, and America developed a defensive psychosis which inevitably led to the removal of Dr. King. He was the symbol— *the unbearable symbol*—of what is wrong with ourselves and our culture.

Because Martin Luther King was a *black* man, and because he articulated so clearly and expressed so perfectly the central message of Christian doctrine, he was for white-oriented America the negation of negation; a contradiction in terms; a paradox *par excellence.* He could not be dismissed as a fool, or as a quack, or as a "Negro cultist" because his credentials in faith and learning were of the highest order, coming as they did from some of white America's most respected institutions. But how do you deal with the negation of a negation? How do you deal with a black man who does not hate, but who knows he is hated; who loves when he knows he is not loved; who wants to live, but whose life is a constant challenge to death; who prays for his abusers; who in a word, says to a society which consigned him to oblivion, "Is this what you meant by the faith?"

One response to the paradox created by King is that we contrived to see ourselves in him—"our better selves," we said hopefully and often and *sotto voce;* and that is symptomatic of *our* tragedy, for what we saw was fantasy. Neither the real Martin Luther King, nor the impossible *ignis fatuus* we sought to make of his love, his courage, and his dignity said much about our efforts except that they were poor. To look in a looking glass is to run the risk of confirming what was always known but never faced:

> *Mirror, Mirror, on the wall*
> ?

Martin Luther King was not the image in the looking glass.

It was inevitable that we would have to kill Martin Luther King, and it was just as inevitable that we would make of him a myth and a legend in preparation. "Whom the gods would destroy, they first make mad." Since Dr. King successfully resisted madness, human society, which is often more subtle and more pragmatic than the gods, began assembling an anecdotal vita. It was imperative that we create *King, the Myth,* because we were unprepared to deal with *King, the Man,* in any way different from our traditional ways of dealing with men who are black. So we created an elaborate mythology to justify an "enlargened perspective" without realizing that since no Blackamerican other than Dr. King could fit that perspective, it was no less sterile and unenlightened than our traditional views about the sources of value in being human.

We were right back where we started from, but the process of mythmaking is itself vitally functional to the way racial accommodation works in this society. It makes possible a kind of ritual participation—a ritual sharing in which blacks and whites create together the social truths they agree to live by. Societies do this without respect to racial accommodation, of course, as in the naming of heroes, the interpretation of significant events, the sanctification of dogma, et cetera; but the American racial rapprochement, where it has existed at all, has traditionally depended upon the mutual acceptance of an inordinate body of deliberate, contrived mythology about everything from sex to salvation. As a consequence, white people and their black counterparts seldom touched base together in the common realities of their mutual existence. Myth has been the language with which we talk past each other and avoid confrontation. When the mythology is about a person, e.g., Martin Luther King, it is used as a vehicle for the displacement of emphasis and the distortion of values. Society may avoid, if it chooses, confronting what is truly significant about what a man is and what he does, by addressing itself to the less crucial issues embodied in the mythological screen which diffuses the impact of his personality. We do not have to be serious about a myth, and if the myth obscures the reality behind it, or in some way qualifies that reality, we do not have to be serious about the reality either. The best of all possible postures is to be able to look over the man *and* the myth with the privilege of delayed option.

In the case of Martin Luther King the chief mythmakers have been the blacks who knew him before the live coal touched his lips, and the whites who heard him prophesy thereafter. It was the blacks—the friends, the relatives, the teachers, the biographers, the classmates, the casual acquaintances—who supplied the anecdotal data (sometimes with the proper local-boy-made-good embellishment); but it was influential white America that

put the peculiar construction on the data supplied, and gave
it the meaning and analysis that shaped the mythological prism
through which America was willing to contemplate Martin
Luther King. Together, the blacks and the whites created something. An understanding. A rapprochement. In the age-old tradition, but with new consequences. The boyhood antics of King
became the salient clues to a singular destiny (after the fact),
and his ordinary collegiate experiences became the sure sign of
Divine intention. Even his ancestors had to be purified by myth
back to the threshold of slavery (but significantly, not beyond)
to make them acceptable progenitors of a unique kind of Blackamerican with which America had somehow to come to terms.
How important is it that King's paternal grandfather was "part
Negro, part Irish" [1] (a confusion of categories to begin with);
and what is the significance of being born into a family of "black
puritans"? [2] Our society gives such accidents an inordinate significance, and that significance has something to do with the
credibility of a man who is to become a black leader in our kind
of a society. It would not do for him to be *totally* black (for
whence the source of his genius?); but being black *can be* respectable if it is relieved with white values (*i.e.,* "puritanism").

Martin Luther King did not have an extraordinary childhood.
The "black puritanism," which was indeed an aspect of respectable black Atlanta, was also an effective insulation sepa-
rating Martin from the forces that might have otherwise contributed to a broader developmental experience. In the Atlanta
in which Martin Luther King grew up, the social structure of
"Negro" Atlanta was rigidly defined by color, money, and profession. The faculties of a half-dozen Negro colleges, the pulpits
of perhaps twice as many major churches, the insurance and
banking institutions, the abundance of black lawyers, doctors,
and businessmen gave Atlanta one of the most substantial black
middle classes to be found anywhere in America. Against this

[1] Reese Cleghorn's essay, p. 113.
[2] Lerone Bennett, Jr., *What Manner of Man* (Chicago: Johnson Publishing Co., 1964), p. 16.

backdrop, the social and economic circumstances of King's development, while not modest, were not exactly singular either, although they are likely to appear so to white Americans accustomed to thinking of all Blackamericans (except the ones they know personally) as having somehow survived the Claude Brown syndrome.[3] King did well in school, but he seems not to have traveled very much until he was out of college. Until then, as the book-oriented, stay-at-home son and grandson of Baptist ministers, his experiences were both prosaic and parochial. Because they were, the more extraordinary would be the challenge of an unextraordinary youth who was destined to become the most extraordinary American of the century.

Martin Luther King was thrust into leadership under the most unpropitious circumstances possible. If he could have chosen the time, it would not have been so soon after he and Coretta were married and had begun a family, or so early in his first fulltime independent pastorate. If he could have chosen the issue, it would not have been one which required black people—who were already tired unto death—to walk. And could he have chosen the place, it would hardly have been Montgomery, Alabama—"the cradle of the Confederacy." But history controls its own options and seldom inquires whether or not we will to play the game. There was nothing in Hegel or Thoreau or Gandhi which could have prepared Martin Luther King to confront the evil and the racial hatred endemic in a people who neither knew nor cared about Hegel or Thoreau or Gandhi. In Montgomery, he was confronting history, not ideology, and the history he was confronting was one which institutionalized white-over-black in every conceivable aspect of human intercourse. It was history and economics; history and fear; history and sex; history and chauvinism. There was no philosophical handbook which applied to the situation in Alabama, for in Alabama, his-

---

[3] Broken homes, absent fathers, slum tenements, narcotic addiction, illegitimacy, etc., etc. *ad infinitum,* as depicted in Claude Brown's *Manchild in the Promised Land.*

tory and nonviolent resistance had never met. When they did meet, at Montgomery, and later at Birmingham and Selma, each time Martin Luther King learned something about nonviolence he had never known before.

The "Great Walk" in Montgomery was a psychological and a practical victory for the black people who lived there, and an important tactical victory for King. It made Dr. King an important black leader, and it confirmed, at least tentatively, what had been for him the theoretical power of nonviolence. But there were larger implications which dwarfed the significance of desegregated buses in Montgomery, and the importance of Martin Luther King's new mandate for leadership as well. There was a certain element of serendipity in the success at Montgomery, which had a potential significance for the whole black struggle. The Great Walk had destroyed a myth and shaped a new history for Blackamericans. *Thousands of black men and women had sacrificed convenience, security, and the "good will" of the white folks to follow a black leader under circumstances that were uncertain, dangerous, and against established tradition and circumspection.* The social dictum that "black people won't follow a black leader" had been institutionalized for centuries in politics, the military, education, labor—wherever it was important to a white hegemony for a black constituency of whatever kind to be under white leadership and control. Perhaps the single important exception was the church, but even in religion the strategy of controlling the black church by controlling its economics (and hence its leadership) was an established practice, albeit one that was not universally successful as is evident by the many instances of strong independent leadership among black clergymen.

The notion that black constituencies were disdainful of black leadership was rooted in a complex mythology that had to do with the black leader's alleged vulnerability and the white man's alleged invulnerability. Martin Luther King demonstrated the power of black men and the vulnerability of white men *and the systems which protect the white mystique of invincibility.* In doing so, he set the stage for the ultimate liberation of black men by freeing them from the paralyzing self-hypnosis induced by accepting at face value the white man's stereotyped projection of the meaning of being black. Black people had forgotten how to believe strongly in themselves, or in each other, or in their leaders. When we consider the awful weight of tradition operating through an implacable social policy of racial denigration, and the abundance of superficial evidence amassed and disseminated in support of that policy, none can wonder why. But by the same token, black people have always had an unwavering *religious* faith. The peculiar genius of Martin Luther King is that he was able to translate religious fervor into social action, thereby creating political leadership under the rubric of his religious ministry at an extraordinary level of involvement and commitment. It had been done before, but never for so sustained a period under such conditions of extreme danger and liability. It may well be the final judgment of history that Martin Luther King's greatest contribution to black freedom was made in Montgomery when he helped black people free themselves from self-doubt and self-abasement. *In Montgomery, black people learned to talk together, pray together, walk together, and stay together.* Having learned how to do that, the ensuing course of events was predictable. No chains can hold a people who believe in themselves and in each other.

The Southern Christian Leadership movement, or something like it, was the inevitable precipitate of the Montgomery experience. From that experience, King emerged the leader of a successful local confrontation with institutionalized racism. But racism was also regional, national, world-wide. It was but one aspect of the wider convolutions of man's inhumanity to man. Montgomery gave King a broader vision of responsibility—and larger ambitions to match his vision. SCLC was the logical step in a progression which would ultimately lead Martin Luther King to see the world as his parish. The March on Washington (which drew 250,000 "blacks and whites together"), the Nobel Peace

Prize, the eventual leadership in the Anti-Vietnam War Crusade, the projected Poor People's Campaign were all confirmations and evidences of his growing concept of a larger calling.

King's understanding of his mission was not shared by large numbers of Blackamericans. From the very beginning, traditional black leadership looked askance at the young minister, and at his methodology. In the first place, he was a preacher, and while clerical leadership was more solidly established in the black experience than any other, it had at times been indifferent, at times self-aggrandizing, and at other times altogether dysfunctional in its accommodation to white paternalism. A developing class of nonclerically oriented leaders feared the emergence of another black preacher who might be co-opted by the white moderates as an instrument for maintaining the *status quo ante* while giving the illusion of "moderation"—moderation itself being conceived as a synonym for as little change as possible over as long a period as could be managed. So while "Montgomery" was applauded by the black rank and file, the implied threat to "established" techniques of civil rights leadership (and to emergent forms then still in the stage of debate or limited experimentation) produced a wariness on the part of existing black leadership and potential leadership. The hope was that Martin Luther King and his impractical *Satyagraha* would soon go away. Martin Luther King had no intention of going away. He had seen the mountaintop, and he fully intended to plant his pennant of nonviolent leadership there.

The essays which make up this profile offer personal interpretations of King's attempt to scale his personal mountain as he saw it. Martin Luther King was not only a Christian humanitarian involved in a cause, he was also a man, and as such, subject to the loyalties, the analyses, and the criticisms of men. In the role he assigned himself, or was assigned by fate or Providence, some men would applaud him, fear him, honor him, love him, misunderstand him, hate him, and idolize him. Some men would agree with him; some would not. But few men could ignore him, and few men did. Of the men who have written about him here, some are black, some are white; some knew him intimately, some hardly at all. But all were his contemporaries, and all were touched to some extent and in some fashion by what he said and by what he did. There were points at which their lives and his were intertwined, and what they have said about Martin Luther King reflects in part their vision of society and of themselves. What they have written offers an exceptional profile of an exceptional moment in the social history of America.

C. ERIC LINCOLN

New York
June 1, 1969

Martin Luther King, Jr., 1929–1968

Martin Luther King, Jr., was born in Atlanta, Georgia, on January 15, 1929, into a family of middle-class Blackamericans. His father, Martin Luther King, Sr., was a Baptist minister; his mother, Alberta Williams King, a schoolteacher. King graduated from Morehouse College in 1948 at the age of nineteen. Three years later he took the Bachelor of Divinity degree at Crozer Theological Seminary in Chester, Pennsylvania, graduating at the head of his class, winning the Pearl Plafkner Award for scholarship, and the J. Lewis Crozer Fellowship as well. He entered the Graduate School of Theology at Boston University in 1951 where he studied briefly with Edgar Sheffield Brightman (until his death) and L. Harold DeWolf. He was awarded the Ph.D. degree in systematic theology in 1955.

While studying at Boston University King met Coretta Scott of Marion, Alabama, who had graduated from Antioch College and was then studying at the New England Conservatory of Music. They were married in 1953, and became the parents of four children, Yolanda Denise, Martin Luther III, Dexter, and Bernice Albertine. Dr. King was pastor of the Dexter Avenue Baptist Church in Montgomery, Alabama, from 1954 until he left Montgomery in 1960. While pastor at Dexter Avenue King was elected president of the Montgomery Improvement Association which organized a year-long boycott against segregated public transportation in Montgomery. The boycott was successful, and Dr. King was catapulted to prominence in the civil rights struggle of Blackamericans. In a very short time he became world-famous for his nonviolent philosophy in seeking social change.

In 1957 King organized what later became the Southern Christian Leadership Conference and was elected its president. SCLC, with offices in Atlanta, was the organizational base for Dr. King's civil rights activities after 1960, when he moved to Atlanta to become co-pastor (with his father) of Ebenezer Baptist Church. King was a principal leader of the historic March on Washington in 1963, and was designated *Man of the Year* for 1963 by *Time* magazine. In 1964 he was awarded the Nobel Peace Prize—the youngest Peace Laureate in history.

For a decade Martin Luther King was world-famous as a leader of Blackamericans in their struggle against discrimination and race prejudice. His campaigns were principally in the South, and he was arrested and jailed on numerous occasions. His life was threatened frequently. His home was bombed. His confrontations with the raw violence of the police in Birmingham and Selma, Alabama, directed world-wide attention to the racism that characterizes much social behavior in America and contributed to the developing image of America as an extraordinarily violent society.

In the spring of 1967, in speeches at the Chicago Coliseum and at Riverside Church in New York, King associated himself with the Vietnam peace movement. His public statements on Vietnam alienated him from other black leaders and resulted in a considerable erosion of his black constituency, who felt that their leadership was being co-opted and that attention was being deflected from the civil rights fight by the peace movement. He was praised and damned in the nation's press for this new venture outside the racial struggle.

In the midst of plans for a "Poor People's March on Washington," Martin Luther King made the second of two trips to Memphis to rally support for the garbage collectors there who were on strike for better wages and improved working conditions. While in Memphis, he was murdered by an assassin firing from ambush as King stood on a balcony of the Lorraine Hotel talking with friends and members of his staff. It was the fourth of April, 1968.

C.E.L.

MARTIN LUTHER KING, JR.

★

A Man with a Hard Head

Death came looking early for Martin Luther King, and it kept looking through most of his thirty-nine years to the final appointment on the balcony of a Memphis motel.

The grim search began long before the bombings of his home, the attempted shotgunnings, the stabbing in New York by a deranged woman of his own race, the seventeen jailings, the torrent of mail which years ago quite accurately predicted the terrible headlines of the day that is now upon us: "This isn't a threat but a promise—your head will be blown off as sure as Christ made green apples."

No, it was long before, when only a handful of people in this world knew little Martin Luther King, Jr., then referred to around the house as "M.L." or "Mike." He was five and in the house where he'd been born on January 15, 1929, a comfortable thirteen-room two-story house at 501 Auburn Avenue, Atlanta, Georgia.

The boy was leaning against an upstairs banister. Suddenly he plunged headfirst over it to the floor twenty feet below, then bounced through an open door into the cellar. He got up, nothing

---

From Jerry Tallmer, "Martin Luther King, Jr., His Life and Times," *New York Post* (April 8, 1968), p. 37.

broken, nothing scratched. Nor was anything broken or scratched
—except the bicycle—when, a few years later, a car hit his
bike from behind and hurled M.L. to the sidewalk. Nor when
the same thing happened again six months later and young King
flew to the ground over the handlebars. Nor when he was caught
hard on the side of the head by a baseball bat that had slipped
from the fingers of younger but bigger brother A.D. (Alfred
Daniel), who would say [later]: "He was up right away, and
arguing that I was out because I'd missed on a third strike.
M.L.'s got a hard head, all right."

Trudging to work in 1956 during the historic Montgomery,
Alabama, bus boycott led by King, an elderly Negro woman
was told of one of those boyhood incidents. "The Lord had his
hand on him even then," she replied. "He was saving him for us.
No harm could come to him."

The remark was conveyed to King, who concurred. "Well,"
he said, "I guess God was looking out for me even then. He must
have given me a hard head just for that purpose."

Martin Luther King lived with death all his mature life; he had
long since adjusted to it; he admitted he did not like it any better
than the next man, but he was ready for it; as long ago as 1957,
in Montgomery, on the weekend when twelve sticks of dynamite were found, unexploded, on his porch, he spoke words
almost identical with those he would speak on the night in 1968
before he died: "Tell Montgomery that they can keep shooting
and I'm going to stand up to them; tell Montgomery they can keep
bombing and I'm going to stand up to them.

"If I had to die tomorrow morning I would die happy because
I've been to the mountaintop and I've seen the Promised Land,
and it's going to be here in Montgomery. The old Montgomery
is passing away."

In the midst of death we are in life, and life in Atlanta was
far from being all grim for young M.L.

There was little or no economic deprivation. His mother Alberta had been a teacher. "She had been sent to the best avail-

able school and college," King was later to write, "and had, in
general, been protected from the worst blights of discrimination."
Her father was the Reverend Dr. Daniel Williams, for twenty-
seven years the pastor of Ebenezer Baptist Church in Atlanta
and one of the South's outstanding preachers. The man who
did know what deprivation and discrimination were all about
was Martin Luther King, Sr., son of a sharecropper, husband to
Alberta, successor at Ebenezer Baptist to Dr. Williams.

To "Daddy" King, Martin Luther, Jr., "always was manly, even
as a child."

The boy was also a bit of a hellion, though he didn't drink
or smoke or swear; and a bit of a Don Juan.

Says brother A.D.: "He had his share of girlfriends, and I
decided I couldn't keep up with him. Especially since he was
crazy about dances and just about the best jitterbug in town. . . .

"I decided when I was nineteen that I was going to get married
and settle down, but not that M.L. He kept flitting from chick to
chick. I don't think he ever kept one regular girlfriend for more
than a year—two at most."

M.L. was also a natural take-charge type in sports and social
conduct. "He could outwrestle anybody in our gang and he knew
it," says a boyhood companion. In basketball they called him a
"will-shoot," because no matter who was where on the court,
he'd go ahead and shoot rather than pass.

"Also, because of his shrimpy size"—King at full growth
stood a muscular 5-foot-7—"we started him out on our back-
yard football team as a quarterback. But he wound up as the full-
back—shrimp size and all because he ran over anybody who
got in the way."

In later years King was to be reported as maintaining that all
his life he "never liked to fight, even when . . . provoked."
In the seventh grade, it was further reported, the school bully
"kicked me down the school steps, but I didn't retaliate. Whenever I was pushed to the limit and fought back, I always regretted
it. It's always been a part of me, I guess."

Could be. But members of the old crowd from Atlanta put a slightly different interpretation on it. They say M.L. had a patented phrase of physical challenge, as follows: "Well, let's go to the grass." Martin Luther, Jr., or "Tweed," as they also called him because he liked good clothes, would police the school and club dances.

"He'd see you dancing too close to a girl or giving her a hard time," according to the recollections of one acquaintance, "and he'd come over and try to joke you out of it. If you kept it up, he'd tell you flatly to stop it. And if you still kept on, you could expect: 'Let's go to the grass.'

"Nobody ever called his hand, as far as I remember."

With a laugh now:

"The rest of the world is wondering how he got that (passive resistance) way so young, and we all wonder how he got that way so quick."

M.L. was so bright a child that his parents slipped him into grade school at the age of five, a year below the local legal limit.

"And then," according to his father, "he had to let the cat out of the bag. He always was a talkative chap, you know. So he shot his mouth off and told them that he was only five while the other children were six, so they booted him right out of class."

The boy was a voracious reader. "You just wait and see," he would tell his mother, "I'm going to get me some big words." The first and, at the time, only Negro high school in Atlanta was Booker T. Washington. King skipped two grades at Booker T. and at fifteen enrolled at Morehouse College, a branch of the Atlanta University System. His sister Christine had entered Spelman College two years earlier. They graduated in the same week in 1948.

At first, much to his father's regret, Martin Luther, Jr., hadn't wanted to become a minister. He thought of being a doctor, a lawyer. He was to say later that he had found—he, who would be Martin Luther King!—had found the "emotionalism" of the

Negro church not altogether to his taste. He wondered whether religion "could be intellectually respectable as well as emotionally satisfying." However, he was persuaded into a career in the ministry by Benjamin Mays, president of Morehouse College ("I perceived immediately that this boy was mature beyond his years"), and while still at Morehouse, young King was ordained in his father's church and elected co-pastor there upon his graduation.

Next came graduate work at Crozer Theological Seminary, Chester, Pennsylvania, with King as one of six Negroes in a student body of one hundred.

At Crozer he topped the field in everything, was president of the senior class, won a fellowship to go for a Ph.D. at the university of his choice. He chose Boston University.

At Crozer he opened the door into the great world of ideas, philosophy, social philosophy; had immersed himself in the seminal contributions of Aristotle, Plato, Hegel, Kant, Rousseau, Locke, Ricardo, Adam Smith, Karl Marx, Paul Tillich, Reinhold Niebuhr.

And one other: Martin Luther ("Here I stand; I can do no other, so help me God").

And yet another: Jesus of Nazareth.

And then another: Mohandas K. Gandhi.

On his fellowship King went up to Boston University in 1951 to take his Ph.D. in systematic theology. He also took courses in philosophy at Harvard. He began getting job offers from Negro churches, schools, universities, both in the North and the South. His plans did not contemplate either marriage or a quick return to the South.

Then, in Boston, he met a beautiful and brainy girl from Marion, Alabama, named Coretta Scott. She was a soprano, studying voice at the New England Conservatory of Music; she likewise had no plans for marriage or for a return to the South.

But within an hour of their first meeting, as he was driving

her back to class, he suddenly said: "You know, you have everything I ever wanted in a woman. We ought to get married some
day."

They were married by his father, June 18, 1953, on the spa-
cious lawn of the house of Obie Scott, Coretta's father, a tough-
spirited, self-made businessman in trucking, groceries, a filling
station.

Two months later Martin Luther King, Jr.—"after being in
school twenty-one years without a break"—completed the residential requirements for his Ph.D. He received a letter from a
church in Montgomery, Alabama, "saying that they were without a pastor and that they would be glad to have me preach when
I was again in that section of the country"—the Dexter Avenue
Baptist Church, diagonally across Capitol Square from the high-
domed Montgomery Statehouse on the steps of which, on February 18, 1861, Jefferson Davis had taken the oath of office as
President of the Confederate States of America.

LERONE BENNETT, JR.

✪

When the Man and the Hour Are Met

A museum piece of the South's "Lost Cause," Montgomery, Alabama, was chosen by a puckish fate to be the myth-event of the New Cause. The city, which was the first capital of the Confederacy, seemed in 1954 to be a most unlikely place for great events. Schizoid, looking both to the past and to the future, organized around and defined by symbols of defeat and Negro degradation, the city curled around a hairpin bend at the head of the Alabama River. In 1954, there were eighty thousand white citizens. There also lived in Montgomery at the time fifty thousand Negroes. But they were neither citizens nor subjects. To most white people in Montgomery, the Negro populace was composed of objects, tools, instruments, *things* to be manipulated, dominated, and endured.

The Negro community of Montgomery had been subjected over the years to a series of galling indignities. Particularly annoying to Negro leaders was the Montgomery City Lines, a Northern-owned bus company which reportedly insulted Negro citizens though Negro customers contributed almost 70 per cent of the company's revenue. As in practically all Southern cities, bus

From Lerone Bennett, Jr., *What Manner of Man: A Biography of Martin Luther King, Jr.* (Chicago: Johnson Publishing Co., Inc., 1964, 1968), pp. 55-86. Reprinted by permission of Johnson Publishing Co., Inc.

passengers in Montgomery seated themselves on a segregated, first-come, first-served basis with Negroes seating themselves from the rear forward and whites taking seats from the front backward. In Montgomery, however, unlike some of the more enlightened Southern cities, the first four seats were reserved for the exclusive use of white patrons. Worse, the driver was empowered to order Negroes sitting in the foremost section to yield their seats to white customers. This system, which was a flagrant and open reminder of white supremacy, could not work without a certain amount of tension and unpleasantness. Negro passengers would testify later that it was not unusual for drivers to call them "niggers," "black apes," and "black cows." Nor, it seems, was it unusual for drivers to require Negroes to pay their fares at the front door, get off, and reboard the bus through the rear door. Occasionally, it was said in court, while Negro passengers were going through this complicated ritual, the bus would drive off, leaving them stranded in the middle of the street.

Vernon Johns, Martin Luther King's predecessor at Dexter Avenue Baptist Church, and E. D. (Ed) Nixon, a tough, fearless veteran of Asa Philip Randolph's nonviolent crusade of the forties, had tried desperately to rouse the Negro populace against these and other abuses. All to no avail. By all accounts, the Negro population in 1954 was slumbering fitfully in an uneasy placidity. The Negro population just then was riven geographically and ideologically. And, as always happens when men possess the name of power without the validating instruments, the leaders had fallen into the debilitating habit of fighting each other instead of their oppressors.

To this city, in no whit different from thousands of other Southern towns, came Martin Luther King, Jr., in September, 1954. His charge, the red-brick Dexter Avenue Baptist Church, sat, ironically, at the foot of the mall of the Alabama State Capitol in downtown Montgomery. Near this spot one hundred years before, William Yancey had introduced Jefferson Davis, the new president of the Confederacy, with the words: "The man and the hour have met." In this same place, in the shadow and ambience of the earlier deed, a new man and a new moment began to approach each other.

Such are the demands of fame that it is likely that the period between September 1, 1954, and December 5, 1955, was one of the happiest—if not the happiest—periods in the life of Martin Luther King, Jr. In the days before the boycott, the young pastor and his gracious, charming wife were supremely happy. The couple moved that fall into the big white frame parsonage at 309 South Jackson Street. The Reverend Mr. King unpacked his books, put them on the shelves in his study, and turned from books to face the world.

Following in his father's footsteps, King immediately installed a system of church financing at Dexter similar to the successful Ebenezer program. (There were no regular collections. Financial contributions were collected outside the sanctuary.) As the weeks wore away, rounding the curve of winter, King tightened his control over the church and began to feel the inner joy of a man who finds within himself unsuspected reservoirs of leadership. From the beginning, King stressed social action, organizing a social and political action committee within the church and urging every member to become a registered voter and a member of the NAACP. Although King had a passion for social justice, his approach to the racial problem at that time was rigidly conventional. He leaned apparently toward the NAACP protest approach, but he also championed the gradualistic tactics of organizations like the interracial Alabama Council on Human Relations. This group, which King served as vice-president, held monthly meetings in the basement of his church.

Throughout this period, King continued to work on his thesis, writing several hours in the early morning and returning to the task for several hours each night. (He completed the thesis in the spring and was awarded the Ph.D. degree in systematic theology on June 5, 1955.) No less important were the hours he spent polishing his sermons. By the summer of 1955, he had earned a richly deserved reputation as a preacher and speaker. Far more fateful and decisive, however, to the subsequent development of his career were events that happened in the outer world. On May 31, 1955, the Supreme Court ordered school desegregation with "all deliberate speed." In the wake of this event, White Citizens Councils sprang up over the South and the atmosphere turned sultry, darkening with thunderheads of unrest. There then followed an atrocity that cauterized almost all Negroes and prepared them for more radical departures. On August 28, Emmet Till, a fourteen-year-old Chicago boy who was vacationing with relatives near Money, Mississippi, was kidnapped and lynched. The effect of all this on King, as on so many other Negroes, was explosive. To be sure, King did nothing. Still, he was forced by stirrings within and provocations without to make an agonizing reappraisal of the Negro situation.

One observes with interest that the things King did not do during this period were far more important than what he did. The Negro leadership group in that season was faction-ridden and torn with controversy. King's inherent decency and a natural instinct of prudence prevented him from identifying with any particular faction to the exclusion of the other. With consummate skill, he picked his way through the undeclared battlefield, winning admiration and later, when it counted, the votes of moderates, activists, and conservatives.

Another nonact which preserved King for posterity was the declination of a chance to run for the presidency of the local NAACP branch. Members of the branch asked him to run for the position in November, less than a month before the boycott began. King saw no reason why he should not, but Coretta urged him to turn it down. She said that his first duty as a new pastor was to organize his church. Since he was already attending meetings day and night, she suggested that the NAACP presidency would be "too much." King, who sometimes defers to his wife's judgment, recalled the incident later, saying: "Coretta's opposition probably resulted in one of the luckiest decisions of my life."

For when the bus protest movement broke out, I would hardly have been able to accept the presidency of the Montgomery Improvement Association without lending weight to the oft-made white contention that the whole thing was an NAACP conspiracy."

Into this quiet and conventional life—an hour of philosophical reading in the morning, visits to the sick and infirm, and the usual clerical round of marrying, baptizing, and burying—came a day in December. The day, Thursday, December 1, promised to be no better, and no worse, than any other day. King rose early, as was his wont, read for an hour, breakfasted, and went about the business of the Lord. W. A. Gayle, the mayor, rose and went to his office in City Hall. That morning, Rosa Parks, a handsome Negro seamstress in rimless glasses, caught a bus and rode to her job at the Fair department store. In the big frame house on South Jackson, Coretta Scott King changed the baby and put away the breakfast dishes. Time passed, the clock moved, and Montgomery went about its business, livestock, lumber, cotton, fertilizer, the Negroes doing the dirty work, the whites commanding. Cows were killed, buses ran, money was made, prayers were said, babies fed, sins committed, dreams shattered—and through it all, Montgomery marched on to danger, and to destiny.

It was a pleasant day, but unseasonably warm for December. When the downtown stores closed, Negroes and whites thronged the streets, eagerly eyeing the windows, their minds running on to Christmas. There was considerable activity at this hour in Court Square, where, in the days of the Confederacy, Negro slaves had been auctioned. Now, as the early evening haze gathered, a Montgomery City Lines bus pulled through this square and proceeded to its next stop in front of the Empire Theater. On this bus were twenty-four Negroes, including Rosa Parks, who was sitting behind the white section which was filled with twelve white passengers. Six whites boarded the bus at the Empire Theater stop, and the driver left his seat and asked the Negroes in the foremost section to get up and give their seats to the white patrons. This was an ancient custom which excited no undue comment. Three Negroes rose immediately, but Rosa Parks remained seated. The driver again asked her to yield the seat and Rosa Parks, a sweet-tempered, gentle woman, again refused. The driver then summoned police officers, who arrested Rosa Parks for violating the city's segregation ordinances. Because of an extraordinary convergence of forces, because her moment was a crossroad of forces that had been decades in preparation, Rosa Parks's arrest did what no other event, however horrible, had been able to do: it unified and focused the discontent of an entire Negro community. By doing this, by proving that it could be done, the arrest released dammed-up deposits of social energy that rolled across the face of the South and the North. There was, first of all and most important of all, a one-day boycott. The one-day boycott stretched out to 382 days. The 382 days changed the spirit of Martin Luther King, Jr., and King, thus transformed, helped to change the face and the heart of the Negro, of the white man, and of America. Viewed thus, as a sensitizing social symbol, the Montgomery bus boycott was a myth-event comparable, in a different era and on a smaller scale, to the French Revolution, of which Kant prophetically said: "Such a phenomenon in history can never be forgotten, inasmuch as it has disclosed in human nature the rudiment of and the capacity for better things which, prior to this, no student of political science had deduced from the previous course of events."

With Montgomery, an epoch came to an end. To be sure, a new epoch did not begin immediately. There was an interregnum, a period of diffuse groping and stumbling. No one knew then, not even King, which road to take, but it was clear to many that one road, the road of submission and accommodation, had been closed, perhaps forever.

Why did all this happen?

Why, to go back to the beginning, did Rosa Parks refuse to move?

Martin Luther King, Jr., said later that Rosa Parks had been "tracked down by the *Zeitgeist*—the spirit of the times." Rosa Parks, a former secretary of the local NAACP branch, gave a more prosaic answer. "I don't really know why I wouldn't move. There was no plan at all. I was just tired from shopping. My feet hurt." At the point where these two answers coincide is the truth of Montgomery. In the hour of its beginning, the Negro rebellion was a result of an intersection of pain—the pain of feet and the deeper, unstated, pain of the heart—and what William James called "the receptivities of the moment." There had been pain before, but no Southwide explosion. There had been bus boycotts before (in Harlem in 1941 and in Baton Rouge in 1953), but no Southwide movement. What made Rosa Parks's pain significant and the Montgomery bus boycott compelling was the ambience of the age. Hegel and James apart, Negroes were ready for a new shuffle of the cards. Events—the interior migration of the thirties and forties and the convulsion of the fifties—had prepared them. Basic to an understanding of Montgomery, and of King, is an understanding of this fact: Negroes had already changed. They only needed an act to give them power over their fears, an instrument to hold in their hands, and a man to point the way. Montgomery furnished all three, giving Negroes not only an act but also a remarkable fisher of men and a new ideology, nonviolence. Man and method were products and not causes of the event. It is a point of immense significance that the act preceded both the man and the idea. King did not seek leadership in Montgomery; leadership sought him. He did not choose nonviolence; nonviolence chose him, imposing itself on him, as it were, as an interior demand of the situation. We can see, with the benefit of hindsight, that it was King, really, that the *Zeitgeist* was seeking. "Tracked down" and "chosen" by the times, King transcended the occasion, changing the times and transforming a diffuse uprising into a mass movement with passion and purpose. As a catalytic agent, he created a revolutionary point of departure, a new tissue of aspirations and demands. As a magnet and exemplar-myth, as an invitation to a new way of life, King attracted and released the energies of men and women of varying viewpoints.

Beyond all that, King must be seen as a leader who solved a technical problem that had worried Negro leaders for decades. As a powerless group dominated by a powerful majority, Negroes could not stage an open revolt. To go into the streets under those conditions with open demands for change was suicidal. As I have indicated elsewhere, King and the sit-in students solved the technical problems by clothing a national resistance movement in the disarmingly appealing garb of love, forgiveness, and *passive* resistance.

To understand the magnitude of King's accomplishment, it is necessary to understand how he did it, and how much it cost him and others. King, significantly, was marginal to the germination of the Montgomery plot. As pastor of the most influential church in the community, he was, of course, consulted in the feverish hours that followed the Thursday arrest of Rosa Parks. But E. D. Nixon, a Pullman porter, seems to have taken a leading role in the first phase of the controversy which, by Friday night, consumed the attention of diverse strata of the Montgomery Negro community. It was Ed Nixon who arranged Rosa Parks's bail. It was Nixon, King said in his autobiography, who suggested that *something* should be done. After a great deal of telephoning between, among others, the Women's Political Council, Negro professionals, and Negro preachers, including King and Rev. Ralph D. Abernathy of the First Baptist Church, it was decided to stage a one-day bus boycott. Mimeograph machines, without which it is almost impossible to stage a modern rebellion, clanked, and mysterious leaflets appeared on the streets with an anonymous appeal:

Don't ride the bus to work, to town, to school, or any place Monday, December 5.
Another Negro woman has been arrested and put in jail because she refused to give up her bus seat. . . .

Come to a Mass Meeting, Monday at 7:00 P.M., at the Holt Street Baptist Church for further instruction.

Monday morning came, December 5. King and Coretta rose earlier than usual. A bus stopped a few feet from their door and they were anxious to see the first act in this new and uncharted drama. At this hour, King and other leaders of the Negro community believed they would be lucky to get 60 per cent cooperation. Somewhat apprehensive, fearing a negative response, King and Coretta waited impatiently for the first bus, which usually passed their house at six o'clock. King was in the kitchen when Coretta shouted: "Martin! Martin! Come quickly!" King ran to the living room and Coretta pointed to the big orange bus which was inexplicably, gloriously empty. King could hardly believe his eyes but caution checked his joy. It would be better perhaps, he said, to wait for the second bus. But it, too, was empty, or almost; and so was the third. Excited now, envisioning the beginning of a new day, King jumped into his car and drove around the city, scanning the windows of empty buses. An inexpressible joy welled up within him and he told himself that "a miracle" had happened. So it had. That morning, Negroes walked, rode mules, and drove wagons. The boycott was almost totally effective and it would remain so from that December to the next.

One-day social "miracles" are rare; two-day social "miracles" are almost inconceivable, even to ministers. That morning, after Rosa Parks was convicted of violating the city segregation code and fined ten dollars and costs, King and other leading members of the leadership class began to explore the possibilities of a structure that could draw the "miracle" out. Since a mass meeting had already been scheduled for the Holt Street Baptist Church at 7 P.M., the leadership group decided to hold an organizational meeting at 3 P.M. in the Mount Zion AME Church. At this meeting, it was decided to extend the boycott until the company met certain minimal demands. An *ad hoc* organization, the Montgomery Improvement Association, was formed and Martin Luther King, Jr., was elected president without a dissenting vote. King and others have suggested that King was selected because he was new in the community and was not identified with any faction of the bitterly divided leadership group. It has also been suggested that King was named because almost no one wanted to be identified publicly as the leader of a new departure with an uncertain future.

With only a few minutes remaining before the night mass meeting, King went home to prepare an outline for what he has called "the most decisive speech of my life." It was now six thirty, and King had only twenty minutes or so to prepare for a venture nothing in Hegel or Rauschenbusch had prepared him for. As the minutes ticked by, he was overwhelmed by a sense of inadequacy. The enormity of the thing, a full-scale Negro rebellion in a Southern town, rose up and smote him in the eyes. As he has done in almost every crisis situation since, King decided through prayer. Then he turned to the outline of his speech only to come face to face with a problem that has always haunted Negro leadership, the problem, as King cogently put it, of how "to make a speech that would be militant enough to keep my people aroused to positive action and yet moderate enough to keep this fervor within controllable and Christian bounds?" King decided finally—and this is a key to his racial philosophy—"to face the challenge head-on," by attempting "to combine two apparent irreconcilables," the militant and the moderate approaches.

When King arrived at the mass meeting, the church was packed and three or four thousand people were standing outside waiting to monitor the proceedings on loudspeakers. This huge crowd voted unanimously to boycott the buses until their demands were met. With billowing enthusiasm, they sang-shouted "Onward Christian Soldiers" and waited patiently as the young Dr. King was introduced. King, speaking without manuscript or notes, reviewed the long train of abuses Negroes had endured on Montgomery buses. He did not quote Gandhi that night, but he did quote Jesus and, remarkably, Booker T. Washington. "Our method," he said, "will be that of persuasion, not coercion. We will only say to the people, 'Let your conscience be your guide.' " He went on to mention the transforming power of love, saying: "Love must be our regulating ideal. Once again we must hear the words of Jesus echoing across the centuries: 'Love your enemies, bless them that curse you, and pray for them that despitefully use you.' If we fail to do this our protest will end up as a meaningless drama on the stage of history, and its memory will be shrouded with the ugly garments of shame. In spite of the mistreatment that we have confronted we must not become bitter, and end up hating our white brothers. As Booker T. Washington said, 'Let no man pull you so low as to make you hate him.' " Then, after the applause died down, King built to a climactic crescendo that would later become his oratorical signature. "If you will protest courageously, and yet with dignity and Christian love, when the history books are written in future generations, the historians will have to pause and say, 'There lived a great people—a black people—who injected new meaning and dignity into the veins of civilization.' This is our challenge and our overwhelming responsibility." As King turned to his seat, the people rose *en masse* in a standing ovation.

So far, so good. There remained now the far more difficult task of inventing and sustaining a structure. In this task, King had the help and support of a doggedly inventive group of aides, most of them ministers, many of them under forty. One of the most talented of this group was Ralph D. Abernathy, a pudgy, pugnacious Baptist minister who selflessly sacrificed his own ambitions in one of the most remarkable acts in the history of Negro leadership. Though markedly different in personality and outlook, King and Abernathy were perfect complements as leaders and as speakers, King taking the high road of philosophy, Abernathy taking the middle road of Baptist fervor, King exalting a crowd with Hegel and Gandhi, Abernathy moving a crowd with humor and earthy examples. Among the other leaders of the boycott directorate were E. D. Nixon, the treasurer, and Fred D. Gray, the young attorney.

Under the impact of these personalities and others, with King serving as an ideologist, spokesman, mediator, and arbiter, the Montgomery Improvement Association became a potent rival of the white city government. Within a short time, a fleet of some three hundred automobiles was making regular runs from forty-six pick-up stations in the community. Equally important, MIA leased space, first in the Negro Baptist Center and finally in the Bricklayers Hall, where Negro Montgomerians trooped with a bewildering variety of problems and requests. To support this immense operation, special collections were taken up in Montgomery Negro churches and at the twice-weekly mass meetings. As word of the boycott spread, donations poured in from all sections of the country and from many countries in Asia and Europe. By the end of the year, the association had disbursed an estimated $225,000.

From the beginning, the Montgomery movement assumed a missionary character. The huge mass meetings, which rotated from church to church, served not only as a means of communication but also as a morale builder. At these meetings, professors, porters, doctors, maids, laborers, housewives, even drunks, abandoned the claims of rank, class, and creed, reaching out to each other in new hope and new faith. Under the impact of the old Negro spirituals, of hand-clapping, shouting, "testifying," and "amen-ing," personality shells dissolved and reintegrated themselves around a larger, more inclusive racial self.

The effect of these meetings on Martin Luther King was no less immediate and obvious. King had tended to look down on the "emotionalism" of the Negro church, but now he began to see that the Negro religious tradition contained enormous reservoirs of psychic and social strength which had never been adequately tapped. And more: King began to accept himself and the Negro people as history had made them, never on that account relaxing the inner demand that he and they should be better. In some such manner, in a church of fire, the re-education, the metamorphosis, of Martin Luther King, Jr., began.

Other transformations were taking place. King had approached the first two negotiating sessions with unwarranted optimism. In truth, the demands of the Negro protestants were modest in the extreme. They asked in the beginning only for courtesy, a first-come, first-served system within the bounds of the segregated system, and the employment of Negro bus drivers on predominantly Negro lines. To King's surprise, city officials and bus officials spurned these "demands," promising only to show "partial" courtesy to Negro customers. It seemed to King and to some neutral observers that some of the officials were more interested in defending the ancient Southern theory that it was not wise, or safe, to give in to a Negro's *demand* as distinguished from a Negro's plea. King had believed that truth would set men free, that Aristotelian logic and the law of the excluded middle would be of some service in the struggle for human justice. Now he saw, with a sinking feeling, that he was wrong, that the issue was not logic but power, that "no one gives up his privileges without strong resistance," and that "the underlying purpose of segregation was to oppress and exploit the segregated, not simply to keep [people] apart."

It was a new man, chastened, who emerged from the negotiating sessions of December 8 and December 18. There was on the opposite side a similar understanding of the tenacity of purpose of the Negro contestants. In the beginning, white Montgomerians—and many Negro Montgomerians—believed that the boycott would eventually unravel at the seams, with the Negro leaders devouring each other like wounded sharks. When this failed to happen, white Montgomery turned mean. The mayor and city commissioners publicly and dramatically joined the White Citizens Council. Finally, on Tuesday, January 24, Mayor Gayle announced what was called a "get-tough" policy. "We have pussyfooted around on this boycott long enough," the mayor said, "and it is time to be frank and honest. . . . The Negro leaders have proved they are not interested in ending the boycott but rather in prolonging it so that they may stir up racial strife. The Negro leaders have proved that they will say one thing to a white man and another thing to a Negro about the boycott. . . . [They] have forced the boycott into campaign between whether the social fabric of our community will continue to exist or will be destroyed by a group of Negro radicals who have split asunder the fine relationships which have existed between the Negro and white people for generations. . . . What they are after is the destruction of our social fabric. . . . The white people are firm in their convictions that they do not care whether the Negroes ever ride a city bus again if it means that the social fabric of our community is destroyed so that Negroes will start riding buses again."

There then followed a series of incidents that strained Montgomery's "social fabric" to the breaking point and projected Martin Luther King into the national spotlight. In the early days of the boycott, it was by no means certain that King would emerge as the leader of the movement. Speculation tended rather to revolve around Ralph Abernathy, Fred Gray, and other professionals who had been in the community longer than King. Forty-five days after the boycott began, Tom Johnson, a Montgomery reporter, asked editorially, "Who is the acknowledged boycott leader?" Johnson said that it "seemed" to be King, but the question could only be answered, as it was answered, in an act.

On Thursday afternoon, January 26, as a direct result apparently of the "get-tough" policy, King was arrested on a charge of driving thirty miles an hour in a twenty-five mile zone. Two policemen searched the young pastor, pushed him into a patrol car, and drove away. King, who had never been arrested before and who had not the vaguest idea of the location of the city jail, noticed that the car drove away from the downtown section where he assumed the jail was located. For a moment he panicked, sure that the officers were carrying him to an isolated spot for mayhem or even murder. He was therefore relieved when the car arrived at the jail where he was thrown into a cell with drunks, thieves, murderers, and vagrants.

If, as Tolstoy said, "nobody knows what kind of government it is who has never been in prison," then the first arrest of Martin King must certainly be listed as one of the most educational experiences of his life. Stunned into speechlessness, King surveyed the crowded cells, noticing the dehumanizing atmosphere, the men lying sprawled on mattresses, slats, even the floor; the open, revoltingly nauseous toilets, and everywhere the psychic fever of men dehumanized by being caged in such conditions or by caging men in that condition. King told himself and would later tell others that "no matter what these men had done, they shouldn't be treated like this." Fortunately, King did not remain long in jail. When a large number of Negroes assembled before the jail, the jailer decided that justice would be served if King were permitted to sign his own bond. Just before King left the jail, one of his cellmates said: *"Don't forget us when you get out."*

Four days later, on Monday, January 30, while King was addressing a mass meeting, a bomb was thrown on the porch of his home. When the bomb landed, Coretta, who was talking to the wife of a church member in the living room, told herself that it was only a brick. But "somehow," she said, "I felt that we should go to the back." When they were halfway to the back, the bomb exploded, splitting a pillar on the porch, shattering the front windows and filling the living room with a hail of broken glass. To Coretta, the blast sounded as though it had blown the whole front of the house away. She could feel the cold air surging through the house, and she thought, "Well, it finally happened." Her next thought was of her nine-week-old baby, sleeping in a bassinet in the back room. For a moment, she paused, not knowing quite what to do, trying to think of someone to call. Then she and Mrs. Roscoe Williams went into the bedroom. At that moment, the doorbell rang. "My first thought," Coretta King said, "was that they are coming in now. And for a split second,

I got a little panicky wondering what to do about the baby. Finally, a voice said: 'Is anybody hurt?' I knew then they were friendly callers. I went up front. . . . There was smoke everywhere. Then the telephone started ringing. Somebody answered and a woman said: 'Yes, I did it. And I'm just sorry I didn't kill all you bastards.' Then people from all over town started gathering."

When King arrived, some fifteen minutes later, the house was ringed by an angry Negro crowd armed with guns, rocks, rods, knives, sticks, and Coca-Cola bottles. As he pushed his way through the crowd, he heard a Negro bystander tell a white policeman: "Now, you got your .38 and I got mine; so let's battle it out." King went into the house, which was filled now with policemen, firemen, and other guardians of law and order, including the fire chief and Mayor Gayle. He talked briefly with his wife, looked in on the baby, and returned to the front where the crowd was trembling on the verge of a violent and apocalyptic spasm. By now, it was nine thirty or thereabouts, and more than one thousand Negroes were milling in the street in front of the house. King stood on the front porch for a moment, studying the crowd. At his side were the mayor and other city officials, their faces graven with anxiety and apprehension. It was clear to almost everyone that Montgomery was on the verge of a blood bath and it seemed then that there was nothing anyone could do about it. Shouts, threats, curses rent the air. Only a spark was needed to inflame the crowd, which had been driven to the edge of desperation by repeated acts of insult. Uneasily aware of that fact, King raised his arms. "Don't get panicky," he said. "Don't do anything panicky at all. Don't get your weapons. He who lives by the sword will perish by the sword." As the crowd fell silent, wondering at these words coming from the lips of a man whose wife and child had narrowly escaped serious injury and perhaps death, King rushed on: "We are not advocating violence. I want you to love our enemies. Be good to them. Love them and let them know you love them. I did not start this boycott. I was asked by you to serve as your spokesman. I want it to be known the length and breadth of the land that if I am stopped, this movement will not stop. If I am stopped, our work will not stop, for what we are doing is right. What we are doing is just and God is with us." As King finished, cries of "amen" and "God bless you, son" floated up from the crowd, which began to disperse, its anger deflected, dissipated.

This moment changed the course of the protest and made King a living symbol. He and other members of the boycott directorate had spoken before of love and forgiveness. But now, *seeing the idea in action,* fleshed out by pain, paid for by anguish, millions were touched, if not converted. The parable of the porch went out now over the wires of the news media and King's name became a token to almost all American Negroes. Of greater immediate consequence, however, was the impact of the event on the Montgomery movement, of which King now became leader, not only by election but also by the acclamations of committed hearts.

Though King spoke persuasively that night of love and forgiveness, he was not yet a Gandhian. Later that night, in a quieter moment, the claims of manhood reasserted themselves. Reliving the moment, realizing that his wife and baby could have been killed, he was filled with rage. The indignity of it, the insult of it, the "viciousness of people" who would deliberately, consciously, cold-bloodedly perform a series of operations designed to snuff out his life, and the lives of his wife and nine-week-old baby: all this overwhelmed him and drove him to the "verge of corroding hatred." Lying in bed, King wrestled with himself and overcame himself, saying: "You must not allow yourself to become bitter." Still, King was more than half receptive when someone suggested that self-defense was the better part of valor. With friends, he went to the sheriff's office and applied for a gun permit. The application was finally denied. By that time, however, King was convinced that even self-defense was wrong. He came to this view by a roundabout route. Contrary to the common impression, he did not enter the Montgomery struggle with a vision of battle. Somewhere in the back of his mind, of course, were the seeds of his 1950 perusal of Gandhism. But it would be an error to conclude from this that the King of 1955 was a Gandhian. The truth is at once more prosaic and more striking: *Martin King convinced himself and, in convincing himself, he convinced others.*

In the beginning, nothing apparently was further from the minds of Montgomery resistants than Mahatma Gandhi. King and other leaders urged Negro boycotters to remain calm and peaceful but they relied primarily on the words of Jesus and the traditional Negro leadership rhetoric that Negroes could never win in America with violence. Although the leaders stressed peaceful protest, they also believed apparently in the Western tradition of self-defense, as witness King's application for a gun permit.

Interestingly enough, in his first major interviews with Robert E. Johnson, a college classmate who was the managing editor of *Jet,* and Tom Johnson, a white Montgomery reporter, King did not mention Gandhi at all. In the Tom Johnson interview, published January 19, 1956, in the Montgomery *Advertiser,* King said he was motivated chiefly by the "social gospel." "Besides the religious philosophers," Tom Johnson reported, "King was particularly interested in the German philosophers Kant and Hegel. The latter, his favorite, fathered the 'dialectical process' which holds that change is the cardinal principle of life and that in every stage of things there is a contradiction which only the 'strife of opposites' can resolve."

Paradoxically, the idea for an opening to Gandhi seems to have come from a Southern white woman. Soon after the boycott began, Juliette Morgan, a white Montgomery librarian, remarked, in a letter to the editor of the Montgomery *Advertiser,* on the similarities between the Montgomery struggle and Gandhi's crusade. The leaders, who were moving in a similar direction, seized on this idea and began to use Gandhi as an authority in their frequent appeals for restraint. The Gandhi idea caught on, particularly and at first almost exclusively with the large number of Northern and European reporters who flocked to the scene.

The opening to Gandhi was facilitated by two factors: King's propensity—largely because of his philosophical training and his original choice of himself as a symbolic being—for large ideas and concepts; and the further fact that the movement was already based on the solid rock of the Negro religious tradition. What King did now—and it was a huge achievement—was to turn the Negro's rooted faith in the church to social and political account by melding the image of Gandhi and the image of the Negro preacher and by overlaying all with Negro songs and symbols that bypassed cerebral centers and exploded in the well of the Negro psyche.

Nonviolence, as we have seen, was not a new idea in the ghetto or in America. Ninety-eight years before King was born, and some eighty years before Gandhi's first campaign, William Lloyd Garrison, the white abolitionist, made what was perhaps the first sustained attempt to use passive resistance as an instrument of liberation in a major social conflict. Garrison used much the same phrases Gandhi and, later, King would use. "The history of mankind," he said, "is crowded with evidences proving that physical coercion is not adapted to moral regeneration; that the sinful disposition of man can be subdued only by love; that evil can be exterminated from the earth only by goodness; . . . that there is great security in being gentle, harmless, long-suffering, and abundant in mercy; that it is only the meek who shall inherit the earth, for the violent who resort to the sword are destined to perish with the sword."

Nonviolence was not only ancient; it was also a submerged, though far from articulate, element in the world view of the Negro leadership class, which could not visualize any practical alternative. "We must condemn physical force and banish it from our minds," James Weldon Johnson said. "But I do not condemn it on any moral or pacific grounds. The resort to force remains and will doubtless always remain the rightful recourse of oppressed peoples. Our own country was established upon that right. I condemn physical force because I know that in our case it would be futile." Though, as this quote indicates, the nonviolent strain in the Negro leadership tradition was more practical than theoretical, the graveyard of Negro leadership was by 1956 replete with the bones of men who had attempted to establish an American passive resistance movement based on Gandhian methodology. The matter was discussed seriously in the twenties after Gandhi launched his Indian campaign. In a 1924 symposium in *The Crisis,* the NAACP journal, several Negro leaders and intellectuals debated the possibilities of a duplication on American soil of Gandhi's struggle. E. Franklin Frazier, the Negro sociologist, seems to have expressed the majority view, saying there would be a "blood bath" if a Gandhi arose to lead Negroes. As a sociologist, Frazier was contemptuous of the redemptive power of love. "If the masses of Negroes can save their self-respect and remain free of hate, so much the better for their moral development. [But] I believe it would be better for the Negro's soul to be seared with hate than dwarfed by self-abasement."

Despite these negative assessments, the idea of an American Gandhi persisted, fueled by the glowing reports of Howard Thurman, then dean of the Howard University Chapel, and other Negroes who made pilgrimages to India and to Gandhi. Finally, in the turbulent forties, Asa Philip Randolph electrified Negro America with a broad-scale attempt to create a mass-based civil disobedience movement. Stimulated by John L. Lewis' success with sit-down strikes and massive unrest in Negro ghettos, Randolph called for a "nonviolent goodwill direct action campaign," including school and bus boycotts, mass marches on city halls and the White House. Buoyed up by the response, Randolph staged in 1942 a series of mass meetings of a size and intensity unparalleled in the ghetto. Then disaster struck. On the eve of the proposed "civil disobedience campaign," America erupted in the violent riot season of 1943. Chastened, Randolph and his aides "postponed" the campaign and it was never revived.

Though the "American Gandhi," as Randolph was called, failed in his main objectives, he did activate new charges of energy, influencing Bayard Rustin, Daisy Bates, E. D. Nixon, and others. More concretely, the new idea was institutionalized with the founding in 1942 of CORE [Congress of Racial Equality]. This organization grew out of a memorandum, "Provisional Plan for Brotherhood Mobilization," which James Farmer, a young pacifist, submitted to A. J. Muste and the Fellowship of Reconciliation on February 19, 1942. Farmer proposed a "creative" application of Gandhian tactics to the American race problem, avoiding, however, "an uncritical duplication of the Gandhian steps in organization and execution." The heart of his plan was a national mobilization extending over a five- or ten-year period "after which, it is to be hoped, relentless non-cooperation, economic boycott, civil disobedience, et cetera, will be thrown into swing wherever and whenever possible." CORE, with Farmer as its first national director, succeeded in staging a small "freedom ride" in 1947 and integrated public facilities in several Northern and border states, but the "relentless non-cooperation . . . et cetera" Farmer envisioned had to await the maturing of events and of Martin Luther King, Jr.

All these currents, which had been swirling for years beneath the surface of Negro life, began to converge on Montgomery and Martin Luther King, Jr., in the early months of 1956. By that time, two Negro-Americans—Adam Clayton Powell in *Marching Blacks* (1945) and Howard Thurman in *Jesus and the Disinherited* (1949)—had written books on nonviolence and the Negro struggle. (King read or reread at least one of these books, *Jesus and the Disinherited,* after the boycott began.) The Fellowship of Reconciliation and CORE also had considerable experience with nonviolent direct action and soon after the boycott began, members of these groups, Bayard Rustin and A. J. Muste among others, drifted into town with advice and patterned programs.

As the boycott wore on, King plunged ever deeper into Gandhism. A post-boycott trip to India, in 1959, solidified his commitment to the cause. Even more decisive perhaps in the transformation of King was a ministry of pain. The pressures on King and his wife grew apace as his fame spread. In 1956–1957, the frame house on South Jackson Street became a vortex of swirling forces that threatened to engulf the minister and his young wife. Day and night the phone jangled, bringing oftentimes violent and abusive threats. Wherever King went, wherever he traveled, in Montgomery or in the Northern cities to which he went often now to make fervently received speeches, the demands of developing fame claimed him, turning, twisting, altering his life in a spiraling pattern of pressure. Hovering over all, subtly shaping and distending all was the ever-present possibility of sudden and violent death. Stretched taut on the rack of himself, having no time to sort out, analyze and organize the new experiences through which he was going, King came one night in January, 1956, to the end of his personal rope. The air was thick with doubts and very real dangers then, and King, sitting dejected in the kitchen of his home, told God that he couldn't go any further alone. "I am here taking a stand for what I believe is right," he said, "but now I am afraid. The people are looking to me for leadership, and if I stand before them without strength and courage, they too will falter. I am at the end of my powers. I have nothing left. I've come to the point where I can't face it alone." Into King's kitchen, or so it seemed to him at any rate, came "the presence of the Divine," and he thought he heard the "quiet assurance of an inner voice saying: 'Stand up for righteousness, stand up for truth; and God will be at your side forever.'" This "vision," which bore the mark not of Gandhi but of the Negro Baptist tradition was, as King admitted, a turning point in his life. Having reached the end of himself, he now began to experience the beginning of himself. After that experience, King said in his autobiography, "My uncertainty disappeared. I was ready to face anything."

Building on the Gandhi tradition, learning not so much from words as words fed by the blood of experience, King now transformed himself and the Montgomery movement, giving men, women, children, and himself a new vision of struggle and a new vision of the possibilities of man. King has said that the *experience* of Montgomery "did more to clarify my thinking on the question of nonviolence than all the books that I have read." He also said that the spirit of the Montgomery movement came from Jesus, the technique from Gandhi.

The Montgomery struggle continued throughout the year of 1956 but it was won, really, at the point where King and, through him, the Negro population cast off fear, saying with their spirit and, most importantly, with their bodies, that they were ready to *lose* everything in order to win. Not understanding the depth of change in the Negro community, the white power structure made extraordinary blunders. On February 21, for example, the Montgomery County Grand Jury indicted some ninety of the leading boycott participants on a charge of violating a 1921 statute which made it a misdemeanor for anyone to hinder lawful business without "just cause or legal excuse." Within forty-eight hours King and other leading pastors were arrested. The mass arrest of practically all the Negro ministers of Montgomery, as almost anyone could have predicted, unified the Negro community as it had never been unified before; and the trial of King, as a test case for the other indicted Montgomerians, served only to increase his stature, locally and nationally.

During the four-day trial, the Negroes of Montgomery thronged the courtroom, wearing cloth crosses bearing the legend: "Father, forgive them." When King was convicted on March 22, he and Coretta emerged from the courtroom, smiling triumphantly. On the courthouse steps, the young couple was hailed by a large crowd of demonstrators, shouting: "Long live the King! We ain't gonna ride the buses no more."

All the while, on another level, the legal level, things of consequence were unfolding. Under the impact of events, the movement jettisoned its original demands and opened an attack on segregation *per se*. On February 1, four Negro women asked the federal court to ban bus segregation in Montgomery. On June 4, the court ruled that statutes requiring bus segregation in Montgomery were illegal. The case was immediately appealed to the United States Supreme Court. Before that tribunal could hand down a decision, Montgomery officials made a grab for victory that almost succeeded, asking a state court to enjoin the Montgomery Improvement Association from operating an illegal transit system. This move, of course, imperiled not only the car pool but also the movement. On Tuesday, November 13, King and his aides, their spirits drooping, waited forlornly in a Montgomery courtroom for the inevitable decision outlawing the car pool. During a lull in the proceedings, King noticed a stir at the prosecution table. At that moment, Rex Thomas, an Associated Press reporter, handed King a piece of paper on which these words were written:

The United States Supreme Court today affirmed a decision of a special three-judge U.S. District Court in declaring Alabama's state and local laws requiring segregation on buses unconstitutional.

The word sped through the crowd. From somewhere in the courtroom came the booming voice of an anonymous Negro: "God Almighty has spoken from Washington, D.C." The next night, Wednesday, November 14, some ten thousand Negroes, holding simultaneous meetings in two churches, voted to end the boycott. King asked his followers to go back to the buses "with humility and meekness." "I would be terribly disappointed," he said, "if any of you go back to the buses brag-

ging, 'We, the Negroes, won a victory over the white people.
. . .' " Of the 382-day struggle which he would later call "one
of the greatest in the history of the nation," King said: "All along,
we have sought to carry out the protest on high moral standards
. . . rooted in the deep soil of the Christian faith. We have carefully avoided bitterness. [The] months have not at all been
easy . . . Our feet have often been tired and our automobiles
worn, but we have kept going with the faith that in our struggle we had cosmic companionship, and that, at bottom, the
universe is on the side of justice. [The Supreme Court decision was] a revelation of the eternal validity of this faith,
[and] came to all of us as a joyous daybreak to end the long
night of enforced segregation in public transportation."

On Friday, December 21, after receipt of the Supreme Court
order, the Montgomery buses were integrated, with King and a
party consisting of E. D. Nixon and the Reverend Glenn Smiley, a
white minister, leading. After a spasm of violence, including
the bombing of four Negro churches and the homes of Ralph
D. Abernathy and other leaders, Montgomery came to a grudging peace with Martin King's *Zeitgeist*.

It is a point of immense interest that the Montgomery movement began in irony and ended in irony. It began not as a protest against segregation but as a demand for more equal treatment within the "separate-but-equal" system; and it ended not
as a triumph of passive resistance but as a confirmation of the
NAACP theory that lawyers are the Negro's best friend. And
yet, when all this is said, one fact remains: Montgomery transcended lawyers. There was an incident at the mass meeting
celebrating the end of the struggle that is very illuminating in
this general connection. The Reverend Robert Graetz, the only
white man in the leadership of the movement, decided that night
to read the scripture according to Paul: "When I was a child, I
spoke as a child, I understood as a child, I thought as a child.
. . ." At this point, there was a vast uproar. All over the floor
now, men and women were on their feet, waving handkerchiefs

and weeping. It was only with great difficulty that Graetz completed the sentence.

> . . . But when I became a man, I put away childish things.

The Negro people had grown, tremendously; and so had Martin Luther King, Jr. In the days ahead King and the Negro people would grow together, reciprocally influencing each other, King contributing to the radicalization of the Negro people and the growing radicalization of the Negro people pushing King to new postures, the whole process pushing upward and outward in an ascending curve of resistance.

When the Montgomery boycott ended, King was only twenty-seven years old. A little below average height, his oblong face purified by a long looking on death and on evil, King presented a picture of deliberative determination. Like Booker T. Washington, who was famous at thirty-nine, and Frederick Douglass, who was internationally known at twenty-eight, King stood on the heights at an early age. Despite his age, King, like Douglass, was well prepared for the task assigned him by history. An excellent orator, getting better with every delivery, King had an ability, rare in Negro leadership circles, to articulate and dramatize ideas. He also had a superb sense of history. Moreover, King had, as he had just demonstrated in Montgomery, an unexcelled ability to pull men and women of diverse viewpoints together and to keep their eyes focused on the goals. It was said on the debit side that King was deficient in administrative ability. He himself admitted that details bored him, a fact which does not concern us here. It cannot be said too often that administration is one thing, and leadership another. Brilliant administrators are born several times every day; a man with King's genius, with his ability to move men and motivate them, is born once a generation, if not once a century. If King were an administrator, if he had been blessed and cursed with the bureaucratic sensibility, a sensibility given to caution and an overemphasis on the rituals of paperwork, he would not have triumphed in Montgomery and we would not be discussing him here. What is important is that King, like Franklin Delano Roosevelt, demonstrated in Montgomery and later a rare talent for attracting and using the skills and ideas of brilliant aides and administrators. Of greater weight than the charge of administrative fumbling was the criticism, that grew in force in the sixties, that there was a certain softness, a certain fuzziness and lack of focus in King's leadership, a deficiency that stemmed, or so the critics said, from the fact that he tended to make ends of his means.

King emerged from the boycott as a national leader with a popular backing of a depth and intensity unknown in America since the days of Booker T. Washington. His increasing weight in the world of men was obvious even before the end of the boycott. On May 17, 1956, for example, he was invited to speak at the Cathedral of St. John the Divine in New York City. In August, he appeared before the platform committee of the Democratic National Convention. By the spring of 1957, he was one of America's most sought-after speakers and his name was known in almost every corner of America. *Time,* the leading white-oriented news magazine, and *Jet,* the leading Negro-oriented news magazine, had run cover stories on him. Long and generally approving articles had appeared in almost every large American periodical and most major newspapers abroad. The general tenor of these articles can be gauged by the *Jet* article which said King had become "a symbol of divinely inspired hope," "a kind of modern Moses who has brought new self-respect to Southern Negroes."

The trickle of tributes became a flood in 1957. In May, King became the youngest person and the first active pastor to win the Spingarn Medal, which is awarded annually to the person making the largest contribution in the field of race relations. The next month, in June, he received the first of his scores of honorary degrees. Particularly pleasing to King was the citation from Morehouse, his alma mater. Speaking with great feeling, Benjamin E. Mays said:

You are mature beyond your years, wiser at twenty-eight than most men at sixty; more courageous in a righteous struggle than most men can ever be; living a faith that most men preach about and never experience. Significant, indeed, is the fact that you did not seek the leadership in the Montgomery controversy. It was thrust upon you by the people. You did not betray that trust of leadership. You led the people with quiet dignity, Christian grace, and determined purpose. While you were away, your colleagues in the battle for freedom were being hounded and arrested like criminals. When it was suggested by legal counsel that you might stay away and escape arrest, I heard you say with my own ears: "I would rather spend ten years in jail than desert the people in this crisis." At that moment, my heart, my mind, and my soul stood up erect and saluted you. I knew then that you were called to leadership for just such a time as this. . . . On this our ninetieth anniversary, your alma mater is happy to be the first college or university to honor you this way.

Then, his voice trembling with emotion, Benjamin E. Mays executed one of the oratorical flourishes that had drawn King into the ministry ten years before. "See," Benjamin Mays said, quoting Emerson, "how the masses of men worry themselves into nameless graves when here and there a great soul forgets himself into immortality."

All this was heady wine which could have destroyed a man with less balance. Despite his stolidity, King did not escape—no one could have escaped—unscathed. He is said to have complained in 1957 that he hadn't read a new book, thought a new thought, or made a new speech in a year. More significantly, he confessed to the inevitable crisis of identity. He was not in January of 1957 the same man he was in January of 1956. But who was he? And what did he want now, now that he could have almost anything he wanted? Offers by the dozen poured into the South Jackson house in the days after the boycott, ten-, fifteen-, twenty-thousand-dollar-a-year offers, the pastorship of a large Northern white church, professorships and even a deanship of major white universities. Even more tempting were opportunities to earn more than $75,000 a year as a professional lecturer. "Frankly," King told J. Pius Barbour, an old friend, "I'm worried to death. A man who hits the peak at twenty-seven has a tough job ahead. People will be expecting me to pull rabbits out of the hat for the rest of my life."

Fame being marketable, many men came to Montgomery to tell King who he was and where he should want to go. King, as usual, listened patiently and kept his counsel, waiting for events to speak to him. Either through events or through the working of his exquisitely tuned personal radar, he decided finally that he was, first, a pastor, and, second, a Negro leader or, at least, a Southern Negro leader. He said then and would say later that the second was an extension and not an addition to the first.

During the year which was now behind King but which somehow would never leave him, traits in his character had hardened and new sensitivities had emerged. As a result of his immersion in the church of fire, King had come to radically different conclusions about the nature of the Negro struggle. A key concept in his new orientation was the idea of confrontation, the idea of bringing out into the open submerged evils, of *forcing* face-to-face meetings of man and man, of community and community, individually as in the refusal of a single individual to accept segregation, collectively as in the open challenge by a Negro community of the fiats and fears of a white community. The idea that nothing substantial would happen in the field of race relations if men and communities were not *forced* to face evils was stated with great eloquence by Asa Randolph in the forties, but King carried it to a higher stage of development, making the "showdown situation" the central component of the Negro's new vision of battle. Like Randolph, he believed direct action indispensable for racial progress. "Pressure, even conflict," he said, "was an unfortunate but necessary element in social change." Abandoning the mainstream Negro leadership tradition, which shied away from conflict and considered direct appeals to the masses inflammatory, King called for a total mobilization of all the resources in the Negro com-

munity—"the no D's and the Ph.D.'s." He stressed, moreover, the responsibility of every individual to history in the
making. Every individual, according to King, had a right, nay, a
duty, to break or ignore unjust laws. Any man who accepted segregation involved himself, tragically, in his own degradation.

A practical idealist, fervent in exhortation but cool and cir-
cumspect in action, King fashioned his neo-Gandhian philosophy over a four-year period extending through the fall of 1961.
Like James Farmer, he argued against an "uncritical duplication"
of Gandhism. The Gandhian program as it evolved during the
Indian struggle included collective civil disobedience, *hartals,*
work stoppages, etc., based on an absolute turning away from
the government and a refusal to recognize its authority or even
its existence. King stopped far short of collective civil disobedience. In 1957, he only advocated the right of individuals acting as individuals to violate "unjust local laws" that conflicted
with national laws. "Every man," he said, "has a right and personal responsibility to break, ignore, and resist certain local
laws—no matter what the personal consequences are—in order
to abide by the national law." As for collective action similar
to the Montgomery struggle, King said: "All cities have conditions that could lead to the kind of thing we are doing in Montgomery. I would not, however, advocate the indiscriminate use
of the boycott as a weapon. Whenever it is tried, the Negro must
be sure that it is well organized, strategically wise, and in an
area where counter-boycotts cannot be used against them." Despite the limitations King placed on passive resistance, his contention that Negroes had a right to disobey local segregation
laws had revolutionary implications.

With the formation of the Southern Christian Leadership
Conference (SCLC), King became an institution. Sixty Negro
leaders, most of them preachers, from ten Southern states
founded the organization at a meeting in Atlanta's Ebenezer
Baptist Church on January 10–11, 1957. The next month at a
meeting in New Orleans the organization, which was then

known as the Southern Conference on Transportation and Nonviolent Integration, changed its name and elected King president. SCLC in its original call to battle reflected King's ideas, calling upon all Negroes, "to assert their human dignity" by refusing "further cooperation with evil." "But far beyond this," the organization said, *"we call upon them to accept Christian love in full knowledge of its power to defy evil. We call upon them to understand that nonviolence is not a symbol of weakness or cowardice, but as Jesus demonstrated, nonviolent resistance transforms weakness into strength and breeds courage in the face of danger."*

In its formative years, the organization, as its first name indicated, was concerned primarily with segregation in transportation facilities and voter registration. Some of the more theoretical sit-in students would say later that the Montgomery idea was aborted before it reached full development. While there is some truth in this, it is surely true also that the foundation of the movements of the sixties was laid by King's first strides in the darkness of the new departure.

Future consequence apart, King's ideas had immediate effects. With the crystallization of King's ideas in the Southern Christian Leadership Conference and their diffusion through articulate strata of the Negro community, a sense of urgency penetrated Negro leaders. Lewis W. Jones has called attention to this fact in an important essay on the Tuskegee movement. "In the spring of 1957," he wrote, "strong sentiment developed among Tuskegee Negroes to 'do something about our situation.' Outspoken persons within and without the Tuskegee Civic Association talked about something 'similar to the action taken in nearby Montgomery regarding the public transportation boycott.' " This feeling—the feeling that it was necessary "to do something"—and its corollary—the implicit threat that if Negro men of power did not "do something" somebody else would—opened fissures in several Negro communities and prepared the way for a displacement of accommodating Negro leadership. More significantly, young Negro preachers began to view themselves through the prism of the King image. The grand outcome was a series of bus boycotts in Tallahassee, Atlanta, and other communities. When, in January, 1959, Atlanta's buses were desegregated, the Reverend William Holmes Borders said, "Thank you, Montgomery. Thank you, Martin Luther King, Jr." King's influence was also perceptible in Little Rock, where Daisy Bates, a state NAACP leader, outmaneuvered state and city officials and kept nine Negro children in a school which had become a national battleground.

The adulation which King received in 1957 cannot be explained entirely by King's acts. It must be explained, at least in part, by what men and women saw in King. For some fifty years, Negroes had been expecting a leader. Now, as King's image rose on the horizon, Negroes of all ranks and creeds pooled their psychic energy and projected it onto King, anxiously asking themselves, anxiously asking King, with every gesture, every glance: "Art thou he who should come or should we seek another?"

No serious student of King's life can help being struck by what can only be called the genius of his unconscious. Like all great men, he seems to have a talent for appearing at the right fork on the right road. It was his good fortune in 1957 to appear on the national scene at a time when lines of forces that had been gathering since his birth were coming to an intersection. Since the early twenties, American Negroes had been gathering fury against their situation, and impersonal socio-economic forces—urbanization, a developing middle class, the rise of the welfare state, etc.—had heightened their hopes and sharpened their sensitivities. Postwar developments, particularly the Supreme Court decision of 1954 and the crumbling of European colonialism, had dangerously increased Negro aspirations. Now, in 1957, in the wake of Southern resistance to the Supreme Court decision and a deepening economic crisis in Northern ghettos, Negroes were becoming increasingly restive over mainstream leadership tactics of protest and appeal. And out of this there began to emerge the feeling, nebulous at first but always waxing clearer, that another line had to be found. A feeling began to creep from Negro to Negro in these years, from ghetto to ghetto, a dawning sense, a fiery hope, that things did not have to be that way forever, that someway, *somehow* life could be better. For having sensed that hope, long before he knew what to do with it, and long before others could name it, Martin Luther King, Jr., earned the right from 1957 on to speak for the Negro, and for man. . . .

WILLIAM ROBERT MILLER

The Broadening Horizons:
Montgomery, America, the World

As the [Montgomery] boycott drew to a close, it was hard to suppress a certain exultation—a feeling if not of triumph, at least of having endured. Nineteen fifty-six had been a year of hope and unprecedented solidarity—and strain. Yet when the victory was achieved, Martin Luther King had been filled with the vision of a new age dawning. December 21 had been a day of days. On that day the Montgomery *Advertiser* observed that "acceptance of this significant change in Montgomery's way of life came without any major disturbance." Many hopeful incidents were reported. On one bus, two white passengers found themselves sitting behind a Negro. One said to the other, "I see this sure isn't going to be a white Christmas." The Negro turned around with a good-natured smile and said firmly, "Yes, sir, that's right." Other passengers smiled, too, and even the man who had spoken slipped into a sheepish grin. For a week, the Christmas spirit mellowed the air—and with it came a slacken-

---

ing of attendance at the Montgomery Improvement Association mass meetings, a decline in zeal and urgency, a diminution in the readiness of King's colleagues to accept his leadership.

To King, the letdown was depressing. After Christmas had come the disorders, followed by suspension of evening bus service. Scurrilous leaflets appeared, denouncing him personally. He brooded over what had come to pass. But at the great week-long MIA institute, Martin had called for a Southwide meeting of the leaders of the proliferating movement to be held in Atlanta at his father's church beginning on Wednesday, January 10. Martin and Ralph Abernathy arrived in Atlanta the night before. At 2 A.M., the telephone rang. It was Mrs. Abernathy, telling her husband of the nightrider bombings that had just struck their home and virtually demolished Graetz's, had damaged two churches, including Abernathy's, and destroyed two others. No one had been injured. Abernathy and King were stunned. Together they prayed for strength to carry on.

Remembering last January 30, Martin pictured angry mobs gathering at the scene of each explosion. Anxiously, he made several phone calls to make sure no riots had broken out and to urge his colleagues to do whatever was needed to maintain order. After four or five hours of telephoning, the two ministers, leaving Coretta to take her husband's place at the conference, flew back to Montgomery to survey the wreckage. Martin was amazed that the crowds did not erupt into violence—he knew the cost of suppressing his own anger. The morning paper sternly condemned the bombings; an editorial translated the issue from one of segregation into one of safety. Other influential white voices, too, went on record against the terrorism.

Despite his exhaustion, Martin felt it his duty to put in an appearance at the Atlanta meeting. There the mood was enthusiastic. Among the sixty present were such prominent ministers as C. K. Steele of Tallahassee, Fred Shuttlesworth of Birmingham, Matthew McCollum of Orangeburg, and William Holmes Borders of Atlanta's Wheat Street Baptist Church—key activists from all over the Deep South. They had indeed gone ahead, in King's absence, with discussions of nonviolent community organization, leadership training, publicity media. They resolved to fashion a coordinated strategy at future conferences, and a continuing organization was set up for this purpose, which came to be called the Southern Christian Leadership Conference. Martin Luther King arrived just in time to be elected its president.

Gloom hung over Montgomery when he returned. The bus company had discontinued all service on orders of the city commissioners. It looked as if the Citizens Council and the Klan had robbed from the blacks their hard-won victory. Another long struggle might be looming ahead, a struggle not to broaden the gains already won but merely to retrieve what now seemed lost. Literally exhausted, Martin had no heart for it. He felt miserably inadequate, unable to rise to the responsibilities now thrust upon him by this the harsh caprice of history. In the catacombs of his soul, he relived the drama of conscience and guilt. The dark subconscious feelings of fourteen years ago swept over him again. Uncontrollably, he felt again the blame for his grandmother's death—not for causing it, certainly, but for failing to prevent it. It was bound, in some obscure way, to the very root of his being. Brooding was useless but he was helpless against it, and somewhere, in this tangle of emotions, he felt inescapably that Jesus would not have let his followers down in this way. The sense of failure posed for Martin a personal, psychological crisis of staggering proportions. All resilience had vanished; he felt a shattered man.

In this state of mind, he attended the mass meeting on January 15—his twenty-eighth birthday. As he prayed with the audience for God's guidance, he suddenly blurted out, "Lord, I hope no one will die as a result of our struggle for freedom in Montgomery. Certainly I don't want to die—but if anyone has to die, let it be me!"

"No! No!"—the audience was in an uproar. Martin tried to

continue but could not. He stood in the pulpit, his mind reeling. In a moment, two ministers were at his side. "Come, Martin, sit down," said one. He stood immobilized for several minutes. Finally, the paralyzing tension lifted and he was able, with their aid, to sit down. A flood of relief came, much as it had when, at the age of twelve, he had leaped from the window. His composure returned quickly as people came up to express their solicitude after the meeting, and when he got home, he slept soundly.

The year of the bus boycott finally ended on January 28, but not without one last incident. On the night of the twenty-seventh, a bundle of dynamite was deposited on the King's porch. No one was home, and there was no explosion. The next day, five white men were arrested. None of them was ever convicted, but the terrorism abruptly ceased.

Fourteen months earlier, Martin Luther King had been the promising young minister of a Negro church in Montgomery. Quickly, he had become the acknowledged spokesman of a city-wide movement which almost immediately gained national and world attention. By mid-1956, he was famous. The fame, the responsibility, the suddenness—all contributed to the burden under which he collapsed on his twenty-eighth birthday. The opportunities from which he had chosen in 1954 seemed shadows by comparison with the functions and duties that now inundated him. "I'm worried to death," he told his friend J. Pius Barbour. "A man who hits the peak at twenty-seven has a tough job ahead. People will be expecting me to pull rabbits out of a hat for the rest of my life." Indeed, they expected more. An article in *Jet* magazine hailed him as "a symbol of divinely inspired hope" and "a kind of modern Moses who has brought new self-respect to Southern Negroes." He could easily have earned $75,000 a year on the lecture circuit or settled into the pastorate of a large and predominantly white church in a Northern metropolis, and his voice would continue to be heard by millions.

But his destiny seemed to take another path. He would remain in Montgomery for a while. The Dexter Avenue church
would suffice as a base for his wider activities, and these too
would be centered in the South—that was his homeland, the
place where the struggle must first be waged. That was where
the action was in 1957, and indigenous leadership was essential to it. The Southern Christian Leadership Conference, born in
the crucible of the Southern struggle, could address itself increasingly to the national scene in those terms. Hence, among
its first acts was an appeal to President Eisenhower to "come
south immediately, to make a major speech in a major Southern city urging all Southerners to accept and to abide by the
Supreme Court's decisions as the law of the land." This request,
and similar requests to Vice-President Nixon and Attorney-
General Brownell, encountered polite refusals or silence. At
SCLC's second meeting on February 14 in New Orleans, these
overtures were repeated even more forcefully. The President
was asked to call a White House conference on civil rights, and
was admonished further that "if some effective remedial steps
are not taken, we will be compelled to initiate a mighty
Prayer Pilgrimage to Washington."

Meanwhile, on February 10, the Race Relations Sunday message of the National Council of Churches was read from pulpits
throughout the country. Titled "For All—A Nonsegregated
Society," and written by Dr. King, it called for action "to banish
segregation from every area of American life."

Meanwhile, too, the Dexter Avenue Baptist Church, recognizing the Kings' need for an interlude of rest, voted the pastor
and his family $2,500 for a trip abroad, to which the MIA added
another $1,000. Martin and Coretta decided to use it for a
visit to the Gold Coast, which was soon to achieve its independence. They arrived in New York on March 3 to join an American contingent that included Ralph Bunche, A. Philip Randolph, and Adam Clayton Powell. Vice-President Nixon was
the official U.S. representative, but Prime Minister Kwame

Nkrumah had made a special point of inviting black American leaders as well. The journey, which took two days, including stopovers in Lisbon and Monrovia, proved great fun. During the flight to Lisbon, Dr. King had the treat of sitting at the controls, and he jovially reported to his traveling companions, "If I just had a few more lessons, I think I could fly us all to Accra by myself."

Martin and Coretta had never been outside the United States, and they enjoyed Lisbon's old-world charm under the guidance of Adam Powell. At Monrovia, they were met at the airport by Romeo Horton, a Morehouse man now president of a Liberian bank. But the high point came when they reached Accra, where they lodged with an English family at Achimota College, and proceeded to the independence ceremony. A crowd of fifty thousand gathered at the polo grounds on the evening of March 5. At the stroke of midnight, Nkrumah stood in his colorful African robes and proclaimed, "The battle is ended. Ghana, our beloved country, is free forever." The British colonial flag was hauled down and the Ghanaian flag was hoisted amid great shouts from the crowd: "Freedom! Freedom! Ghana is free! Ghana is free!" For Martin and Coretta the moment was profoundly felt, the proclamation of freedom in a land from which their ancestors had been abducted and enslaved. And in the days of celebration and relaxation that followed, they were happy to be constantly in the midst of free black people who controlled their own destinies. They knew of the nonviolent "positive action" by which Nkrumah had led his country to independence. When they lunched with him privately, he told them how heartened he had been by the news of the Montgomery struggle. Martin, in turn, drew from this encounter great encouragement and an enhanced sense of his destiny as a leader.

The undercurrent of fatigue persisted, however, and before they left Ghana, both Martin and Coretta had suffered for several days with tropical fever. The specter of death that had

haunted Martin before now appeared in a new guise—his illness became much more serious than Coretta's—but they both
weathered the crisis. On their return trip, they detoured through
Nigeria, then went on to Rome, Geneva, Paris, and London.
Back in New York on March 25, Martin stopped to confer
with Roy Wilkins, director of the NAACP, and A. Philip Randolph. While in Ghana, Richard Nixon had invited Dr. King to
come and see him in Washington, but the Administration still
remained silent on the request for a White House conference.
The three black leaders agreed to meet again on April 5, and
they did gather then, with some seventy associates, at the Me-
tropolitan Baptist Church in Washington, D.C. The following
six weeks vibrated with activity. Roy Wilkins, the most conservative of the three, set up the program, and the NAACP under-
wrote the major part of the expenses. Thus, the Prayer Pilgrimage for Freedom got under way. Under the Reverend Thomas Kil-
gore as national director and Ralph Abernathy as associate director for the South, special organizers Bayard Rustin and Ella
Baker swept immediately into action. On the morning of May
17, about thirty-seven thousand marchers from all parts of the
country, most of them churchgoing Negroes, assembled at the
Lincoln Memorial. Among the crowd were a few celebrities—
Jackie Robinson, Sidney Poitier, Harry Belafonte, Sammy
Davis, Jr.—and perhaps three thousand white people.

The program got under way at noon with speeches by A.
Philip Randolph, Mordecai Johnson, Roy Wilkins, and Adam
Powell; the Howard University chorus, Philadelphia's interracial
Fellowship Chorus, and Mahalia Jackson sang; SCLC boycott
leaders Steele, Shuttlesworth, Borders, and Davis gave testimo-
nies. It was 3 P.M. when Randolph introduced Martin Luther
King. The crowd stood and cheered, then a hush fell as his rich
baritone rang out: "Give us the ballot—and we will no longer
plead to the federal government for the passage of an anti-
lynching law. . . . Give us the ballot—and we will transform
the salient misdeeds of bloodthirsty mobs into the abiding good

deeds of orderly citizens. Give us the ballot—and we will fill our legislative halls with men of good will! Give us the ballot —and we will get the people judges who love mercy. Give us the ballot—and we will quietly, lawfully implement the May 17, 1954, decision of the Supreme Court." Listening to this sermon-like speech, the audience, schooled in the Negro church, quickly caught the beat, adding their voices to his as he called out each time, "Give us the ballot!" As he moved into a different rhetoric, they chorused "amen" as he assailed the Eisenhower administration for being "too silent and apathetic" and Congress as "too stagnant and hypocritical." He sounded a challenge to white moderates, jabbing at their "quasi-liberalism, based on the principle of looking sympathetically at all sides." He called for strong leadership from Southern white liberals and from Ne-groes. He spoke of the Montgomery campaign and how it had withstood white terrorism. "We must never be bitter," he said. "If we indulge in hate, the new order will only be the old order. . . . We must meet hate with love, physical force with soul force." He exhorted the marchers to return home in that spirit and work for civil rights.

By all accounts, it was a moderate speech, emphasizing con-ventional goals and methods. The right to vote—what could be less controversial? But the Crusade for Citizenship which King announced shortly thereafter in the name of SCLC represented a strong acceleration of the NAACP's previous efforts to se-cure the ballot. In addition, it showed a mature recognition of the realities of power. Martin Luther King did not raise the slogan of "black power," but nonetheless this was the objective—to give black people political control over their destinies. When the slogan did emerge seven years later, the soil it rose from had been plowed by SCLC organizers. Nonviolent courage played a continuous, if not often dramatic part in the voter reg-istration and education program that formed the core of SCLC's activities.

The Prayer Pilgrimage stood as an important milestone. The

governors of California, Iowa, Maryland, and Missouri designated May 17 as Pilgrimage Day, as did the mayors of Los Angeles and New York City. One step toward the great march to
come six years later had been taken. And Martin Luther King
emerged as a national figure giving his first speech to a national
gathering. It was fitting that in the same month he was awarded
the NAACP's Spingarn Medal for his contributions to race relations—and that he later purchased two $500 life member-
ships in the NAACP, one for himself, and one in the name of
the Montgomery Improvement Association. King might well
differ with Roy Wilkins and the NAACP on matters of strategy,
but he made it his policy not to promote division among the
forces working for racial equality. On many occasions he deferred to Wilkins and others to be assured of their support—
gestures criticized by those who wanted an emphatic program
of nonviolent direct action.

   Among the many accolades that came his way at this time
were the annual award of the National Religion and Labor Foundation, which he shared with Senator Herbert Lehmann and
Father John LaFarge, S.J., and honorary degrees from the Chicago Theological Seminary, Howard University, and Morehouse College. The Morehouse event found him surrounded
by his parents, Coretta, Chris, and A.D. [Martin's brother], as
well as old schoolmates and teachers. Martin felt deeply moved
when Benjamin Mays, whom he admired so much, addressed
him at the convocation: "You are mature beyond your years,
wiser at twenty-eight than most men at sixty; more courageous
in a righteous struggle than most men can ever be; living a faith
that most men preach about and never experience. . . . 'See,'
said Emerson, 'how the masses of men worry themselves into
nameless graves when here and there a great soul forgets himself into immortality.' "

   Soon after the Prayer Pilgrimage, Martin King and Ralph
Abernathy had a two-hour conference with Vice-President Nixon
and pressed the requests SCLC had made earlier. The chief

result was a White House conference attended on June 23 of the following year by King, Randolph, Wilkins, and Lester B. Granger of the National Urban League. The nine-point program which Randolph presented on behalf of the group was politely received, but it had no apparent effect on the administration's policies.

The year between those two events appeared outwardly uneventful for the movement. Martin King made more than two hundred speeches in 1957, while still wearing the several hats of the Dexter pastorate, the MIA and SCLC presidencies, and the larger role of charismatic leader under which all these were subsumed. Coretta's second pregnancy had begun on one of those hectic and harrowing January nights, and in September, Martin became the proud father of his first son and namesake, Martin Luther King III. The MIA's second annual Institute of Nonviolence, held in December, was poorly attended and generally accounted a failure, perhaps because Martin's attention had been pre-empted by the triennial meeting of the National Council of Churches in St. Louis on December 4. In addition, the MIA's ongoing program had greatly dwindled and was now virtually confined to voter education. During this period too, with the continuous aid of his friend Lawrence Reddick, Dr. King managed to carve out enough time to respond to what many had urged—he wrote his own account of the Montgomery bus boycott. At the same time, he assisted Reddick in preparing a biography of himself that would follow his own book by a few months. In February, both tasks were substantially completed, and the manuscript of *Stride Toward Freedom* was delivered to the publisher. Work on Reddick's *Crusader Without Violence* continued at intervals throughout 1958.

Both books clearly show that Martin King's commitment to nonviolence was growing rather than abating. From time to time, he put forth tentative proposals for direct action—massive stand-ins in voting booths, for example, and sit-ins in white schools—but these ideas evoked little response from his colleagues. He welcomed the continuing efforts of the Fellowship of Reconciliation, and in 1958 he became a FOR member, confirming his by now deep-going commitment to pacifism as well as to the strategic validity of nonviolence as a method. In February, 1958, the FOR opened a Southern regional office in Nashville. Its secretary, a young Negro Methodist minister studying at Vanderbilt University, James M. Lawson, joined with Glenn Smiley and Ralph Abernathy in a reconciliation team which for two months visited communities in eight Southern and a few Northern states, holding seminars and workshops at Negro churches and colleges. They took with them copies of a newly published FOR "comic book"—*Martin Luther King and the Montgomery Story*—prepared by the FOR staff in consultation with Dr. King and executed by the Al Capp Organization with the aid of a $5,000 grant from the Fund for the Republic. During the next two or three years, some 200,000 copies were distributed, seeding the ground for nonviolence. Also in wide use during this period was a pocket-size FOR leaflet, *How to Practice Nonviolence*. A new edition of Richard B. Gregg's *The Power of Nonviolence* went into production, its revisions including a chapter on the Montgomery Movement and an introduction by Martin Luther King.

Yet the note which King continued to sound most consistently was that of the SCLC Crusade for Citizenship. Twenty-one simultaneous mass meetings were held in key Southern cities on Lincoln's birthday, February 12, 1958. The crusade soon conscripted Ralph Abernathy, who had to drop out of the FOR team. Its announced goal was to double the number of Negro voters, and it served as the occasion for one of King's most forceful speeches:

America must begin the struggle for democracy *at home*. The advocacy of free elections in Europe by American officials is hypocrisy when free elections are not held in great sections of America. To Negro Americans it is ironic to be governed, to be taxed, to be given orders, but to have no representation in a nation that would defend the right to vote abroad. . . .

Let us make our intentions crystal clear. We must and we will be free. We want freedom now. We want the right to vote now. We do not want freedom fed to us in teaspoons over another 150 years. . . .

There is blood on the hands of those who halt the progress of our nation and frustrate the advancement of its people by coercion and violence. But despite this, it is our duty to pray for those who mistreat us. . . .

The ghastly results have not been borne alone by the Negro. Poor white men, women, and children, bearing the scars of ignorance, deprivation, and poverty, are evidence of the fact that harm to one is injury to all. . . . Today, because the Negro cannot vote, Congress is dominated by Southern Senators and Representatives who are not elected in a fair or legal manner. . . .

We Southerners, Negro and white, must no longer permit our heritage to be dishonored before the world. . . . We have the duty to remove from political domination a small minority that cripples the economic and social institutions of our country and thereby degrades and impoverishes everyone.[1]

A growing new militancy occasionally flickered. On Easter Sunday, King and Abernathy led a procession of fifteen black-robed ministers from Dexter to the Alabama Capitol steps to conduct a "service of repentance" for the recent execution of Jeremiah Reeves, a Negro youth who at the age of sixteen had been convicted of raping a white woman. The gathering of some twenty-five hundred Negroes remained orderly. The Klan and the Citizens Council kept their distance. Police and state troopers cooperated, on orders from the mayor and the governor, wisely wishing to avoid disturbances, and indicating the stature that King had now achieved.

In August, King received word of sit-ins in Oklahoma City and Wichita, Kansas, organized by the NAACP Youth Councils

[1] Martin Luther King, "Who Speaks for the South?" *Liberation,* March, 1958, pp. 13-14. The speech was originally made at a meeting in Florida.

there and involving white FOR and CORE members as well as Negroes. A Youth March for Integrated Schools, organized nationally by the ubiquitous Bayard Rustin, had helped to set these local demonstrations in motion, but they remained limited in scope. Nevertheless, the seeds were beginning to sprout.

Asked to appear on the campus of Purdue University, King addressed some three thousand delegates attending the first National Conference on Christian Education of the newly merged United Church of Christ. He based one of his talks, an extended meditation titled "What Is Man?" on the query in Psalm 8, "What is man, that thou art mindful of him?" Man, said King, is first of all "a biological being with a physical body," and "any religion that professes to be concerned about the souls of men and is not concerned about the economic conditions that damn the soul, the social conditions that corrupt men, and the city governments that cripple them, is a dry, dead, do-nothing religion in need of new blood." But man is also a child of God, a "marvelous creation" made in God's image, possessed of spirit and rational capacity which transcend time and space, a being with "the unique ability to have fellowship with God." And man is also a sinner. "We must admit that he has misused his freedom. Some of the image of God is gone. . . . And so in a real sense the 'isness' of our present nature is out of harmony with the eternal 'oughtness' that forever confronts us. We know how to love, and yet we hate. . . .

"In our collective lives," he continued, "our sin rises to even greater heights. See how we treat each other. Races trample over races; nations trample over nations. We go to war and destroy the values and the lives that God has given us. We leave the battlefields of the world painted with blood, and we end up with wars that burden us with national debts higher than mountains of gold, filling our nations with orphans and widows, sending thousands of men home psychologically deranged and physically handicapped.

"This is the tragic plight of man"—tragic because he need

not be prodigal, tragic because man is made for something better. "So long as he lives on the lower level he will be frustrated, disillusioned and bewildered," as was the prodigal son in Jesus' parable after he had "wasted his substance and even his character." Western civilization, like the prodigal son, has "strayed away to the far country of colonialism and imperialism." Prodigal America has likewise strayed, and King depicted a divine voice saying, "You left the house of your great heritage and strayed away into a far country of segregation and discrimination. You have trampled over sixteen million of your brothers. . . . In the midst of all your material wealth, you are spiritually and morally poverty-stricken, unable to speak to the conscience of this world." Dr. King closed the meditation with a prayer of thanks for the inspiration of Jesus' life. "And grant that we will see in that life the fact that we are made for that which is high and noble and good. Help us to live in line with that high calling, that great destiny."

On September 3, he received a shocking reminder of the coarse, vicious reality he had spoken of. As a child, he had once been slapped and called "nigger." As a Christian minister with a Ph.D., he had been threatened, arrested, his home bombed. Now, the recipient of many honors—medals, prizes, honorary degrees—featured on the cover of *Time,* he had spoken as an equal with Nkrumah and Eisenhower. But he had not experienced what to countless black Americans spelled out the meaning of "segregation and discrimination" in everyday terms. Martin and Coretta King went to Recorder's Court with Ralph and Juanita Abernathy where Ralph was to testify against a man who had assaulted him. When a surly guard refused to admit them, Dr. King, confident that Fred Gray, the MIA's attorney, could clarify the situation, asked to speak to him. "Boy," the officer drawled, "if you don't get the hell out of here, you'll *need* a lawyer!" Before King could reply, a voice from behind growled, "Boy, you done done it now—let's go." Two guards seized him in a hammerlock, thrust him down the courthouse steps and

54 WILLIAM ROBERT MILLER

around the corner to police headquarters. Coretta, on the verge of tears, started after them. One of the guards scowled over his shoulder, waving her away. "You want to go too, gal? Just nod your head." She slackened her pace as her husband said quickly, "Don't say anything, darling."

Coretta and the others followed as Dr. King, his arm painfully twisted behind him, was hauled inside the police station. As they forced him to a cell, an officer barked, "Everybody clear out—you too, gal." They shoved him roughly into the cell, barking "Raise your hands, boy!" After they frisked him, one officer tried to knee him in the groin. Another grabbed him by the throat, and both landed a few kicks before the cell door clanged shut. It is probably fair to surmise that when the guards reported their coup in the cause of white supremacy to Commissioner Clyde Sellers, the more sophisticated officer rebuked them for their stupid blunder. Within ten minutes the officers had returned, ushered King to the desk, and permitted him to sign out on bond.

For many months, devotees of nonviolence, including Bayard Rustin, had suggested to King that going to jail would aid the cause more than allowing the white power structure to embroil him in legal maneuvering. Gandhi had repeatedly done this in India with powerful effect, as Martin was reminded in mid-August when he received a visit from Ranganath Diwakar. Diwakar had been one of Gandhi's chief lieutenants in the Quit India campaign of 1942. The author of a handbook on nonviolent action, *Satyagraha,* he had been jailed by the British and had discussed the question of going to jail with Gandhi himself. As Coretta said after the three-day visit of Diwakar and his associates, "We began to think more deeply about the whole philosophy of nonviolence. We talked about how superficial and shallow our knowledge of the whole thing was."

They talked some more when Martin got home from police headquarters. "I've had enough of this thing," he said. On Friday, September 5, the judge found him guilty of refusing to obey an officer, and fined him ten dollars plus costs—the same sum the court had levied against Mrs. Rosa Parks. "Your honor," said King, "I could not in good conscience pay a fine for an act that I did not commit and above all for brutal treatment that I did not deserve." Attorney Fred Gray told the court that his client would serve out the penalty in jail. Taken to a detention room to await transportation to the jail, King was released before the next police wagon came. Someone had paid his fine. That someone turned out to be Clyde Sellers, who issued a statement that he had "elected to spare the taxpayers of Montgomery the expense of feeding and housing [King] during the next fourteen days"—he could not permit the black leader to use the city jail "for his own selfish purposes" as a "publicity stunt."

Meanwhile, some two hundred Negroes, having joined Ralph Abernathy in an impromptu protest march from the courthouse to Dexter Avenue Baptist Church, were engaged in a meeting there when Dr. King unexpectedly arrived and took command. "When I go to jail," he said, "the whole world knows it. I have hundreds of telegrams and I have received telephone calls from nearly every state in the Union. But when one of you goes to jail and suffers brutality, no one knows about it. I am happy that I could suffer just a little bit. . . . It makes me feel a closer part of you. We have a mandate from God to resist evil. . . . We must go out of this meeting with the determination to take a firm and courageous stand against police brutality. We must go out and no longer be afraid to go to jail. This has taught us one thing—we no longer have to fear going to jail." And he pledged never again to pay a fine for any charge arising "from our fight for freedom."

Two weeks later, on Saturday afternoon, September 20, Martin Luther King, busy making public appearances to launch *Stride Toward Freedom,* sat at an improvised desk in the shoe department of Blumstein's, a white-owned store in Harlem, autographing copies of his book for the crowd that clustered around him. Looking up, he saw a heavy-set dark-skinned woman pushing her way toward him. "Are you Mr. King?" she said. "Yes, I am," he nodded.

"Luther King," she muttered, cursing, "I been after you for five years!" As she spoke, she drew a glittering object from her dress. It flashed down hard, and suddenly the startled leader winced in pain as it struck his chest. The woman beat at him with her fists, ranting incoherently. Moments later, the police took her into custody and found a loaded Biretta in her handbag. Martin, in a state of shock, sat in his chair with the handle of an eight-inch steel letter opener protruding from his chest. The store was in an uproar of shrieking, hysterical women. One of them was about to extract the long blade when a man intervened: "Don't touch it. The doctors will take care of it." Wise counsel, for the blade's tip was delicately poised against the aorta. At Harlem Hospital, three surgeons took three hours to remove the letter opener. It was indeed a close call; a cough or sneeze would have pierced King's heart.

Coretta flew up from Montgomery immediately, praying that her husband would be spared, wrestling with a fear that was all too real. She had had to live with it for nearly three years. If the worst came, she would carry on in the struggle they had shared—but with a rush of relief, she found him alive. Messages of good will and concern poured in from all over the world. For nearly two weeks, Coretta served as a buffer between Martin and the numerous would-be visitors. Only close friends and a few dignitaries such as Governor Averell Harriman were permitted to see him. In ten days, seated in a wheelchair, Dr. King held his first press conference. He felt "no ill will toward Mrs. Izola Curry," the woman who had stabbed him. "I hope all thoughtful people will do all in their power to see that she gets the help she apparently needs. . . . The apathetic aspect of this experience is not the injury to one individual. It demonstrates that a climate of hatred and bitterness so permeates areas of our nation that inevitably deeds of extreme violence must erupt. Today it was I. Tomorrow it could be another leader or any man, woman, or child who will be the victim of lawlessness and brutality."

On October 3, Martin Luther King left the hospital, and after a few days of convalescence in New York, he and Coretta returned to Montgomery. Mrs. Curry was examined by psychiatrists at Bellevue Hospital and eventually committed to Mattewan State Hospital for the Criminally Insane.

For four months of convalescence, Martin cut down on his activities, canceling many speaking engagements and maintaining his role as leader on a largely symbolic level. The period was punctuated with sounds of the ongoing struggle. On October 12, the bombing of a Jewish synagogue in Atlanta shocked the nation. Billy Graham, whose Crusade for Christ had prefigured the Crusade for Citizenship and who had warmly introduced King at one of his Madison Square Garden rallies in July, 1957, stated: "Every Christian should take his stand against these outrages." Paul Tillich and other leading churchmen added their voices to the outcry. Even President Eisenhower broke his customary silence on the Southern struggle to deplore this violence.

Despite die-hard resistance, white attitudes began to bend. A *Pulpit Digest* survey of ministers in seventeen Southern states showed that from 50 per cent (South Carolina) to 89 per cent (Kentucky) favored compliance with the Supreme Court ruling of 1954, and only 3 per cent of a total of 765 answers favored open defiance. Nearly all of those favoring school integration, according to the survey, also supported abolishing color barriers in their own churches but felt sure their congregations would not permit it.

In Birmingham, the Reverend Fred L. Shuttlesworth, an SCLC board member, was arrested on October 20, together with twenty other Birmingham Negroes who seated themselves in the reserved-for-whites section of two city buses, and by month's end, a boycott was under way. In more temperate Atlanta, the Reverend William Holmes Borders launched a boycott which brought segregated bus seating to an end in January,

1959, and a genial statement from Borders, an old friend of
Mike King's: "We aren't mad at anybody. We believe in Christian love."

For more than a year, an invitation from Prime Minister
Jawaharlal Nehru had lain on King's desk. Now, with his responsibilities temporarily curtailed, he decided to act on it, with
the aid of grants from SCLC and a Quaker organization, the
American Friends Service Committee. A week after addressing
the annual conference of the War Resisters League in New York
on February 2, he boarded a plane for New Delhi with Coretta
and Lawrence Reddick.

The Kings did not arrive on Sunday, February 8, as expected.
Fewer people, therefore, were on hand at Palam Airport when
they landed on the tenth. Nevertheless, newsmen showed up in
full force, along with James E. Bristol, a leading American exponent of nonviolence who at that time was director of the
Quaker Center in Delhi, G. Ramachandran, and Mrs. Sucheta
Kripalani of the Gandhi National Memorial Fund. Their shoulders heaped with garlands of flowers, the visitors were soon
whisked off to the Janpath Hotel where reporters besieged
Martin with questions. "To other countries," he said, "I may
go as a tourist, but to India I come as a pilgrim. This is because
India means to me Mahatma Gandhi, a truly great man of the
age. India also means to me Pandit Nehru and his wise states-
manship and intellectuality that are recognized the world over.
Perhaps, above all, India is the land where the techniques of
nonviolent social change were developed, that my people have
used. . . . We have found them effective and sustaining—
they work!" To a reporter's question about the tangible gains of
the Montgomery boycott, he replied, "Our real victory is not
so much the desegregation of the buses as it is a new sense of
dignity and destiny." Thirty-five Southern cities, he added, had
voluntarily abolished bus segregation since the boycott.

Indian Communists had recently won elections in Kerala
State, the nation's most Christian province. Why, asked the news-

men, hadn't Negroes pressed for a similar course in the American South? "The basic reason," King replied, "is that the American Negro has faith that he can get justice within the framework of the American democratic setup."

The Kings' itinerary was constantly crowded. Before their first day was over, they had lunched with Rajkumari Amrit Kaur, taken tea with Sarvepalli Radhakrishnan, the noted philosopher and Vice-President of India, attended receptions in their honor at the Quaker Center and the Gandhi Smarak Nidhi, and dined with Prime Minister Nehru, who obligingly rearranged his schedule to accommodate the Kings' late arrival. The next morning, before breakfast, they laid a wreath on Gandhi's tomb (*samadhi*)[2] and knelt there for a long time in prayer. On Thursday, they spent the morning discussing nonviolence with Ramachandran, chairman of the Gandhi Smarak Nidhi. In the afternoon, Martin addressed the Delhi University Student Union, challenging them to put an end to prejudice and tyranny throughout the world through nonviolent action. They called on President Rajendra Prasad, a visit especially memorable for a walk through the luxuriant Moghul Gardens, a park teeming with multihued flowers in full bloom. Coretta was frequently asked to sing, and she did so again this evening after she talked with a group of African students at the Quaker Center, while Martin met with *sarvodaya*[3] workers at the Nidhi.

Jayaprakash Narayan, one of Gandhi's lieutenants in the struggle for India's freedom, was a major exponent of *sarvodaya*. The Kings traveled by plane, train, and jeep to visit his austere *ashram* at Sokhodeora. It was their first encounter with rural India, and, amid peasants and villagers whose way of life had

[2] Strictly speaking, a *samadhi* is not a place of entombment; the Gandhi Samadhi is the place where the Indian leader was cremated on January 31, 1948. It is located in Rajghat, between Delhi and New Delhi, in a beautiful garden where services of prayer are held every Friday evening.

[3] *Sarvodaya* or "nonviolent socialism" is a major feature of the Gandhian constructive program, involving committed social service and the development of cooperatives similar to the Israeli *kibbutzim*.

changed very little in several centuries, they were surprised
to find Japanese scholars and technicians who had come to
Jayaprakash's retreat center to study his experiments in de-
centralized, grass-roots democracy. A great favorite with the
children there, too, Martin King hardly could take a step without one or two of them holding onto his hand. Years later, in
Chicago, he would remember this visit.

From Sokhodeora, they pushed on by train and truck to
Shantiniketan, or "abode of peace"—the ashram of the great
poet Rabindranath Tagore. It was here, at the Visvabharati, a
center of world cultures, that Mordecai Johnson had come for
the World Pacifist Meeting, a fact that made the visit meaningful to Martin as he thought back to 1950 when he heard Johnson's talk in Philadelphia. He and Coretta were moved by the
choral songs of welcome and farewell, and they were once again
struck by the internationalism of this out-of-the-way place—
their hosts included the great Chinese scholar Tan Yun Shan.
In this regard, it reminded them somewhat of Monteagle, Tennessee, where people from far away came to visit the High-
lander Folk School, an institution that had more in common with
its Danish counterparts than with its Appalachian neighbors.

Calcutta, where they arrived on February 15, was full of
contrasts. One evening, they dined in their luxurious suite at
the Grand Hotel; the next evening was spent discussing problems of poverty and wages with labor leaders. Martin never
forgot the sight of thousands of emaciated refugees who still
thronged Calcutta's streets nearly a decade after the massacres
and the partition that uprooted them from what came to be
Pakistan. The consequences of such intergroup strife haunted
him. Among those he met in Calcutta were Nirmal Kumar Bose,
who had been Gandhi's personal secretary, and others closely
associated with the independence movement. Coretta was
thrilled by a visit to the All-India Radio Studios where, for the
first time, she listened to *ragas* and *talas* and examined instruments such as the sitar, the sarod, the tamboura, and the mri-

dangam, in those days little known in America. She could hardly have dreamed then that one day black Americans like Richie Havens would make such instruments their own. She was fascinated by the unusual timbres and intricate rhythms of the unfamiliar music.

After three days in Calcutta, the Kings flew nearly a thousand miles south to Madras, India's third-largest city. For the next week or so, in the intense tropical heat, they lived among many dark-skinned people, descendants of the Dravidian races who lived there long before the Aryans brought Hinduism down from the north. South India had many ancient Hindu temples and also many churches, some of them dating back to the missionary voyage of St. Thomas in the first century. They visited some of those temples, like the one elaborately carved out of solid rock at Mahabalipuram, and paid a brief but meaningful visit to C. Rajagopalachari, the aged statesman whom Gandhi called "the keeper of my conscience." Wherever he went, Martin discussed Gandhi's ideas with men who had known Gandhi and seen those ideas in action—and, what is more, who had, like Rajagopalachari, actually translated those ideas into action, men who were makers of their nation's history. Martin reflected that it was a little like having lunch with George Washington, then tea with John Adams, supper with Jefferson, and an evening chat with Tom Paine. Yet these veterans of India's struggle greeted him as one of their own, an apostle of nonviolence.

One of Gandhi's ideas which came to fruition only after his death was the concept of the *Shanti Sena,* or "peace army," patterned after the small groups of volunteers which Gandhi led on his peace missions to strife-torn regions in the first year of independence and partition. At Gandhigram ("Gandhi Village"), Martin and Coretta were saluted by five hundred members of the Shanti Sena dressed in spotless white *khadi* (homespun cloth). It was Friday, and the Kings were fortunate to be present for the weekly prayer service, with readings from Hindu,

Muslim, Judaeo-Christian, and Buddhist texts. Like Sokhodeora, Gandhigram was a kind of pilot community for its founder's ideas on economics and education. Here they saw tangible examples of Gandhi's program with its emphasis on manual village industry and the equal distribution of both work and income. This was the only place on their itinerary where King's speech had to be translated into Tamil, the local language.

From Gandhigram, they traveled south the next morning, stopping at three villages along the way to Madurai. The first was a *Harijan* village of outcastes, or untouchables—Gandhi had renamed them *harijani*, "children of God." The village was impoverished but hospitable—Martin and Coretta were served raw coconut in one of the *harijan* huts. Mrs. Sundaram Ramachandran, wife of the secretary of the Gandhi Smarak Nidhi, not only arranged the visit but served as guide and interpreter. She next took them to two *Gramdan* villages. *Gramdan,* she explained, was part of Vinoba Bhave's *bhudan* ("land gift") movement. Vinoba, a close disciple of Gandhi who was often called "the walking saint" because he often trudged along village roads like an ancient *sadhu* on his mission, was regarded by many as the Mahatma's spiritual heir. His own version of *sarvodaya* was based on securing gifts of land from large landholders and turning it over to poor peasants. As in feudal Europe, few peasants in India owned their own land—many lived like Mississippi sharecroppers. *Gramdan* meant the gift of an entire village, releasing its inhabitants, in effect, from feudal economic bonds and enabling them to govern themselves and share equitably in the fruits of their labors. Mrs. Ramachandran took the Kings to two such villages. They arrived in the second in time for lunch and ate as millions of poor Indians do, seated on the ground, with banana leaves serving as their dishes. Arriving in Madurai late in the afternoon, they visited the ancient, towering Hindu temple there, and in the evening Martin addressed a meeting at the new Gandhi Smarak Nidhi museum. Whether or not regarded as a prophet in his own country, he was treated as one here. The Gandhi Smarak Nidhi was virtually an alumni association of the nonviolent struggle for India's independence —its board of trustees included Nehru, Rajagopalachari, Birla, Morarji Desai, and many others. The President of India was a former chairman. As their guests, the Kings were assured a warm welcome and the opening of many doors. And everywhere they went, people plied Martin with questions.

At Trivandrum, capital of Kerala State, a crowd bearing bouquets and garlands greeted them at the airport. Chief Minister Namboodiripad, recently returned from several weeks in Moscow, gave a luncheon in Martin King's honor, and arrived half an hour early to chat with him alone. That evening, the visitors were taken to the Gandhi shrine at Kanniyakumari, the southernmost tip of India. They sat on the rocks beside the shrine for more than an hour, contemplating, on the clear horizons of the Indian Ocean, the exquisite sunset to their right and the rising of a full moon to their left. Next morning, King, Reddick, and Bristol swam on the tropical beach before breakfast. That evening, Martin addressed an overflow crowd. Gandhi, he said, had blazed a trail for all mankind, and only this trail led to enduring justice and enduring peace. In an age of thermonuclear weapons, he said, "the choice is no longer between nonviolence and violence, but between nonviolence and nonexistence."

Heading north again, the Kings spent three days in Bangalore, visiting both cottage industries and large factories. The Governor of Mysore State accompanied them on a visit to the All-India Cattle Show, where they saw, among other displays, an $8,000 prize bull who seemed very proud of his pedigree. At the Institute of World Culture on February 26, one well-attended meeting began at 8 A.M. Two weeks earlier, Martin wouldn't have believed anyone would show up at such an hour.

They left that afternoon for Bombay, where they met R. R. Diwakar with whom Martin had a good discussion of *satyagraha,* Gandhi's concept of nonviolence. Diwakar, chairman of the

Gandhi Smarak Nidhi, showed the visitors through the Mani Bhavan, a simple building where Gandhi had once lived, still kept as it had been during his lifetime. Here, too, Martin and Coretta viewed the hour-long documentary film of Gandhi's life and work, *Voice of India,* now all the more memorable because they had met so many people and visited so many places that they recognized in the film. They were also deeply moved by the pitiable sight of starving refugees in the Bombay streets, and it was in Bombay that Martin made the most stirring speech of the whole trip, speaking of the suffering and degradation of human beings still so prevalent in 1959 and urging his listeners to be courageously "maladjusted" to this state of affairs.

Early on March 1, they flew to Ahmedabad and from there were taken by car to Gandhi's *ashram* on the Sabarmati River. The Sabarmati ashram had been founded by Gandhi upon his return to India from South Africa. From this center of his activities for eighteen years, he began his famed Salt Satyagraha,[4] vowing never to return to Sabarmati until India had won her independence. Martin and Coretta had the feeling that they were indeed on hallowed ground as they joined some six hundred residents, mostly *harijani,* in prayer. Continuing north to a small village near Kishingharh, they met Jayaprakash Narayan again, and Vinoba Bhave, both of whom were there for an All-India Shanti Sena Conference. Martin fell ill before he could address the conference, but he recovered in time to accompany Vinoba on his *padayatra* (foot march) for a few miles. Vinoba greeted him with a warm embrace and explained to Martin and Coretta how his *bhudan* movement had grown to embrace *gramdan* and *shanti sena.* To Martin's request for a message to take back to the United States, Vinoba, an accomplished Hindu scholar, replied modestly, "It would be presumptuous on my part to give a message to a Christian nation."

[4] *Satyagraha,* or "soul force," refers to technique or to a nonviolent campaign—here, Gandhi's 1930 march to the sea to obtain untaxed salt in defiance of British law.

Returning to Delhi, the visitors stopped en route for a full day of sightseeing at Agra, the former residential capital of the Moghuls. They spent the morning at the Taj Mahal, the fabulous seventeenth-century tomb of the Empress Mumtaz Mahal. How ironic, they thought, for twenty-two years of labor and so much architectural skill to be expended on such an awesome and undeniably beautiful edifice for a single dead person while millions lived in want. That afternoon, they passed through the 75-foot-high sandstone walls of the sixteenth-century Agra Fort and wandered through the many rooms of the great palace inside.

The day after they arrived in Delhi, they spent several hours with Pyarelal Nayar, the author of several books on Gandhi's life and the history of his movement, and Pyarelal also introduced them to many people who had known Gandhi. They devoted most of their last week in India, based at the Quaker Center, to discussing all that they had seen. Their whirlwind tour had taken them around the entire coast of India. They had traveled outside the United States only once before, when they visited Ghana. These four weeks in India constituted a real pilgrimage, full of unforgettable impressions that left them both imbued with the spirit of Gandhi as never before. Even more than their brief meeting with Nkrumah in Accra, the weeks in India left Martin with an inescapable sense of his stature on the world stage. He felt so much more a part of world history and human destiny. This growth, and his realization of it, would have broad implications in the months and years ahead.

The Kings and Dr. Reddick left Delhi early in the morning of March 10. The day before, they had held a press conference at the Gandhi Smarak Nidhi. "We have learned a lot," said Martin Luther King.

We are not rash enough [he continued] to presume that we know India—vast subcontinent with all of its people, problems, contrasts

and achievements. However . . . we venture one or two generali-
zations.

First, we think that the spirit of Gandhi is much stronger today than
some people believe. There is not only the direct and indirect influence
of his comrades and associates but also . . . the work of the Gandhi
Smarak Nidhi and the movement led by the sainted Vinoba
Bhave. . . .

Secondly, I wish to make a plea to the people and government of
India. The issue of world peace is so critical that I feel compelled to
offer a suggestion that came to me during the course of our conver-
sations with Vinobaji.[5]

The peace-loving peoples of the world have not succeeded in per-
suading my own country, America, and Soviet Russia, to eliminate
fear and disarm themselves. Unfortunately, as yet America and the
Soviet Union have not shown the faith and moral courage to do this.
Vinobaji has said that India or any other nation that has the faith and
moral courage could disarm itself tomorrow, even unilaterally.

Having demonstrated that a nation could win its independence
nonviolently, said King:

India may have to take the lead and call for universal disarmament,
and if no other nation will join her immediately, India should declare
itself for disarmament unilaterally.

Such an act of courage would be a great demonstration of the spirit
of the Mahatma and would be the greatest stimulus to the rest of the
world to do likewise. Moreover, any nation that would take such a
step would automatically so draw to itself the multitudes of the earth
that any would-be aggressor would be discouraged from risking the
wrath of mankind.

It seemed strange, as they boarded the plane the next morning, to see Jim Bristol waving goodbye—and Swami Vishwan-
anda, too—for he and Bristol had been their constant companions. As the Swami later wrote, "Some of us were very silent; the
relationship that had developed was too sacred. When the heart

[5] The -*ji* suffix is often added to Indian names as a mark of respect, as
in Vinobaji, Gandhiji, etc.

speaks, the tongue is silent. Our eyes searched the skies until the plane that carried the Kings . . . disappeared over the horizon."

Black Americans were restive when Martin King returned from India. Nearly five years had passed since the Supreme Court had decreed the end of segregated schooling, and, indeed, a number of other rulings favoring equal treatment for Negroes had been handed down. Progress was visible. For each city wracked with struggle, a score of others had quietly let down the bars. The Southern white power structure was learning, as their Northern cousins already knew, that they need not have segregation statutes in order to "keep the niggers down." A gesture here, a token there, could mollify white consciences. Desegregation did not necessarily mean integration. White resistance, as officials in Montgomery had been among the first to learn, could even include a measure of courtesy toward prominent black agitators—the crude extremism of the Klan, whose image and tactics were deplored as "oafish" by such men as Grover Hall, editor of the Montgomery *Advertiser,* was passé.

But close examination of American life and mores at the time of Martin King's return disclosed very little actual integration, even in the citadels of liberalism. On the rosters of leading organizations committed to the principles of equality, in the offices of Americans for Democratic Action or the American Civil Liberties Union, how many black persons could one find? In any "integrated" school, at most, one found only a token cluster of black students, often shunned by their white classmates. White America had barely begun to recognize the malaise which permeated every pore of the body politic and inhabited the white psyche, tinging the attitudes of the most guileless and well-meaning. America's self-discovery had barely begun.

Revolutions are born not of hopeless despair but of a spark of desperate hope. Change begets the demand for more and faster change, spiraling upward and gaining in acceleration at each disclosure of a new possibility. The Negroes' wartime gains

were slim. So were those that followed the Montgomery boycott. The Civil Rights Act of 1957 contributed a mere pittance
toward securing equality. But each represented a step forward,
and added together, they gave a certain solidity to a growing
expectation, a leverage on the future. Each fell short of the
mark, whetting the Negroes' insistence on their *full* rights as
citizens and emboldening them to redouble their efforts in their
next surge toward the long-deferred goal. White people did not
understand this. Viewed externally, the black man seemed a
glutton. Half a loaf means something quite different to a starving man than it does to a man already corpulent with inequitable
affluence. The fat man could justly say that the Negroes
"never had it so good," but he was blind to the significance of
his own remark. If Negroes had it so good that they had begun
to realize how deprived they really were, they would soon demand all that was rightfully theirs, without too tender a regard
for Mister Charlie's inconvenience.

Such was the dynamic of history at work in 1959. The second Youth March for Integration, on April 18, was followed a
week later by the lynching of Mack Parker in Poplarville, Mississippi, and a rising demand that his killers be punished. Out
of this clamor, new voices of black militancy began to rise—the
voices of Elijah Muhammad, leader of the black Nation of Islam,
and his brilliant and fiery lieutenant, Malcolm Little, who, under the name Malcolm X, rejected appeals to "the conscience
of white America" and excoriated Martin Luther King for advocating defenselessness in the face of the perfidy of "blue-
eyed devils." What Malcolm X said made sense to thousands
who thronged to hear him on street corners in the black ghettos
of the North, and he posed a serious challenge to Martin
Luther King's leadership of the nationwide movement for freedom,
although he made no inroads on King's native grounds in the
South.

Another challenge, however, arose in Monroe County, North

Carolina, where local NAACP president Robert F. Williams formed an armed guard which exchanged gunfire with Klansmen and police. Williams, a Marine Corps veteran, asserted that Monroe County Negroes had tried nonviolence and appeals to state and federal authorities, all to no avail. "The Montgomery bus boycott," he wrote, "was a great victory for American democracy," but not the prescription for every situation. "If Mack Parker had had an automatic shotgun," he argued, "he could have served as a great deterrent against lynching."

"The struggle for civil rights," Martin Luther King observed, "has reached a stage of profound crisis. . . . Full integration can easily become a distant or mythical goal . . . and in the quest for social calm a compromise [may be] firmly implanted in which the real goals are merely token integration for a long period to come." Such a compromise had been inflicted in 1878, but Negroes would not accept another. Negroes today, he noted, would rather resort to arms, as Robert Williams had done. "When the Negro uses force in self-defense," said King, "he does not forfeit support—he may even win it, by the courage and self-respect it reflects. . . . It is unfortunately true that however the Negro acts, his struggle will not be free of violence initiated by his enemies, and he will need ample courage and willingness to sacrifice to defeat this manifestation of violence. But if he seeks it and organizes it, he cannot win. . . .

"There is more power in socially organized masses on the march than there is in guns in the hands of a few desperate men," he continued. "Our enemies would prefer to deal with a small armed group than with a huge, unarmed but resolute mass of people." Gandhi, he said, counseled his followers in the struggle against the British, "Never let them rest." "Our powerful weapons are the voices, the feet, and the bodies of dedicated, united people moving without rest toward a just goal. Greater tyrants than Southern segregationists have been subdued and defeated by this form of struggle. We have not yet used it, and it would be tragic if we spurned it because we have failed to perceive its dynamic strength and power."

The nonviolent movement continued its plowing and sowing. In July, a three-day Institute on Nonviolence and Segregation at Spelman College in Atlanta was co-sponsored by SCLC, CORE, and the Fellowship of Reconciliation. Randolph, Reddick, Rustin, Lawson, Richard Gregg, and William Stuart Nelson all spoke. In August, the MIA readied its forces for a September school-integration drive that was paralleled by SCLC affiliates elsewhere, and on September 5 in Miami, CORE began a two-week workshop in nonviolent strategy and tactics, emphasizing the sit-in technique it had employed in Northern cities since 1942.

During the summer, Martin Luther King's SCLC colleagues suggested that the time had come for him to move to Atlanta. Ella Baker, a dark-skinned and very beautiful veteran NAACP field secretary, had played a major part, along with Bayard Rustin, in organizing SCLC in 1957. In 1958, she had set up a permanent office in Atlanta to which Dr. King commuted from time to time. It was growing increasingly obvious that if SCLC was to play its destined role in the years ahead, it would require an Atlanta-based staff, and its president must be prepared to spend more time there as well.

Martin's brother A.D. had long since worked out his differences with their father. Giving up his job as a life insurance salesman, he had returned to Morehouse. When Martin moved to Montgomery, he accepted his father's invitation to step in as assistant pastor of Ebenezer Baptist Church. Now A.D. was ready to move on and was considering the pastorate of the First Baptist Church in Birmingham. Martin, Sr., eager to welcome his namesake back as co-pastor, understood that SCLC would have a certain priority on the latter's time and energies.

Martin and Coretta were reluctant to take the step. Both of them had sunk their roots in Montgomery, but Coretta realized as much as he did that the move was inevitable. Ralph Abernathy would be moving, too, for the same reason. On Sunday, November 29, Dr. King told his congregation that he was unprepared to preach and turned the pulpit over to another minister. Then, before giving the benediction, he asked the church members to remain for a brief period while he announced his plans. He needed, he said, "to reorganize my personality and reorient my life. . . . I can't stop now. History has thrust something upon me which I cannot turn away. . . . I would like to submit my resignation as pastor of Dexter Avenue Baptist Church to become effective on the fourth Sunday in January." After the formalities were concluded, everyone joined hands and sang "Blest Be the Tie That Binds." And feeling its knot in his heart, Martin's eyes flooded with tears.

The next day, he issued a statement to the press, dated for release on Tuesday morning. "The time has come," the statement said, "for a bold, broad advance of the Southern campaign for equality. After prayerful consideration, I am convinced that the psychological moment has come when a concentrated drive against injustice can bring great, tangible gains. We must not let the present strategic opportunity pass. Very soon our new program will be announced. Not only will it include a stepped-up campaign of voter registration, but a full-scale assault will be made upon discrimination and segregation in all forms. We must train our youth and adult leaders in the techniques of social change through nonviolent resistance. We must employ new methods of struggle involving the masses of the people."

Martin Luther King and the
Republican White House

For his share in the big "next step," King decided that the time
had come to pick up the bid that Vice-President Nixon had extended to him in Ghana. Such a meeting would have Eisenhower's
blessings, for Sherman Adams had written to King that "the President . . . is pleased to know that you will be meeting with the
Vice-President. . . ."

Nixon was a good man to see. For one thing, the newspapers
had him at various times as "Acting President" and "heir apparent." For another thing, his report on his good-will tour of Africa
had been widely quoted and praised in the Negro press as well
as in the American press in general. "We in the United States,"
he urged, "must come to know, to understand, and to find common ground with the peoples of this great continent." Nixon
called for economic and technical assistance to the Africans and
a firm policy of nondiscrimination. On this he said, "We cannot
talk equality to the peoples of Africa and Asia and practice in-
equality in the United States." This was what Negro leaders had

From pp. 198-202, 215-225, *Crusader Without Violence* by L. D. Reddick. Copyright © 1959 by Lawrence Dunbar Reddick. Reprinted by permission of Harper & Row, Publishers.

been saying all along. They were pleased that the nation's number-two man was standing with them on the relationship of foreign and domestic racial practice.

King could have seen Nixon alone; instead, he took along his "right arm," Abernathy. The two boycott veterans trudged up Capitol Hill on Thursday afternoon, June 13 [1957]. Nixon, accompanied by James P. Mitchell, Secretary of Labor, met them at the Formal Room of the Capitol. It was 3:25 P.M. Some seventy-odd pressmen were there waiting. While photographs were being taken, Nixon, easy and informal, kidded King that the picture would look better if Coretta were there. This done, the photographers hurried away, but the newsmen said that they would wait until the interview was over and get statements.

With the preliminary public relations out of the way, the four conferees retired to the Vice-President's office. The conference was scheduled to last for an hour, but Nixon said immediately, "Take plenty of time; there is no rush," and invited everybody to draw up his chair a little closer.

Abernathy and King had worked out some points that they intended to make. Some of their friends had also given them some briefing, warning them to beware of Nixon's "noncommittal charm."

King started things off. He began to describe the situation in the South, for he and his colleagues had said repeatedly that Washington surely would do more, if it but knew. He told of the bombings, intimidations, disfranchisement, corruption of the legal system, and the various pressures put upon those who would be courageous.

Then Abernathy picked up the discussion and characteristically described the conflict situation more bluntly. He said that Negroes were resolute and so were white segregationists; Negroes meant to have their rights *now* and would not be hoodwinked or frightened from them. At the same time, he continued, their opponents were equally determined "that the house that they have ruled for so long will not pass from under their control."

In between these two active and opposing groups, Abernathy explained, were most white Southerners. They were not members of the White Citizens Councils or the Ku Klux Klan. Perhaps they preferred segregation but would go along with the law, if those in authority made it clear that the law really meant "desegregate." Abernathy said that he was sure that the President did not realize what the situation was or else he would have spoken out, adding with a smile that the Vice-President had spoken out more clearly than had the President.

Nixon smiled, too, but came to the President's defense, quietly and pleasantly. The President, he pointed out, was not making as many speeches as was the Vice-President and thus did not get around to all of the subjects. Moreover, the President had called together the Republican members of Congress and told them that he did not believe in platform hypocrisy and that civil rights was in the Republican platform.

The discussion then moved directly to the civil rights debate then raging in Congress. Nixon thought that a civil rights bill would pass the House and had a fifty-fifty chance of getting through the Senate.

When King said that neither party had done much to push the bill, Nixon referred to insincere legislators who played politics by introducing civil rights bills that they knew had no chance of passing, just so they could say back home, "You see, I'm for civil rights." He praised the President and the Republicans for favoring a bill that had some reality about it that had a chance of becoming law.

Nixon then went back to the subject of the South, asking about the cooperation that came from white preachers there. King and Abernathy answered that privately many of them endorsed the Supreme Court's decision but feared to do so publicly; more would come out and take a stand if the President and Vice-President would speak up strongly for the court decrees.

Then King put the concrete proposition up to the Vice-President: What about coming south and making a speech for law and order? Nixon agreed that the general idea was good but had questions about the best way to carry it out. If he came south at the request of Negroes, he said, he would be speaking to Negroes. This reasoning seemed odd, but King and Abernathy let the point pass. Nixon thought that perhaps he could come south naturally in connection with the work of the Committee on Government Contracts that he had worked with for a long while.

Mitchell then took over and gave a rather lengthy description of the committee's operations and the way it sought to persuade concerns that held contracts with the federal government to abide by the clauses prohibiting discrimination in employment on the basis of color, creed, or national origin.

Mitchell said that the committee had difficulty whenever it tried to break new ground. It was, for instance, hard to get Negroes into the "air industry." Stewardesses had to go through a lengthy training period before they were assigned, and a pilot had to work his way up from training school to co-pilot first. A Negro had to be not merely good but excellent before the airlines would agree to let him fly a plane.

Then the conversation faded back to Nixon's personally coming along with the committee on its schedule of hearings in the South.

Later, Abernathy said that he felt like interrupting at this point and suggesting that Nixon either come south and make a report to the President as he did on the Hungarian refugees or come south and make a good-will tour as he had done abroad. But Abernathy held himself back. He did not wish to break up the interview by pressing too hard. After all, he reminded himself, he was really an extra at the conference.

Nixon asked where in the South it would be most appropriate for him to appear if he could make just one stop. King suggested Atlanta or New Orleans. Atlanta seemed a good choice to both the Vice-President and the Secretary of Labor, for the Committee on Government Contracts would be there soon.

Finally, the conversation came back to the question of the

President. What would he do? Nixon thought that maybe Mr. Eisenhower himself would like to hear firsthand about conditions in the South. Accordingly, Nixon suggested that it might be well to wait until the civil rights fight in Congress was concluded and then if King would send him a memorandum on it, he would help arrange a meeting for him and others with the President.

The talk had gone on for two hours and ten minutes. Everybody had indeed taken his time. The Vice-President and the Secretary of Labor had apparently been genuinely interested. King and Abernathy felt good about the interview although they did not get all that they had wanted.

As King and Abernathy emerged from Nixon's office, a tall, brown-skinned stranger appeared suddenly and attempted to whisk them away. This man was Bayard Rustin. He hurried the two boycott leaders down a corridor and out a side door, toward a waiting automobile for a quick getaway.

But the newsmen, who had been waiting for them to emerge, caught sight of the three fast-moving figures and gave chase. But there was no stopping Rustin, who was King's public relations representative. Slamming the car door shut, he shouted that there would be no statements from King until the press conference that he was setting up for six o'clock at the Raleigh Hotel. The reporters were furious.

Later at the press conference, King spoke less about the conversation with Nixon than about his own plans, which grew only in part out of the recent interview. He said that he appealed to the Vice-President to do three things: first, come south and speak; secondly, urge all Southerners to support the law as interpreted by the Supreme Court; thirdly, call together Republicans in Congress and urge them to fight for the enactment of the civil rights bill. He then added that he was recommending to Negroes that they "hold unswervingly to nonviolence in word, thought, and deed," for if they did, they would win.

He got a good press on this, but there were a few journalists whom he had not enchanted. One of them, Louis Lautier of the

National Negro Newspaper Publishers Association, gave King his first real roasting in the Negro press. It would not be his last.

Lautier's piece appeared in most of the Negro weeklies for June 22. The *Afro* carried it on page one, under a big picture of King and Nixon shaking hands. The three-column lead for the story read, "Was King Ready?" with the subhead: "Opportunity with Nixon Seen Missed." The first paragraphs said:

> The Rev. Martin Luther King, Jr., leader of the Montgomery (Ala.) bus boycott, is an estimable young man and excellent pulpit orator, but he is not yet ready for the political big-time.
>
> At his press conference here, after he and the Rev. Ralph D. Abernathy, another leader in the bus boycott, talked with Vice-President Nixon for more than two hours, he showed that he has more homework to do if he is to become a political as well as a spiritual leader.

Lautier added that King answered specific political questions with generalities, and that Secretary of Labor James P. Mitchell gave the reporters more of the meat of the Nixon conference than did King himself.

. . . . . .

As King became less tied down by the MIA he became more and more involved in the program of SCLC. This furnished a broad base for activating the whole South and an appropriate platform from which any national action that he thought necessary could be taken.

The SCLC still dreamed the great dream of registering millions of dark-skinned Southerners and had ready ideas as to how this could be done. But the implementation came more slowly. Big conferences and mass meetings were easier.

The SCLC met in Memphis in mid-November of 1957, but it was December before the central office was opened, and then with only a temporary commitment from Miss Ella Baker as director. Bayard Rustin would lend a hand in an emergency but afterward he would be off, following his star to another great cause in some corner of the world. For example, on the morning of April 4, 1958, CBS in its *World News Roundup,* reporting on a mass march on Trafalgar Square, London, in protest against nuclear bomb tests, said, "And the leader of the parade is an American Negro, Bayard Rustin."

King called his SCLC board together in Atlanta in January, 1958, urging full attendance, for "this will be our last meeting before the mammoth kick-off for the Citizenship Crusade on Wednesday, February 12."

And so, last-minute plans were made. Leaflets were printed; news releases issued; and instructions were sent out to local committees. The big idea was to have giant mass meetings in twenty Southern cities—all on Lincoln's birthday.

When February 12 came, the pulpit orators had their audiences singing and shouting. If the SCLC had only the setup to crystallize the enthusiasm! The general morale effect was good but actually the names of few new voters would get on the books during the next month or so. The crusade, however, did stimulate local groups that already had workers in the field.

On April 30, the SCLC board met again. The long search for an executive director was ended. The Reverend John L. Tilley, who had done a splendid job of voter registration in Baltimore, made plans to move into the Atlanta office with Miss Baker, who was now designated as associate director.

The board also set plans for an open conference in Mississippi for May 29. This was daring, for to many Negroes and their friends "Mississippi" has an evil sound, with loud echoes of plantations and white man bosses and the painful cries of Emmet Till and his brothers. Moreover, in 1956 the Governor of Mississippi had warned King to stay away.

In due course May 29 came and the conference was held as scheduled. Actually, some of the conferees who had thought that going into Mississippi was an act of bravery afterward were loud in their praises of the department of the police, newsmen, and white Mississippians they encountered. The news stories on the activities of the conference deserve to be described as "objective" and no case of the expected brutality of local or state "peace" officers was reported. Governor Coleman did not interfere with Dr. King, and Mississippi Negro leaders came out to the meeting in force. The bulletin of the SCLC described the Clarksdale assembly as "best meeting yet—in attendance, enthusiasm, and sense of direction." This was the most "down-to-earth" conference the SCLC had ever held; there were fewer speeches, more field reports and analysis. At last it seemed that the organization had "found" itself.

In terms of national affairs, the conference shot a single arrow into the air. It scored a direct hit. Its target was the White House. This was a letter to President Eisenhower saying:

Amid continued violence in the South and the dreadful prospect that some areas may close schools rather than obey Federal Court Orders to desegregate in September we urgently renew our request that you grant an immediate conference to Negro leaders in an effort to resolve these problems. . . . Since quite some time ago you promised to meet with Negro leaders and because the present climate of lawless defiance threatens to produce incidents that will shame America at home and abroad when school opens in September, we respectfully request an immediate audience.

About a week later, the answer came back. It was a telephone call from the White House: Yes, the President did find it possible to see Dr. King and a few others. Please come to Washington so that the particulars of the conference could be worked out.

This was great news! King would be in Washington on June 9. On the way, he stopped to receive two more honorary degrees: Doctor of Laws from Morgan State College, Baltimore, Maryland, and Doctor of Humane Letters from Central State College, Xenia, Ohio.

Mrs. King continued to match strides, so to speak, with her husband, making "Woman's Day" talks at churches in Denver and Dayton, and singing at Birmingham.

In Washington, King met with White House aides Rocco Sicili-

ano and E. Frederic Morrow and a member of the staff of the
United States Attorney General. At this preliminary meeting,
the date for the White House session was set at June 23,
11:15 A.M. King got the impression that the interview with
the President would last for fifteen minutes.

The next question was, who should come? King's first thought
had been to suggest the names of his top colleagues of SCLC,
for the White House bid had come in response to that organization's requests. But he felt that the conference might be so significant that a national rather than a strictly Southern representation
should be made. So King suggested his fellow co-chairmen of
the Washington pilgrimage, A. Philip Randolph and Roy Wilkins.

Randolph was acceptable but there was some objection to
Wilkins from the White House representatives on the grounds
that perhaps the President would not want to talk with anyone
who had spoken of him the way Wilkins had at the Negro "sum-
mit" conference. This was a meeting of some four hundred
heads of organizations, scholars, and others, that the National
Negro Publishers Association had held in Washington on May
12 and 13. Almost every Negro leader had been there except
Martin Luther King. And he was absent because he had a long-
standing commitment to the American Jewish Congress which
was meeting at the same time in Miami.

President Eisenhower spoke to the publishers and their guests
for twelve minutes. First, he urged his mutual security, defense,
and foreign aid program. Then he came to civil rights, saying:

. . . every American, if we are to be true to our constitutional heritage, must have respect for the law. He must know that he is equal
before the law. He must have respect for the courts.

He must have respect for others. He must make perfectly certain
that he can, in every single kind of circumstance, respect himself.

In such problems as this, there are no revolutionary cures. They are
evolutionary. I started in the Army in 1911. I have lived to see the
time come when in none of the armed services is practiced any kind
of discrimination because of race, religion, or color.

In the federal government this same truth holds steady. . . . But I do believe that as long as there are human problems . . . we must have patience and forbearance.

I do not decry laws, for they are necessary. But I say that laws themselves will never solve problems that have their roots in the human heart and in the human emotions.

The "patience and forbearance" advice did not go down easily with the delegates. For one, Roy Wilkins said:

I understand the President of the United States gave you some startling advice this afternoon. I guess from where he sits, this makes sense. If you were President, you would want everything to go smoothly. You wouldn't want anyone to kick up a fuss—labor, Democrats, the Negro. If you could convince the Negro that he was being impatient, I guess you would do so. From where Mr. Eisenhower sits, I suppose this makes sense. I don't sit there.

This was mild in comparison with comments of others. Almost every Negro newspaper that editorialized on the conference rejected "patience and forbearance."

King asked the White House men if they had seen his criticism of the President. They said that they had. King had called Eisenhower's words "potentially dangerous," adding that they would only "encourage those who have defied the Supreme Court decisions and who have created the climate of tension and crisis culminating across the South." Then he indicated in his indirect way that if Wilkins did not come he himself would not come. So Wilkins was declared acceptable.

Then the aides brought up the name of Lester B. Granger, who was thought to be a rather conservative liberal and perhaps a Republican. He was thoroughly acceptable to King, who remembered him from the celebration in Ghana and had occasionally encountered him in and about New York before and since.

The preliminaries concluded, King notified Randolph, Wilkins, and Granger that they would be receiving invitations from the White House. Everybody was delighted and agreed that the four of them should put their heads together before going in to talk with the President. The best day for this would be June 22, the Sunday before the Monday of the White House visit.

Meanwhile the news leaked out that Eisenhower would meet with several Negro leaders. Congressman Adam Powell assumed that this was the meeting that he had been promised by the White House as far back as the time when the Little Rock issue first flared. Powell made an announcement to the press and actually named the persons that he felt should compose the delegation. The White House promptly let it be known that this was not Powell's meeting and that Powell himself would not be in the group, though King, Randolph, Wilkins, and Granger would.

Back in Montgomery, King and his advisors went to work. This time there would be no charge of homework undone. Accordingly, a six-page memorandum was put together and sent airmail to Randolph, Wilkins, and Granger. In turn these three prepared memoranda supplementing and correcting King's and brought them along to the planning session of Sunday, June 22, at the headquarters of the Washington NAACP. King arrived at 9 P.M. and found the other three already there. It was a real work session, lasting until 4 A.M.

At first, Wilkins was a little reluctant to have things cut-and-dried. He himself was a master at improvisation and naturally favored feeling out the situation, sensing the flow of things as the conversation with the President proceeded, pushing wherever possible, retreating wherever necessary. In this way, he felt, more would be gained. But the others thought that a set plan should be drawn; however, if the talk took a special direction of its own, then the plan might be thrown aside and the topic of the moment followed. Thus agreed, the men then laid out their memos on the table. King had also a dozen telegrams from various other persons whom he had asked for suggestions. So, far into the early morning hours the men talked, wrote, and rewrote until they had hammered out a seven-page statement. Later Granger would say everybody had agreed to every word of it.

The men also determined the procedure they would follow in talking with the President. Randolph would lead off, making the opening statement; then King, Wilkins, and Granger would each discuss three of the nine points of the joint memorandum. Copies of the document would be made available to the President and the press.

Feeling that they had done a good night's work, the men separated, dashing off to catch a few hours of sleep. As King went away, he felt satisfied with the evening's labor, for everyone had got along well together. He had expected this from his two old pilgrimage colleagues, Randolph and Wilkins. He was delighted to find that it was also true of Granger, for this was the first time that King had had close contact with him.

Lester Blackwell Granger was a social welfare expert. His name was synonymous with the National Urban League, of which he was executive secretary. Until a few years ago, almost all of Granger's problems seemed to dissolve when confronted by his ability and charm. He was a success as a tennis champion, an artillery lieutenant in the First World War, and a social worker. He had attended mixed schools for most of his education, and while at Dartmouth was a schoolmate of James V. Forrestal, later Secretary of the Navy and Secretary of Defense.

It was Granger, more than any other single individual, who gave expert advice on the integration of Negro and white servicemen in the Navy under Forrestal. Everybody in Washington who knew Granger liked him, as did his fellow social workers all over the country, who elected him president of the National Conference of Social Work.

But ten years ago, Granger's good fortune deserted him—at least temporarily. He was stricken with cancer and about the same time began having trouble with his board of directors at the National Urban League. Only his close friends knew about his illness but the revolt of his board finally broke into the newspapers. Some of his most prominent Negro members—such as Kenneth Clark, the psychologist, and Ted Brown, AFL-CIO research specialist—issued public statements and resigned. Their charges were that the League's board was self-perpetuating and undemocratic and that this made it easy for a clique of wealthy men—some of whom were in real estate—to sabotage any real programs of integration, especially in the housing field.

Miraculously, Granger survived both of these attacks. He is today one of those fortunates who have been cured of cancer because it was detected early. Granger also regrouped his board and projected a harder-hitting program for the League.

In June of 1958 he was sixty-one, balding, and graying. His step was no longer spry. A line or two marked the Granger smile. But he was still very much himself—sincere and affable, and not wanting people to mistake his pleasantness for conservatism.

The conferees met on time: 10:30, June 23, in the outer office reception room of the White House. There was ample time (forty-five minutes) for the exchange of stray thoughts that had come to them since they had parted. They were told that they would have thirty minutes with the President. They agreed that they would not quote him directly afterward, leaving him free to make his own statement in words of his own choosing. Morrow, Siciliano, and Attorney General William P. Rogers came in. Everybody was chatting amicably when the signal came (11:15) that "Gentlemen, the President will see you now."

The conferees took seats fanning out from the President's big desk in a broken circle, King sitting directly opposite the chief executive. After the preliminaries were over, Randolph, according to plan, began. He was completely at ease; his first White House conference had taken place back in the days when he was with a delegation, led by the fiery Monroe Trotter, during the Coolidge administration. Randolph, omitting the preamble of the joint statement, read aloud the nine points:

1. The President of the United States should declare in a nationwide pronouncement, prior to September, that the law will be vigorously upheld with the total resources at his command.

2. Much emphasis has been laid on the need for restoring communication between white and colored Southerners who are troubled by a common fear of reaction. The President can well set the example in this matter by convoking a White House Conference of constructive leadership to discuss ways and means of complying peaceably with the Court's rulings.

3. Information, resources, and advice of the appropriate government agencies addressed to the problems of integration should be made available to all officials and community groups seeking to work out a program of education and action.

4. The President should request both parties to lay aside partisanship so that the Congress can enact a civil rights bill which will include Part III originally in the 1957 bill, in order that constitutional rights other than voting rights may be enforced by the United States Attorney General. Lack of adequate and clear statutory authority has made the federal government a mere spectator in the disgraceful maneuverings at Little Rock.

5. We urge the President to direct the Department of Justice to give all legal assistance possible under the law, including the filing of a brief as a friend of the court and appearance of counsel, in the appeal from the [Judge Harry] Lemley decision in the Little Rock case.

6. The President of the United States should direct the Department of Justice to act now to protect the right of citizens to register and vote. In the nine months since the enactment of the 1957 Civil Rights Act, overt acts have been committed against prospective Negro registrants in some areas and numerous complaints have been submitted to the Department, but to date, not a single case has reached a court of law. Unless immediate action is undertaken, thousands of Negro citizens will be denied the right to cast a ballot in the 1958 elections.

7. The President should direct the Department of Justice to act under existing statutes in the wave of bombings of churches, synagogues, homes, and community centers; also in the murderous brutality directed against Negro citizens in Dawson, Georgia, and other communities.

8. In order to counteract the deliberate hamstringing of the new Civil Rights Commission, the President should recommend to the Con-

gress the extension of its life for at least a full year beyond its present expiration date.

9. The President should make it clear both in statement and in act that he believes in the principle that federal money should not be used to underwrite segregation in violation of the federal constitutional rights of millions of Negro citizens, and that this principle should be applied whether in matters of federal aid to education, hospitals, housing, or any other grants-in-aid to state and local government. In support of national policy, the federal government should finance continuation of public schools where state funds are withdrawn because of integration.

The President seemed to listen intently. Then, each man, on cue from Randolph, took up a section of the document, elaborating and explaining. The President followed them closely, occasionally frowning or smiling and asking a question here or there as the exposition went along.

King observed that the conference with the President seemed to transform the personalities of two of his colleagues. Wilkins, the man whom the administration shrank from meeting because he personified that horned devil NAACP, turned out to be the most moderate of the conferees. On the other hand, Granger was the most aggressive. Apparently, he was not going to have anybody think that he was holding back or being soft. In his column in the *Amsterdam News* for May 24, he had written: "President Eisenhower's 'Patience and Forbearance' message to Negro leadership assembled at Washington, D.C., could not have been more poorly timed, from the standpoint of the government and our Afro-American population." Granger repeated this to the President, who flushed for a moment, then recovered his composure.

King was also surprised to find that the President did not know that Negroes were greatly displeased with his administration for not supporting the Supreme Court's integration decrees more strongly. King wondered what the President's advisors had told him on this score.

The President spoke generally, saying in broad terms that he believed in law and order and that all Americans should have their rights. But he would not be drawn into any definite commitment as to what he would do. He would not even comment on the current Little Rock situation.

The President spoke briefly of some of the things that his administration had done for the benefit of all Americans, including Negroes. Attorney General Rogers took over at this point, extending the President's remarks.

By this time, thirty minutes for the interview had stretched into fifty. As the group was breaking up to leave, the President again expressed faith and optimism. At a moment when King was near him, Mr. Eisenhower said with a sigh, "Reverend, there are so many problems . . . Lebanon, Algeria . . ."

The Presidential aides preferred that the Negro leaders not release their nine-point statement to the press, but they did. Wilkins was designated as spokesman to the waiting journalists, photographers, and TV men. According to protocol, he concentrated upon what the Negro leaders had said rather than on what the President had said to them. Wilkins expressed encouragement from the talk. But the reporters would not be put off with generalities. One of them asked: "Did you come away with the impression that the President would do anything about your suggestions?" Wilkins' answer was that if the President had immediately agreed to the requests of the four leaders they would not have thought that he meant it.

Then the newsmen turned to Randolph, who said:

The conference has put a new hope into the hearts of colored people, that as a part of the great American family they have greater assurance of belonging to this family as equals in order that they may utilize their gifts, talents and genius to make America great and strong.

Some of the papers merely used this quote and let it go at that. But the *Afro* commented editorially: "Come, come, Philip. You can talk plainer than that. What did the man say?"

King talked about re-establishing communication between Negroes and whites of the South. Granger said next to nothing at this time.

The *Amsterdam News* ran the headline: "Successful Meeting: Ike Says 'Nothing.' " The *Courier* expressed mixed emotions:

The question therefore arises as to what this conference accomplished except to possibly re-emphasize what is on the whole country's mind; which is all to the good, of course, but how much good? Even the most skeptical persons, however, will agree that it was better to have had it than not to have had it, because conceivably something good may come out of it.

Under the caption "Did Ike Charm Negro Leaders?" Louis Lautier wrote that

The President apparently turned on the Eisenhower charm and pacified four top colored leaders who conferred with him at the White House, Monday. After the conference none of the quartet uttered a single word in criticism of Mr. Eisenhower. Particularly noticeable was the about-face attitude of Roy Wilkins, executive secretary of the NAACP, and the Rev. Martin Luther King, leader of the Montgomery, Ala., bus boycott movement.

Earl Brown, Democrat, in his column in the *Amsterdam News* for July 5, concluded that "the conference was so meaningless that it may have been better if it had not been held at all."

Brown's fellow *Amsterdam News* columnist, Lester B. Granger, gave his estimate of the meeting he had attended: "People . . . are still asking—by phone, letters, or in casual encounters—was the meeting worthwhile? The answer is still the same, 'It depends on what you were expecting.' " Granger then went on to say that no "realist" should have looked for "definite commitments" from the President. However, the "plain-talking, face-to-face" discussion with the President demonstrated the unity of Negro leaders on civil rights. "Perhaps this will be the most lasting effect. . . ."

Back in Montgomery, King looked over his press clippings.

From coast to coast the daily as well as the weekly newspapers had featured the June 23 interview. One of the curious and perhaps revealing contrasts in the treatment of the story was furnished by *The New York Times* and the Montgomery *Advertiser*. Both papers of June 24 ran the story on page 1. But in the very spot—top, left of center—where the *Times* placed the photograph of the President and the Negro leaders, the *Advertiser* placed a picture of a handcuffed Negro criminal suspect. This was not a story of local origin but came in from New York. The *Advertiser* put the picture of Eisenhower and the Negro leaders at the bottom of its second page, a good place to hide almost anything. The *Times* story had the lead: "4 Negro Leaders See Eisenhower," the *Advertiser*: "Ike Silent on Negroes' Plea." Students of the influence of the social environment on the treatment of news—and vice versa—may find these contrasts worthy of study. However, they should know that Lester Granger cursed both papers for he was, no doubt inadvertently, left off the AP wirephoto that both the *Times* and the *Advertiser* used.

A week or so after June 23, King was asked to give his considered evaluation of the White House talk. He spoke of two positive results: First, the excellent press that gave the nine points to the nation. The American people thus got a chance to learn what was on the minds of Negro Americans and what they expect of their government; secondly, the President learned this, too. Whatever he might do or not do immediately or in the future could no longer be explained or explained away by the charitable consideration that perhaps "Ike just didn't know."

Looking back, even Wilkins agreed that it was a stroke of wisdom that the Negro leaders did prepare a document that they could present to the White House—and to the world.

And so the Reverend Dr. Martin Luther King reached a climactic point in his career. To share a conference with the President of the United States on one of the great problems of the nation is no mean achievement for a young man under thirty. . . .

★

The Highroad to Destiny

I first met Martin Luther King, Jr., nearly three years ago now, in Atlanta, Georgia. He was there on a visit from his home in Montgomery. He was "holed up," he was seeing no one, he was busy writing a book—so I was informed by the friend who, mercilessly, at my urgent request, was taking me to King's hotel. I felt terribly guilty about interrupting him but not guilty enough to let the opportunity pass. Still, having been raised among preachers, I would not have been surprised if King had cursed out the friend, refused to speak to me, and slammed the door in our faces. Nor would I have blamed him if he had, since I knew that by this time he must have been forced to suffer many an admiring fool.

But the Reverend King is not like any preacher I have ever met before. For one thing, to state it baldly, I liked him. It is rare that one *likes* a world-famous man—by the time they become world-famous they rarely like themselves, which may account for this antipathy. Yet King is immediately and tremendously winning, there is really no other word for it; and there he stood, with an inquiring and genuine smile on his face, in the open door of his hotel room. Behind him, on a desk, was a wilderness of paper. He looked at his friend, he looked at me, I was introduced; he smiled and shook my hand and we entered the room.

I do not remember much about that first meeting because I was too overwhelmed by the fact that I was meeting him at all. There were millions of questions that I wanted to ask him, but I feared to begin. Besides, his friend had warned me not to "bug" him, I was not there in a professional capacity, and the questions I wanted to ask him had less to do with his public role than with his private life. When I say "private life" I am not referring to those maliciously juicy tidbits, those meaningless details, which clutter up the gossip columns and muddy everybody's mind and obliterate the humanity of the subject as well as that of the reader. I wanted to ask him how it felt to be standing where he stood, how he bore it, what complex of miracles had prepared him for it. But such questions can scarcely be asked, they can scarcely be answered.

And King does not like to talk about himself. I have described him as winning, but he does not give the impression of being particularly outgoing or warm. His restraint is not, on the other hand, of that icily uneasy, nerve-racking kind to be encountered in so many famous Negroes who have allowed their aspirations and notoriety to destroy their identities and who always seem to be giving an uncertain imitation of some extremely improbable white man. No, King impressed me then and he impresses me now as a man solidly anchored in those spiritual realities concerning which he can be so eloquent. This divests him of the hideous piety which is so prevalent in his profession, and it also saves him from the ghastly self-importance which, until recently, was all that allowed one to be certain one was addressing a Negro leader. King cannot be considered a chauvinist at all, not even incidentally, or part of the time, or under stress, or subconsciously. What he says to Negroes he will say to whites; and what he says to whites he will say to Negroes. He is the first Negro leader in my experience, or the first in many generations, of whom this can be said; most of his predecessors were in the extraordinary position of saying to white men, *Hurry,* while saying to black men, *Wait.* This fact is of the utmost importance. It says a great deal about the situation which produced King and in which he operates; and, of course, it tells us a great deal about the man.

"He came through it all," said a friend of his to me, with wonder and not a little envy, "really unscarred. He never went around fighting with himself, like we all did." The "we" to whom this friend refers are all considerably older than King, which may have something to do with this lightly sketched species of schizophrenia; in any case, the fact that King really loves the people he represents and has—*therefore*—no hidden, interior need to hate the white people who oppose him has had and will, I think, continue to have the most far-reaching and unpredictable repercussions on our racial situation. It need scarcely be said that our racial situation is far more complex and dangerous than we are prepared to think of it as being—since our major desire is not to think of it at all—and King's role in it is of an unprecedented difficulty.

He is not, for example, to be confused with Booker T. Washington, whom we gratefully allowed to solve the racial problem singlehandedly. It was Washington who assured us, in 1895, one year before it became the law of the land, that the education of Negroes would not give them any desire to become equals; they would be content to remain—or, rather, after living for generations in the greatest intimacy with whites, to become— separate. It is a measure of the irreality to which the presence of the Negro had already reduced the nation that this utterly fantastic idea, which thoroughly controverts the purpose of education, which has no historical or psychological validity, and which denies all the principles on which the country imagines itself to have been founded, was not only accepted with cheers but became the cornerstone of an entire way of life. And this did not come about, by the way, merely because of the venom or villainy of the South. It could never have come about at all without the tacit consent of the North; and this consent robs the North, historically and actually, of any claim to moral superiority. The failure of the government to make any realistic provision for the education of tens of thousands of illiterate former slaves had the effect of dumping this problem squarely into the lap of one man—who knew, whatever else he may not have known, that the education of Negroes had somehow to be accomplished. Whether or not Washington believed what he said is certainly an interesting question. But he *did* know that he could accomplish his objective by telling white men what they wanted to hear. And it has never been very difficult for a Negro in this country to figure out what white men want to hear: he takes his condition as an echo of their desires.

There will be no more Booker T. Washingtons. And whether we like it or not, and no matter how hard or how long we oppose it, there will be no more segregated schools, there will be no more segregated anything. King is entirely right when he says that segregation is dead. The real question which faces the Republic is just how long, how violent, and how expensive the funeral is going to be; and this question it is up to the Republic to resolve, it is not really in King's hands. The sooner the corpse is buried, the sooner we can get around to the far more taxing and rewarding problems of integration, or what King calls community, and what I think of as the achievement of nationhood, or, more simply and cruelly, the growing up of this dangerously adolescent country.

I saw King again, later that same evening, at a party given by this same friend. He came late, did not stay long. I remember him standing in the shadows of the room, near a bookcase, drinking something nonalcoholic, and being patient with the interlocutor who had trapped him in this spot. He obviously wanted to get away and go to bed. King is somewhat below what is called average height, he is sturdily built, but is not quite as heavy or as stocky as he had seemed to me at first. I remember feeling, rather as though he were a younger, much-loved, and menaced brother, that he seemed very slight and vulnerable to be taking on such tremendous odds.

I was leaving for Montgomery the next day, and I called on King in the morning to ask him to have someone from the Montgomery Improvement Association meet me at the airport. It was he who had volunteered to do this for me, since he knew that I knew no one there, and he also probably realized that I was frightened. He was coming to Montgomery on Sunday to preach in his own church.

Montgomery is the cradle of the Confederacy, an unlucky distinction which no one in Montgomery is allowed to forget. The White House which symbolized and housed that short-lived government is still standing, and "people," one of the Montgomery ministers told me, "walk around in those halls and cry." I do not doubt it, the people of Montgomery having inherited nothing less than an ocean of spilt milk. The boycott had been over for a year by the time I got there, and had been ended by a federal decree outlawing segregation in the buses. Therefore, the atmosphere in Montgomery was extraordinary. I think that I have never been in a town so aimlessly hostile, so baffled and demoralized. Whoever has a stone to fling, and flings it, is then left without any weapons; and this was (and remains) the situation of the white people in Montgomery.

I took a bus ride, for example, solely in order to observe the situation on the buses. As I stepped into the bus, I suddenly remembered that I had neglected to ask anyone the price of a bus ride in Montgomery, and so I asked the driver. He gave me the strangest, most hostile of looks, and turned his face away. I dropped fifteen cents into the box and sat down, placing myself, delicately, just a little forward of the center of the bus. The driver had seemed to feel that my question was but another Negro trick, that I had something up my sleeve, and that to answer my question in any way would be to expose himself to disaster. He could not guess what I was thinking, and he was not going to risk further personal demoralization by trying to. And this spirit was the spirit of the town. The bus pursued its course, picking up white and Negro passengers. Negroes sat where they pleased, none very far back; one large woman, carrying packages, seated herself directly behind the driver. And the whites sat there, ignoring them, in a huffy, offended silence.

This silence made me think of nothing so much as the silence which follows a really serious lovers' quarrel: the whites, beneath their cold hostility, were mystified and deeply hurt. They had been betrayed by the Negroes, not merely because the Negroes had declined to remain in their "place," but because the Negroes had refused to be controlled by the town's image of them. And, without this image, it seemed to me, the whites were abruptly and totally lost. The very foundations of their private and public worlds were being destroyed.

I had never heard King preach, and I went on Sunday to hear him at his church. This church is a red brick structure, with a steeple, and it directly faces, on the other side of the street, a white, domed building. My notes fail to indicate whether this is the actual capitol of the state or merely a courthouse; but the conjunction of the two buildings, the steepled one low and dark and tense, the domed one higher and dead white and forbidding, sums up, with an explicitness a set designer might hesitate to copy, the struggle now going on in Montgomery.

At that time in Montgomery, King was almost surely the most beloved man there. I do not think that one could have entered any of the packed churches at that time, if King was present, and not have felt this. Of course, I think that King would be loved by his congregations in any case, and there is always a large percentage of church women who adore the young male pastor, and not always, or not necessarily, out of those grim, psychic motives concerning which everyone today is so knowledgeable. No, there was a feeling in this church which quite transcended anything I have ever felt in a church before. Here it was, totally familiar and yet completely new, the packed church, glorious with the Sunday finery of the women, solemn with the touching, gleaming sobriety of the men, beautiful with children. Here were the ushers, standing in the aisles in white dresses or in dark suits, with arm bands on. People were standing along each wall, beside the windows, and standing in the back. King and his lieutenants were in the pulpit, young Martin—as I was beginning to think of him—in the center chair.

When King rose to speak—to preach—I began to understand how the atmosphere of this church differed from that of all the other churches I have known. At first I thought that the great emotional power and authority of the Negro church was being put to a new use, but this is not exactly the case. The Negro church was playing the same role which it has always played in Negro life, but it had acquired a new power.

Until Montgomery, the Negro church, which has always been the place where protest and condemnation could be most vividly articulated, also operated as a kind of sanctuary. The minister who spoke could not hope to effect any objective change in the lives of his hearers, and the people did not expect him to. All they came to find, and all that he could give them, was the sustenance for another day's journey. Now, King could certainly give his congregation that, but he could also give them something more than that, and he had. It is true that it was *they* who had begun the struggle of which he was now the symbol and the leader; it is true that it had taken all of *their* insistence to overcome in him a grave reluctance to stand where he now stood. But it is also true, and it does not happen often, that once he had accepted the place they had prepared for him, their struggle became absolutely indistinguishable from his own, and took over and controlled his life. He suffered with them and, thus, he helped them to suffer. The joy which filled this church, therefore, was the joy achieved by people who have ceased to delude themselves about an intolerable situation, who have found their prayers for a leader miraculously answered, and who now know that they can change their situation, if they will.

And, surely, very few people had ever spoken to them as King spoke. King is a great speaker. The secret of his greatness does not lie in his voice or his presence or his manner, though it has something to do with all these; nor does it lie in his verbal range or felicity, which are not striking; nor does he have any capacity for those stunning, demagogic flights of the imagination which bring an audience cheering to its feet. The secret lies, I think, in his intimate knowledge of the people he is addressing, be they black or white, and in the forthrightness with which he speaks of those things which hurt and baffle them. He does not offer any easy comfort and this keeps his hearers absolutely tense. He allows them their self-respect—indeed, he insists on it.

"We know," he told them, "that there are many things wrong in the white world. But there are many things wrong in the black world, too. We can't keep on blaming the white man. There are many things we must do for ourselves."

He suggested what some of these were:

"I know none of you make enough money—but save some of it. And there are some things we've got to face. I know the situation is responsible for a lot of it, but do you know that Negroes are 10 per cent of the population of St. Louis and are responsible for 58 per cent of its crimes? We've got to face that. And we have to do something about our moral standards. And we've got to stop lying to the white man. Every time you let the white man think *you* think segregation is right, you are cooperating with him in doing *evil*.

"The next time," he said, "the white man asks you what you think of segregation, you tell him, Mr. Charlie, I think it's wrong and I wish you'd do something about it by nine o'clock tomorrow morning!"

This brought a wave of laughter and King smiled, too. But he had meant every word he said, and he expected his hearers to act on them. They also expected this of themselves, which is not the usual effect of a sermon; and that they are living up to their expectations no white man in Montgomery will deny.

There was a dinner in the church basement afterwards, where, for the first time, I met Mrs. King—light brown, delicate, really quite beautiful, with a wonderful laugh—and watched young Martin circulating among church members and visitors. I overheard him explaining to someone that bigotry was a disease and that the greatest victim of this disease was not the bigot's object, but the bigot himself. And these people could only be saved by love. In liberating oneself, one was also liberating them. I was shown, by someone else, the damage done to the church by bombs. King did not mention the bombing of his own home, and I did not bring it up. Late the next night, after a mass meeting in another church, I flew to Birmingham.

I did not see King again for nearly three years. I saw him in Atlanta, just after his acquittal by a Montgomery court of charges of perjury, tax evasion, and misuse of public funds. He had moved to Atlanta and was co-pastor, with his father, of his father's church. He had made this move, he told me, because the pressures on him took him away from Montgomery for such excessively long periods that he did not feel that he was properly fulfilling his ministerial duties there. An attempt had been made on his life—in the North, by a mysterious and deranged Negro woman; and he was about to receive, in the state of Georgia, for driving without a resident driver's license, a suspended twelve-month sentence.

And, since I had last seen him, the Negro student movement had begun and was irresistibly bringing about great shifts and divisions in the Negro world, and in the nation. In short, by the time we met again, he was more beleaguered than he had ever been before, and not only by his enemies in the white South. Three years earlier, I had not encountered very many people—I am speaking now of Negroes—who were really critical of him.

But many more people seemed critical of him now, were bitter, disappointed, skeptical. None of this had anything to do—I want to make this absolutely clear—with his personal character or his integrity. It had to do with his effectiveness as a leader. King has had an extraordinary effect in the Negro world, and therefore in the nation, and is now in the center of an extremely complex cross fire.

He was born in Atlanta in 1929. He has Irish and Indian blood in his veins—Irish from his father's, Indian from his mother's side. His maternal grandfather built Ebenezer Baptist Church, which, as I have said, young Martin now co-pastors with his father. This grandfather seems to have been an extremely active and capable man, having been one of the NAACP leaders in Atlanta thirty or forty years ago, and having been instrumental in bringing about the construction of Atlanta's first Negro high school. The paternal grandfather is something else again, a poor, violent, and illiterate farmer who tried to find refuge from reality in drinking. He clearly had a great influence on the formation of the character of Martin, Sr., who determined, very early, to be as unlike his father as possible.

Martin, Sr., came to Atlanta in 1916, a raw, strapping country boy, determined, in the classic American tradition, to rise above his station. It could not have been easy for him in the Deep South of 1916, but he was, luckily, too young for the Army, and prices and wages rose during the war, and his improvident father had taught him the value of thrift. So he got his start. He studied in evening school, entered Atlanta's Morehouse College in 1925, and graduated in June of 1930, more than a year after Martin was born. (There are two other children, an older girl who now teaches at Spelman College, and a younger boy, pastor of a church in Noonan, Georgia.) By this time, Martin, Sr., had become a preacher, and was pastor of two small churches; and at about this time, his father-in-law asked him to become the assistant pastor of Ebenezer Baptist Church, which he did.

His children have never known poverty, and Martin, Sr., is

understandably very proud of this. "My prayer," he told me, "was always: Lord, grant that my children will not have to come the way I did." They didn't, they haven't, the prayers certainly did no harm. But one cannot help feeling that a person as single-minded and determined as the elder Reverend King clearly is would have accomplished anything he set his hand to, anyway.

"I equipped myself to give them the comforts of life," he says. "Not to waste, not to keep up with the Joneses, but just to be comfortable. We've never lived in a rented house—and never ridden *too* long in a car on which payment was due."

He is naturally very proud of Martin, Jr., but he claims to be not at all surprised. "He sacrificed to make himself ready"— ready, that is, for a trial, or a series of trials, which might have been the undoing of a lesser man. Yet, though he is not surprised at the extraordinary nature of his son's eminence, he *was* surprised when, at college, Martin decided that he was called to preach. He had expected him to become a doctor or a lawyer because he always spoke of these professions as though he aspired to them.

As he had; and since, as I have said, King is far from garrulous on the subject of his interior life, it is somewhat difficult to know what led him to make this switch. He had already taken pre-medical and law courses. But he had been raised by a minister, an extremely strong-minded one at that, and in an extraordinarily peaceful and protected way. "Never," says his father, "has Martin known a fuss or a fight or a strike-back in the home." On the other hand, there are some things from which no Negro can really be protected, for which he can only be prepared; and Martin, Sr., was more successful than most fathers in accomplishing this strenuous and delicate task. "I have never believed," he says, "that anybody was better than I." That this is true would seem to be proved by the career of his son, who *never went around fighting with himself, like we all did."*

Here, speculation is really on very marshy ground, for the father must certainly have fought in himself some of the battles from which young Martin was protected. We have only to consider the era, especially in the South, to realize that this must be true. And it must have demanded great steadiness of mind, as well as great love, to hide so successfully from his children the evidence of these battles. And, since salvation, humanly speaking, is a two-way street, I suggest that, if the father saved the children, it was, almost equally, the children who saved him. It would seem that he was able, with rare success, to project onto his children, or at least onto one of them, a sense of life as he himself would have liked to live it, and somehow made real in their personalities principles on which he himself must often have found it extremely dangerous and difficult to act. Martin, Sr., is regarded with great ambivalence by both the admirers and detractors of his son, and I shall, alas, shortly have more to say concerning his generation; but I do not think that the enormous achievement sketched above can possibly be taken away from him.

Again, young Martin's decision to become a minister has everything to do with his temperament, for he seems always to have been characterized by his striking mixture of steadiness and peace. He apparently did the normal amount of crying in his childhood, for I am told that his grandmother "couldn't stand to see it." But he seems to have done very little complaining; when he was spanked, "he just stood there and took it"; he seems to have been incapable of carrying grudges; and when he was attacked, he did not strike back.

From King's own account, I can only guess that this decision was aided by the fact that, at Morehouse College, he was asked to lead the devotions. The relationship thus established between himself and his contemporaries, or between himself and himself, or between himself and God, seemed to work for him as no other had. Also, I think it is of the utmost importance to realize that King loves the South; many Negroes do. The ministry seems to afford him the best possible vehicle for the expression of that love. At that time in his life, he was discovering "the beauty of the South"; he sensed in the people "a new determination"; and he felt that there was a need for "a new, courageous witness."

But it could not have occurred to him, of course, that *he* would be, and in such an unprecedented fashion, that witness. When Coretta King—then Coretta Scott—met him in Boston, where he was attending Boston University and she was studying at the New England Conservatory of Music, she found him an earnest, somewhat too carefully dressed young man. He had gone from Morehouse to Crozer Theological Seminary in Pennsylvania; the latter institution was interracial, which may have had something to do with his self-consciousness. He was fighting at that time to free himself from all the stereotypes of the Negro, an endeavor which does not leave much room for spontaneity. Both he and Coretta were rather lonely in Boston, and for similar reasons. They were both very distinguished and promising young people, which means that they were also tense, self-conscious, and insecure. They were inevitably cut off from the bulk of the Negro community and their role among whites had to be somewhat ambiguous, for they were not being judged merely as themselves—or, anyway, they could scarcely afford to think so. They were responsible for the good name of all the Negro people.

Coretta had perhaps had more experience than Martin in this role. The more I spoke to her, the more I realized how her story illuminates that of her husband. She had come from Lincoln High in Marion, Alabama, to Antioch College in Ohio, part of one of the earliest groups of Negro students accepted there. She was thus, in effect, part of an experiment, and though she took it very well and can laugh about it now, she certainly must have had her share of exasperated and lonely moments. The social mobility of a Negro girl, especially in such a setting, is even more severely circumscribed than that of a Negro male, and any lapse or error on her part is far more dangerous. From Antioch, Coretta eventually came to Boston on a scholarship and by this time a certain hoydenish, tomboy quality in her had begun, apparently, to be confirmed. The atmosphere at Antioch had been entirely informal, which pleased Coretta; I gather that at this time in her life she was usually to be seen in sweaters, slacks, and scarves. It was a ferociously formal young man and a ferociously informal young girl who finally got together in Boston.

Martin immediately saw through Coretta's disguise, and informed her on their first or second meeting that she had all the qualities he wanted in a wife. Coretta's understandable tendency was to laugh at this; but this tendency was checked by the rather frightening suspicion that he meant it; if he had not meant it, he would not have said it. But a great deal had been invested in Coretta's career as a singer, and she did not feel that she had the right to fail all the people who had done so much to help her. "And I'd certainly never intended to marry a *minister*. It was true that he didn't seem like any of the ministers I'd met, but—still—I thought of how circumscribed my life might become." By circumscribed, she meant dull; she could not possibly have been more mistaken.

What had really happened, in Coretta's case, as in so many others, was that life had simply refused to recognize her private timetable. She had always intended to marry, but tidily, possibly meeting her husband at the end of a triumphant concert tour. However, here he was now, exasperatingly early, and she had to rearrange herself around this fact. She and Martin were married on June 18, 1953. By now, naturally, it is she whom Martin sometimes accuses of thinking too much about clothes. "People who are doing something don't have time to be worried about all that," he has informed her. Well, he certainly ought to know.

Coretta King told me that from the time she reached Boston and all during Martin's courtship, and her own indecision, she yet could not rid herself of a feeling that all that was happening had been, somehow, preordained. And one does get an impression, until this point in the King story at least, that inexorable forces which none of us really know anything about were shaping and preparing him for that fateful day in Montgomery. Everything that he will need has been delivered, so to speak, and is waiting to be used. Everything, including the principle of nonviolence. It was in 1950 that Dr. Mordecai W. Johnson of Howard University visited India. King heard one of the speeches Johnson made on his return, and it was from this moment that King became interested in Gandhi as a figure, and in nonviolence as a way of life. Later, in 1959, he would visit India himself.

But, so far, of course, we are speaking after the fact. Plans and patterns are always more easily discernible then. This is not so when we try to deal with the present, or attempt speculations about the future.

Immediately after the failure, last June [1960], of Montgomery's case against him, King returned to Atlanta. I entered, late, on a Sunday morning, the packed Ebenezer Baptist Church, and King was already speaking.

He did not look any older, and yet there was a new note of anguish in his voice. He was speaking of his trial. He described the torment, the spiritual state of people who are committed to a wrong, knowing that it is wrong. He made the trials of these white people far more vivid than anything he himself might have endured. They were not ruled by hatred, but by terror; and, therefore, if community was ever to be achieved, these people, the potential destroyers of the person, must not be hated. It was a terrible plea—to the people; and it was a prayer. In *Varieties of Religious Experience,* William James speaks of vastation—of *being,* as opposed to merely regarding, the monstrous creature which came to him in a vision. It seemed to me, though indeed I may be wrong, that something like this had happened to young Martin Luther—that he had looked on evil a long, hard, lonely time. For evil is in the world: it may be in the world to stay. No creed and no dogma are proof against it, and indeed no person is; it is always the naked person, alone, who, over and over and over again, must wrest his salvation from these black jaws. Perhaps young Martin was finding a new and more somber meaning in the command: "Overcome evil with good." The command does not suggest that to overcome evil is to eradicate it.

King spoke more candidly than I had ever heard him speak before, of his bitterly assaulted pride, of his shame, when he found himself accused, before all the world, of having used and betrayed the people of Montgomery by stealing the money they had entrusted to him. "I knew it wasn't true—but who would believe me?"

He had canceled a speaking trip to Chicago, for he felt that he could not face anyone. And he prayed; he walked up and down in his study, alone. It was borne in on him, finally, that he had no right *not* to go, no right to hide. "I called the airport and made another reservation and went on to Chicago." He appeared there, then, as an accused man, and gave us no details of his visit, which did not, in any case, matter. For if he had not been able to face Chicago, if he had not won that battle with himself, he would have been defeated long before his entrance into that courtroom in Montgomery.

When I saw him the next day in his office, he was very different, kind and attentive, but far away. A meeting of the Southern Christian Leadership Conference was to begin that day, and I think his mind must have been on that. The beleaguered ministers of the Deep South were coming to Atlanta that day in order to discuss the specific situations which confronted them in their particular towns or cities, and King was their leader. All of them had come under immensely greater local pressure because of the student sit-in movement. Inevitably, they were held responsible for it, even though they might very well not have known until reading it in the papers that the students had carried out another demonstration. I do not mean to suggest that there is any question of their support of the students—they may or may not be responsible *for* them but they certainly consider themselves responsible *to* them. But all this, I think, weighed on King rather heavily.

He talked about his visit to India and its effect on him. He was hideously struck by the poverty, which he talked about in great detail. He was also much impressed by Nehru, who had, he said, extraordinary qualities of "perception and dedication and courage—far more than the average American politician." We talked about the South. "Perhaps 4 or 5 per cent of the people are to be found on either end of the racial scale"—either actively for or actively against desegregation; "the rest are passive adherents. The sin of the South is the sin of conformity." And he feels, as I do, that much of the responsibility for the situation in which we have found ourselves since 1954 is due to the failure of President Eisenhower to make any coherent, any guiding statement concerning the nation's greatest moral and social problem.

But we did not discuss the impending conference which, in any case, he could scarcely have discussed with me. And we did not discuss any of the problems which face him now and make his future so problematical. For he could not have discussed these with me, either.

That white men find King dangerous is well known. They can say so. But many Negroes also find King dangerous, but cannot say so, at least not publicly. The reason that the Negroes of whom I speak are trapped in such a stunning silence is that to say what they really feel would be to deny the entire public purpose of their lives.

Now, the problem of Negro leadership in this country has always been extremely delicate, dangerous, and complex. The term itself becomes remarkably difficult to define, the moment one realizes that the real role of the Negro leader, in the eyes of the American Republic, was not to make the Negro a first-class citizen but to keep him content as a second-class one.

This sounds extremely harsh, but the record bears me out. And this problem, which it was the responsibility of the entire country to face, was dumped into the laps of a few men. Some of them were real leaders and some of them were false. Many of the greatest have scarcely ever been heard of.

The role of the genuine leadership, in its own eyes, was to destroy the barriers which prevented Negroes from fully participating in American life, to prepare Negroes for first-class citizenship, while at the same time bringing to bear on the Republic every conceivable pressure to make this status a reality. For this reason, the real leadership was to be found everywhere, in law courts, colleges, churches, hobo camps; on picket lines, freight trains, and chain gangs; and in jails. Not everyone who was publicized as a leader really was one. And many leaders who would never have dreamed of applying the term to themselves were considered by the Republic—when it knew of their existence at all—to be criminals. This is, of course, but the old and universal story of poverty in battle with privilege, but we tend not to think of old and universal stories as occurring in our brand-new and still relentlessly parochial land.

The real goal of the Negro leader was nothing less than the total integration of Negroes in all levels of the national life. But this could rarely be stated so baldly; it often could not be stated at all; in order to begin Negro education, for example, Booker Washington had found it necessary to state the exact opposite. The reason for this duplicity is that the goal contains the assumption that Negroes are to be treated, in all respects, exactly like all other citizens of the Republic. This is an idea which has always had extremely rough going in America. For one thing, it attacked, and attacks, a vast complex of special interests which would lose money and power if the situation of the Negro were to change. For another, the idea of freedom necessarily carries with it the idea of sexual freedom: the freedom to meet, sleep with, and marry whom one chooses. It would be fascinating, but I am afraid we must postpone it for the moment, to consider just why so many people appear to be convinced that Negroes would then immediately meet, sleep with, and marry white women; who, remarkably enough, are only protected from such undesirable alliances by the majesty and vigilance of the law.

The duplicity of the Negro leader was more than matched by the duplicity of the people with whom he had to deal. They, and most of the country, felt at the very bottom of their hearts that the Negro was inferior to them and, therefore, merited the treatment that he got. But it was not always politic to say this, either. It certainly could never be said over the bargaining table, where white and black men met.

The Negro leader was there to force from his adversary whatever he could get: new schools, new schoolrooms, new houses, new jobs. He was invested with very little power because the Negro vote had so very little power. (Other Negro leaders were trying to correct *that*.) It was not easy to wring concessions from the people at the bargaining table, who had, after all, no intention of giving their power away. People seldom do give their power away, forces beyond their control take their power from them; and I am afraid that much of the liberal cant about progress is but a sentimental reflection of this implacable fact. (Liberal cant about love and heroism also obscures, not to say blasphemes, the great love and heroism of many white people. Our racial story would be inconceivably more grim if these people, in the teeth of the most fantastic odds, did not continue to appear; but they were almost never, of course, to be found at the bargaining table.) Whatever concession the Negro leader carried away from the bargaining table was won with the tacit understanding that he, in return, would influence the people he represented in the direction that the people in power wished them to be influenced. Very often, in fact, he did not do this at all, but contrived to delude the white men (who are, in this realm, rather easily deluded) into believing that he had. But very often, too, he deluded himself into believing that the aims of white men in power and the desires of Negroes out of power were the same.

It was altogether inevitable, in short, that, by means of the extraordinary tableau I have tried to describe, a class of Negroes should have been created whose loyalty to their class was infinitely greater than their loyalty to the people from whom they had been so cunningly estranged. We must add, for I think it is important, that the Negro leader knew that he, too, was called "nigger" when his back was turned. The great mass of the black people around him were illiterate, demoralized, in want, and incorrigible. It is not hard to see that the Negro leader's personal and public frustrations would almost inevitably be turned against these people, for their misery, which formed the cornerstone of his peculiar power, was also responsible for his humiliation. And in Harlem, now, for example, many prominent Negroes ride to and from work through scenes of the greatest misery. They do not see this misery, though, because they do not want to see it. They defend themselves against an intolerable reality, which menaces them, by despising the people who are trapped in it.

The criticism, therefore, of the publicized Negro leadership—which is not, as I have tried to indicate, always the real leadership—is a criticism leveled, above all, against this class. They are, perhaps, the most unlucky bourgeoisie in the world's entire history, trapped, as they are, in a no man's land between black humiliation and white power. They cannot move backwards, and they cannot move forward, either.

One of the greatest vices of the white bourgeoisie on which they have modeled themselves is its reluctance to think, its distrust of the independent mind. Since the Negro bourgeoisie has so many things *not* to think about, it is positively afflicted with this vice. I should like at some other time to embark on a full-length discussion of the honorable and heroic role played by the NAACP in the national life, and point out to what ex-

tent its work has helped create the present ferment. But, for the
moment, I shall have to confine my remarks to its organ, *The
Crisis,* because I think it is incontestable that this magazine reveals the state of mind of the Negro bourgeoisie. *The Crisis* has
the most exciting subject matter in the world at its fingertips, and
yet manages to be one of the world's dullest magazines. When
the Reverend James Lawson—who was expelled from Vanderbilt University for his sit-in activities—said this, or something
like it, he caused a great storm of ill feeling. But he was quite
right to feel as he does about *The Crisis,* and quite right to say
so. And the charge is not answered by referring to the history of
the NAACP.

Now, to charge *The Crisis* with dullness may seem to be a
very trivial matter. It is not trivial, though, because this dullness
is the result of its failure to examine what is really happening in
the Negro world—its failure indeed, for that matter, to seize
upon what is happening in the world at large. And I have sin-
gled it out because this inability is revelatory of the gap which
now ominously widens between what we shall now have to call
the official leadership and the young people who have begun
what is nothing less than a moral revolution.

It is because of this gap that King finds himself in such a difficult position. The pressures on him are tremendous, and they
come from above and below. He lost much moral credit, for example, especially in the eyes of the young, when he allowed
Adam Clayton Powell to force the resignation of his (King's)
extremely able organizer and lieutenant, Bayard Rustin. Rustin,
also, has a long and honorable record as a fighter for Negro
rights, and is one of the most penetrating and able men around.
The techniques used by Powell—we will not speculate as to his
motives—were far from sweet; but King was faced with the
choice of defending his organizer, who was also his friend, or
agreeing with Powell; and he chose the *latter* course. Nor do I
know of anyone satisfied with the reasons given for the exclusion of James Lawson from the Southern Christian Leadership

Conference. It would seem, certainly, that so able, outspoken, and energetic a man might prove of great value to this organization: why, then, is he not a part of it?

And there are many other questions, all of them ominous, and too many to go into here. But they all come, finally, it seems to me, to this tremendous reality: it is the sons and daughters of the beleaguered bourgeoisie—supported, in the most extraordinary fashion, by those old, work-worn men and women who were known, only yesterday, as "the country niggers"—who have begun a revolution in the consciousness of this country which will inexorably destroy nearly all that we now think of as concrete and indisputable. These young people have never believed in the American image of the Negro and have never bargained with the Republic, and now they never will. There is no longer any basis on which to bargain: for the myth of white supremacy is exploding all over the world, from the Congo to New Orleans. Those who have been watched and judged and described for so long are now watching and judging and describing for themselves. And one of the things that this means, to put it far too simply and bluntly, is that the white man on whom the American Negro has modeled himself for so long is vanishing. Because this white man was, himself, very largely a mythical creation: white men have never been, here, what they imagined themselves to be. The liberation of Americans from the racial anguish which has crippled us for so long can only mean, truly, the creation of a new people in this still-new world.

But the battle to achieve this has not ended, it has scarcely begun. Martin Luther King, Jr., by the power of his personality and the force of his beliefs, has injected a new dimension into our ferocious struggle. He has succeeded, in a way no Negro before him has managed to do, to carry the battle into the individual heart and make its resolution the province of the individual will. He has made it a matter, on both sides of the racial fence, of self-examination; and has incurred, therefore, the grave responsibility of continuing to lead in the path he has encouraged so many people to follow. How he will do this I do not know, but I do not see how he can possibly avoid a break, at last, with the habits and attitudes, stratagems and fears of the past.

No one can read the future, but we do know, as James has put it, that "all futures are rough." King's responsibility, and ours, is to that future which is already sending before it so many striking signs and portents. The possibility of liberation which is always real is also always painful, since it involves such an overhauling of all that gave us our identity. The Negro who will emerge out of this present struggle—whoever, indeed, this dark stranger may prove to be—will not be dependent, in any way at all, on any of the many props and crutches which help form our identity now. And neither will the white man. We will need every ounce of moral stamina we can find. For everything is changing, from our notion of politics to our notion of ourselves, and we are certain, as we begin history's strangest metamorphosis, to undergo the torment of being forced to surrender far more than we ever realized we had accepted.

✪

Crowned with Crises

Since early April [1963], temperatures had been rising inside the racial pressure cooker called Birmingham, Alabama. One muggy afternoon last month the lid blew off.

City Commissioner Eugene (Bull) Connor, deploying police forces to contain demonstration marches, had watched with growing impatience as a noisy Negro crowd filled Kelly Ingram Park, a square block of tall elms, walkways, and green turf in the main Negro business section. Bellowing, laughing, and jeering, the crowd—mostly students—taunted Connor's blue-clad policemen and the firemen sweating in dun-colored, knee-length slickers. Whining shepherd dogs strained at chains held by the cops, while the firemen manhandled big monitor nozzles combining two hoses for high pressure.

"Freedom!" shouted a Negro boy, flailing his arms. "Get white dogs!"

"Let 'em have it," said the Bull.

The firemen moved, and water shot from the nozzles. With a sound like automatic gunfire, a powerful stream rattled rapid-fire over elm trees, whacking off strips of thick, black bark.

From "Martin Luther King, Jr., Apostle of Crisis," *Saturday Evening Post* (June 15, 1963), pp. 15-19.

Then it slammed into a slim, white-clad Negro girl in the distance. She braced against it for a moment, then was knocked over into the dirt.

A group of unruly, drunken Negroes swung their arms and rocks began to fly. One crashed near the police. A bottle fell and shattered. Shouts of defiance came from the milling crowd. Rocks continued to clatter. The dogs whined eagerly. And over the cacophony of other sounds lay the crashing of the big hoses. The only still figures were about two hundred whites watching somberly from across the street. Finally, with the Negroes pushed back, the water was shut off. "God bless America," a reporter mumbled in disgust.

Thus did racial violence come this spring to the most rigidly segregated major city in America. It marked a collision of two power systems, the first represented by Bull Connor, vigorously enforcing laws that preserve the status quo of racial discrimination, the second by Dr. Martin Luther King, Jr., making a carefully planned assault on those laws and that discrimination.

For the crisis in Birmingham did not just happen. The Negro leader lighted a fire under the pressure cooker, well knowing that the "peaceful demonstrations" he organized would bring, at the very least, tough repressive measures by the police. And although he hoped his followers would not respond with violence—he has always stressed a nonviolent philosophy— that was a risk he was prepared to take. Two months earlier his No. 1 staff assistant, the Reverend Wyatt Tee Walker, had explained, "We've got to have a crisis to bargain with. To take a moderate approach, hoping to get white help, doesn't work. They nail you to the cross, and it saps the enthusiasm of the followers. You've got to have a crisis."

King got his crisis in a hymn-singing, rock-throwing crescendo of peaceful marches and violent strife that sent more than twenty-four hundred Negroes to jail, most of them for such offenses as parading without a permit. It was the largest number ever arrested in an American racial protest. And even after he seemed to have won his fight for an agreement easing discrimination, twenty-five hundred Negroes angrily responded to night riders' bombings by three hours of midnight rioting. Scores of cars were crumpled, torches were put to ramshackle stores and two apartment houses, a policeman and a cab driver were stabbed, and about fifty other people were injured. Later that black Sunday, President Kennedy ordered riot-trained combat troops to nearby bases.

In the days that followed, the tension eased, and integration leaders in Birmingham and around the nation tried to assess the results of King's invasion of this Deep South bastion. If the city's white business and political leaders stand by the agreement worked out in unofficial negotiations between white and Negro spokesmen, King will have won significant victories for the city's Negro population. This agreement calls for desegregation within ninety days of some lunch counters and other facilities in a number of downtown department and variety stores, for upgrading of Negro employment and hiring on a non-discriminatory basis, and for the formation of a biracial committee.

On the other hand, co-workers in the civil rights movement, which today teems with dissent and self-criticism, argue that these gains might have been won even without King. After decades of iron-fisted white supremacy, a series of elections in the past year had brought rejection of the old-line leadership, and white-Negro negotiations had established unprecedented rapport. (Speaking of a local Negro leader and head of the Alabama Christian Movement for Human Rights, a white merchant who a year ago grumbled, "I never thought I'd be sitting down with Fred Shuttlesworth," recently volunteered in obvious sincerity, "I'm delighted to know you, Reverend Shuttlesworth.")

Now, however, Birmingham's Negroes face a backwash of troublesome problems. White hoodlums have been aroused. Negro demonstrators may be faced with heavy fines. School authorities suspended or expelled eleven hundred children who left classes to march in the protests. And both the outgoing commission-type administration of Mayor Art Hanes and Commissioners Bull Connor and J. T. Waggoner, and the incoming mayor-council form of government headed by Mayor Albert Boutwell have publicly stated that they were not bound by the white-Negro negotiations. It will be months before anyone knows how much the Negroes won, or whether the battle of Birmingham is over.

For these and other reasons, some integrationist leaders felt that King had blundered in bringing crisis to Birmingham. It was not the right place, they maintained; this was not the right time; and mass marches to fill the jails—a tactic that bears King's personal brand—was not the right tactic. Furthermore, King had gone into Birmingham not only against the advice of these leaders but without even informing them. "That's just arrogant," one said in exasperation.

Other detractors within the desegregation movement have bitterly accused King of tackling Birmingham primarily to raise money and to keep his name and his organization, the Southern Christian Leadership Conference (SCLC), out in front on the teeming civil rights scene.

But despite such criticism, King's magic touch with the masses of Negroes remains. They do not understand the intricacies of his tactics. What they see is a powerful crusader for equality who does something instead of just talking, who sticks lighted matches to the status quo and who is impatient with talk of waiting. Given the increasing unrest among Negroes, King's flare seems likely to spread a trail of little Birminghams through the nation during the next few months.

For King endows this American struggle with qualities of messianic mission. A short man whose thick neck and heavy shoulders convey an impression of height and power, he can fill New York's cavernous Riverside Church with eloquence about "the battering rams of historical necessity," or set rural Negro Baptists in Georgia to clapping and shouting rhythmic responses when he says, "The cloud is dark, but the sun is shining on the other side."

This oratorical blend of intellectual content with the imagery of an old Southern preacher is natural. King, thirty-four, holds a theological degree from Crozer Theological Seminary in Chester, Pennsylvania, and a doctor of philosophy degree from Boston University. But some think his family heritage and home community explain much more about him than his education.

His father, usually known as "M.L., Sr.," was a strong figure in Atlanta for many years before young Martin became famous. The son of a hard-drinking part-Negro, part-Irish Georgia sharecropper, M.L., Sr., came to Atlanta as a largely unlettered young working man. He went to college, became a preacher, married a daughter of a man who had founded Ebenezer Baptist Church, and later became pastor of this politically influential church, as he still is today.

Young Martin grew up as the son of a man of prestige in the community. Except that he was a Negro in a segregated Southern city, it was almost a typical middle-class American setting.

People who knew young Martin noted one characteristic early: He played rough games, but he didn't like a fight. Once the school bully knocked him down a flight of stairs and beat him, but he didn't fight back.

He was sensitive, and twice as a young boy he seemed to lose control of himself in heartbreak. Once A.D., his younger brother, sliding down a banister, knocked their grandmother unconscious. Thinking she was dead, Martin ran to a second-floor window and jumped out, but the fall was only ten or twelve feet and he was not injured. Later, when he was eleven, he learned that his grandmother really had died and took the same jump out the window—again escaping injury.

King's sensitivity and reluctance to fight back physically remain two of his outstanding characteristics. When a two hundred-pound self-styled American Nazi attacked him during a

speech in Birmingham, King took the man's blows and never tried
to retaliate. But his courage is not seriously questioned, even
by those who find other characteristics to criticize. Although he
does get tense and even tighten up in his speech when faced
with arrest—possibly because of arm-twisting mistreatment he
has received from police in the past—he does not let that deter
him from following his chosen path.

Ordinarily he can match Perry Como in languid laziness of
appearance. His broad face has an Oriental aspect, with a down-
curving mustache and oval eyes, and he never seems to hurry.

His most frequent response is "Oh, yeeees." The word
stretches out like a baritone's last four full notes. When he
laughs at someone's trivial humor, the laugh seems just a moment too late, as if he has been contemplating even this.

Many people think he has no sense of humor; yet he can
clown in private, parodying a swinging gospel singer's radio
routine, for instance. But few people ever see such a performance
or realize that, behind a public dignity of ecclesiastical proportions, he is an avid sports fan. Swimming, tennis, and fishing
have been among his own pursuits, but he has little time for
them these days.

His limited time, in fact, is largely spent with his family—his
wife Coretta, a pretty former Alabaman who sometimes sings
soprano in concerts; Yolanda (Yoki), seven; Martin III, five;
Dexter, two; and Bernice Albertine, born March 28. They live
in a large, two-story brick house in one of Atlanta's less fashionable Negro neighborhoods. He is at home about ten days a
month on the average.

More often he is traveling. A recent schedule took him to
Chicago for four speeches on a Sunday, to the University of
Minnesota Monday, back to his Atlanta SCLC office Tuesday
with a church meeting at home that night; Wednesday through
Friday there were meetings with the SCLC staff; Saturday,
counseling at his church and visits to hospitalized members;

Sunday morning, preaching. And then on the road for New York, Connecticut, and Tennessee.

Despite the pace, he almost always appears fresh. His dress leans to brown, gray, and sometimes dark blue; and his suits, which Mrs. King helps choose, usually look more respectable than stylish. He once bought some suits in the $150-$200 price range, with a preference for high-sheen dressy ones, but his taste seems to be more modest now.

Price, however, is not the problem. Testimony from state investigators in an unsuccessful Alabama tax case against King revealed substantial income. For 1958, for example, he reported $25,348—and the state charged him with having made almost twice that much. He attributed the tax case to persecution, and was acquitted of fraud, but he had by then paid some additional tax which the state claimed was due.

King receives one dollar a year from SCLC and six thousand dollars from Ebenezer Baptist Church, which lists him as co-pastor. Most of his income comes from speaking fees, gifts, and books, of which his third, titled *Strength to Love,* has recently been published by Harper & Row.

For these latter sources of income, King naturally must thank his national prominence as a Negro leader; and it is a curious fact that, between crises, his place in the civil rights struggle seems to slip. After his first ascent to fame during the 1956 bus boycott campaign in Montgomery, Alabama, he passed through a period of limbo. "The rest of my life will be anticlimactic," he told a good friend.

But the next year he re-established himself on the national scene when he proposed a "prayer pilgrimage" to Washington, won out against NAACP opposition, and, on May 17, spoke from the steps of the Lincoln Memorial to twenty-five thousand Negroes. "Give us the ballot" was his theme, rolling out like the refrain of an old hymn. "Give us the ballot, and we will transform the salient misdeeds of bloodthirsty mobs into the

abiding good deeds of orderly citizens. Give us the ballot.
. . . ." The crowd boomed its approval, and editor James L.
Hicks of New York City's *Amsterdam News* wrote that King
"emerged from the Prayer Pilgrimage to Washington as the No.
1 leader of 16 million Negroes. . . . At this point in his career,
they will follow him anywhere."

Still, King, who in those days wore a floppy, broad-brimmed
hat, unfashionable wide-lapel suits, and floral-design ties, was
often out of the limelight. In the fall of that same year, 1957, the
Little Rock explosion thrust other leaders into the headlines;
Daisy Bates of the NAACP was the Negro of the hour then.

King slipped further from view after he narrowly escaped
death on September 20, 1958, when a mentally deranged
Negro woman named Izola Curry plunged a letter opener into
his chest as he autographed his first book, *Stride Toward Freedom*, in a Harlem department store. "I've been after you for
six years," she exclaimed. The blade narrowly missed his aorta,
and King probably would have died if he had pulled the blade
out, a doctor said later. Instead, he waited calmly for medical
attention, with the stoical bravery he has shown on other occasions. His recovery was delayed by pneumonia, and for two
years he remained largely out of public view except for a trip
to India to talk to Nehru.

He did not emerge until 1960, with the advent of more crises.
That year he set up offices in Atlanta for SCLC—"Slick," in
the jargon of the movement—which had been largely dormant
since he and his supporters had founded it three years earlier.
But it was the lunch-counter sit-ins in the Carolinas and the
rising restlessness of the Negro students which brought him to
the fore again. Not leadership but agility put him there.

Students from about forty communities where there had
been sit-ins met in Raleigh, North Carolina, in April, to organize;
and because King was, to them, the great symbol of the movement, they asked him to help. Though they had moved ahead
of him in pressing "selective buying" programs—boycotts—he

had quickly adopted this as his own cause. ("He had to run to catch up with them," a friend remembers.) And now, when they organized the Student Nonviolent Coordinating Committee (SNCC), he became its patron saint. SNCC—usually called "Snick"—has since become a grass-roots organization carrying the dangerous burden of direct action in the tough Black Belt areas of the South.

The revolutionary new youth tide that flowed from Raleigh had the effect of thrusting King into the front of a civil disobedience movement now identified with his name, although in actual practice it was a young people's tactic at that time. Mass violation of the law by sit-ins and jail-ins was the banner that impatient students thrust into his hands for the 1960's. It was a sort of "black man's burden," and he was carrying it when he went to jail in Atlanta's sit-ins of 1960.

The Atlanta showdown exemplifies an essential fact about King; Here, as has often been the case, he was the Negroes' symbol and public spokesman; but actually the sit-in campaign was run by the students, and the command of Negro forces dealing with the Atlanta city administration was exercised by the established Negro power structure of Atlanta. On the operating level, King was a major factor only once, when the power of his oratory was needed to persuade a rally of rebellious students to accept the desegregation timetable which the local Negro leaders had negotiated.

Partly because his method is to move about in evangelical fashion, with local people remaining to reap whatever harvest may come, King has been called the Billy Graham of the civil rights movement. Unlike Billy Graham, however, King bears heavy organizational responsibilities, and it is in this realm that he is most criticized.

"I really don't have a great interest in administration," King said one day recently, semireclining in a swivel chair in his simple, cheaply furnished Atlanta office. He tapped a wooden letter opener rapidly in his palm as he thought. "But I have come to see the necessity of that emphasis. I've never thought I couldn't do it. But I have thought my function was creative leadership, without doing the day-to-day detail. In recent months I have tried to strengthen my administrative ability."

Though King and the NAACP—of which he is a member—periodically deny any rivalry, it is obvious that "the N-double-A" is warily watching one plan he mulls over. It is two-fold: First, SCLC would become a membership organization, composed primarily of individual members rather than affiliate organizations, as at present. Second, it would become truly national. In sum, this move would put SCLC into full competition with the NAACP for members, dues, contributions, and general support.

"I will have to face the decision soon on whether I should be limiting myself to the South," King said. "In the North there are brothers and sisters who are suffering discrimination that is even more agonizing, in a sense, than in the South. . . . In the South, at least the Negro can see progress, whereas in the North all he sees is retrogression."

At present, SCLC's most far-reaching and, many civil rights workers think, most useful activity is its citizenship-training program. In an attractive brick building called the Dorchester Center in rural McIntosh, Georgia, SCLC trains people it calls "the noncommissioned officers of the civil rights movement." Most are leaders from small communities, learning how to teach basic literacy, voter-registration processes, and procedures for obtaining government benefits. So far, about six hundred Negroes from all over the South have gone through Dorchester. In Georgia alone, these graduates recently were conducting fifty local classes.

For these and other operations conducted by its staff of forty, SCLC has a 1963 budget of about $450,000, up from $60,000 in 1960, when the staff numbered three. Fees from its affiliates amount to only about $15,000 of this. Dr. King himself raises about $100,000 with rallies, dinners, and other personal appearances. A surprising $150,000 or so comes through the mail, some spontaneously but most in response to appeals from Dr. King to a mailing list of thirty-five thousand people. When a crisis such as Birmingham's comes, an "emergency appeal" may be sent out, and sometimes it adds substantially to the year's budget. For example, the National Maritime Union alone sent King more than $32,000 in the midst of the Birmingham crisis.

About $100,000 of the SCLC budget is a grant by the Field Foundation to the home mission board of the United Church of Christ, which finances the citizenship school that SCLC administers. The remainder of the SCLC budget comes from periodic benefits, concerts, and assorted entertainment.

King's financial reporting worries some people. In contrast to the NAACP, which reports its money handling extensively and likes to emphasize that it must be "as above suspicion as Caesar's wife," SCLC reports little. Its only known published financial statement is a one-page, carbon-copied sheet with a very general listing of income and disbursements in round figures.

Partly because of its laxity in providing reports even to those with whom it deals on a professional level, SCLC seems to have suffered badly as a participant in the foundation-financed Voter Education Project, set up last year to manage voter-registration programs through five participating organizations. SCLC, which had enthusiastically disclosed that it would receive about $90,000 from the fund last year, actually wound up getting less than $25,000. And when the project drew up its tentative 1963 allocations this April, SCLC was down for none.

Others in the civil rights movement are also taking a tough, critical look at SCLC's work in voter registration. And, despite King's statement in an April fund-raising letter that "we are making the main thrust of our work in the area of voter registration," the "specialty of the house" with SCLC remains the mass protest. The ultimate outcome in Birmingham will be a judgment of this tactic, just as Albany was.

The name of Albany has come to have a special meaning in the rights movement. In that busy little city of fifty-eight thousand in the old plantation country of southwestern Georgia, a total of more than eleven hundred Negroes marched to jail with King in December, 1961, and the spring of 1962, demanding desegregation. Thundering applause had nearly drowned out King's rising, falling oratory when he told a meeting of Albany Negroes: "Get on your walking shoes; walk together, children, and don'tcha get weary!"

King himself had been trapped in the kind of emotion that builds up at these meetings. When he went to Albany he did not intend to go to jail or, apparently, to allow his entire prestige to be committed. But by the time he reached the church, earlier speakers had already fired up the crowd. A local Negro leader, Dr. W. G. Anderson, whirled in the midst of an oration about marching to certain arrest and exclaimed, "Reverend King will lead us, won't you, Reverend King?" The answer had to be yes. "I don't think King leads the movement," said a former associate. "It leads him."

Looking back, an executive of another rights group has commented, "As a professional, I was appalled by the lack of planning in the Albany campaign. They just charged off."

Almost everybody outside King's immediate camp thinks the Albany protest was a failure. "Albany can never be the same again," King had said at the time. But the walls of segregation did not come tumbling down anywhere there, and the Negro's lot today is little different except for some new hardships. Slater King, an Albany Negro leader and businessman, thinks the campaign was worth while on the whole, but he estimates that 20 per cent of the work force of Negro maids and cooks lost jobs permanently because of white hostility aroused by the marches.

"Albany is just as segregated as ever," says Police Chief Laurie Pritchett, who is credited with giving King his first major defeat. And Mrs. Ruby Hurley, Southeastern regional direc-

tor of the NAACP, says, "Albany was successful only if the
goal was to go to jail."

Dr. King himself, though he admits he might do things differently now, believes the marches did achieve something. "Negroes
have straightened their backs in Albany," he says, "and once a
man straightens his back you can't ride him anymore." It is a view
that sheds light on the cause of many of his differences with leaders of other rights groups. As one such executive said, "We
[various rights organizations] meet and decide on tactics for
bringing about desegregation. I have the feeling SCLC does not
regard this as the primary objective. For them it's to increase
the self-esteem of the Negro. That calls for different tactics."

Dr. King, having established himself as the foremost practitioner
of the "fill the jails" tactic, now has set up a legal wing that may
be useful when and if thousands more of his followers go to jail.
Contributions to this new Gandhi Society will be tax-exempt
—unlike those to SCLC, a political action group. Dr. King, honorary chairman of the Gandhi Society, acknowledges that it may
enjoy foundation support—some, hopefully, from the Rockefeller Foundation.

The relationship between King and New York Governor
Rockefeller has aroused a good deal of curiosity, especially
since an SCLC official resigned with charges that Rockefeller
was a heavy contributor to King for political reasons. The two
men met at a Harlem rally in 1957 but had little contact until
1960. That year, when King was to speak at a fund-raising
dinner in Albany, New York, the governor greeted him in New
York City and then flew him to Albany in his personal plane.
They had long talks. "I was very much impressed by him and
the strength of his commitment," King recalls. They have
talked since then, King says, but not frequently. "I must say
he has shown a strong concern for civil rights. I do not think
it is wholly political." But King is hard to corner on the question of whether President Kennedy or Governor Rockefeller
has more appeal as a civil rights advocate.

"I don't endorse candidates and will continue to follow this policy," King said, but he added, "I will go to the extent of telling people who ask my advice what I think the candidates stand for."

Even that could be an important endorsement. During the 1960 campaign his father, the Reverend M. L. King, Sr., publicly endorsed John F. Kennedy for President because of the candidate's "call of concern" to young Dr. King's wife Coretta, while her husband was confined at Georgia's Reidsville State Penitentiary. That call, and another by Bob Kennedy to a Georgia judge handling a traffic case against King, are credited by many political observers with swinging enough Negro votes to elect Kennedy.

King's position in the rights movement unquestionably is enhanced by the fact that he has the ear of the President and, for that matter, of figures around the world. He knows African premiers better than he does the influential whites in his own hometown—recently he could not recall the names of two of the most important churchmen in Atlanta, both of whom had lunched with him to talk race relations. Not only is he on speaking terms with many African leaders to an extent few white Americans appreciate, his name is known and revered throughout much of the world. . . .

Jail usually is the place where King catches up on his reading, but in the Birmingham jail a few weeks ago he caught up on some writing. Seven leading Alabama churchmen, some of whom had staked their prestige and positions upon a moderate solution in Birmingham, had openly criticized his actions there. He answered them with a publicly released nine-thousand-word letter which his staff later dubbed *Birmingham Jail Treatise of Martin Luther King, Jr.* It was a telling document. More than ever it split him from the white moderates of the South and suggested that Negroes would plot their own course in the future.

The moderates, he wrote, had "gravely disappointed" him:

I have almost reached the regrettable conclusion that the Negro's great stumbling block in the stride toward freedom is not the White Citizens Council-er or the Ku Klux Klanner, but the white moderate who is more devoted to "order" than to justice; who prefers a negative peace which is the absence of tension to a positive peace which is the presence of justice; who constantly says, "I agree with you in the goal you seek, but I can't agree with your methods of direct action"; who paternalistically feels that he can set the timetable for another man's freedom. . . .

As for his own course, he said, he was the man in the middle in the Negro community. He stood between "a force of complacency" and "one of bitterness and hatred" exemplified by the Black Muslims, and he realized that he should have known that "few members of a race that has oppressed another race can understand or appreciate the deep groans and passionate yearnings of those who have been oppressed. . . ."

More than a "treatise" it sounded like a declaration of black independence in the civil rights crises of the future.

✪

The Letter from Birmingham Jail

The public letter, in the tradition of Emile Zola's 1898 letter to
the President of the French Republic denouncing the Dreyfus
decision and Thomas Mann's 1937 public letter to the Dean of
the Philosophical Faculty of the University of Bonn, has long
been a means of persuasion used by reformers and politicians,
writers, and prisoners. We can now place among the lists of
great public letters Martin Luther King's "Letter from the Birmingham Jail," dated April 16, 1963. On Good Friday of that
year, the Reverend Dr. King, participating in a civil rights march
in Birmingham, Alabama, was arrested, held incommunicado for
twenty-four hours in solitary confinement, and not allowed to
see his lawyers during that time. After eight days of imprisonment, Dr. King accepted bond and was released. While he was
imprisoned, there appeared in the newspapers a plea signed
by eight Alabama priests, rabbis, and ministers urging the
Negro community in Birmingham to withdraw support from
the civil rights demonstrations being conducted there. These
eight clergymen said they were "convinced that these demon-

From Haig Bosmajian, "Rhetoric of Martin Luther King's Letter from
Birmingham Jail," *Midwest Quarterly*, Vol. VIII (January 1967), pp. 127-
143. Reprinted by permission of Midwest Quarterly.

strations are unwise and untimely." Dr. King's now famous
"Letter from the Birmingham Jail" was his answer to them.

The letter, as King has observed, was written "under somewhat constricting circumstances. Begun on the margins of the
newspaper in which the statement [of the eight clergymen]
appeared while I was in jail, the letter continued on scraps of
writing paper supplied by a friendly Negro trusty, and concluded on a pad my attorneys were eventually permitted to
leave me." It was not long before the letter was reprinted in
several national periodicals and distributed across the nation
in single reprints.

"Letter from the Birmingham Jail" was obviously not directed only to the eight clergymen critical of King's civil disobedience in Birmingham and laudatory of the Birmingham
police force for keeping "order" and "preventing violence."
The letter was not directed only to the Negroes of the community who were being asked by the clergymen to withdraw
support from the civil rights demonstrations. "Letter from the
Birmingham Jail" was addressed primarily to the moderate
clergymen and laymen, black and white, in both the North and
the South; King's appeals, however, turned out to be relevant
to all Americans. Just as King was speaking to clergymen and
laymen alike, so too did he himself speak as a Christian and
as an American.

Essentially the letter is a confirmation by King of his own
case; the letter, however, must also be, and is, a refutation. It
is refutative in the sense that King attempts to deal with the
accusations and arguments presented by the eight clergymen.
Apparently King felt that their attacks might have significant
consequences, for he does not delay at all in his refutation. The
eight clergymen had stated in their letter that the people of Birmingham were "now confronted by a series of demonstrations
by some of our Negro citizens, directed and led in part by outsiders." From the outset of his public letter, King turns his at-

tention to this worn-out "outsider" charge. That he found it necessary to justify his involvement in the civil rights activities in Birmingham is in itself a commentary on his audience, the eight clergymen, the "moderates," the Church in particular, Americans in general. He was, of course, dealing with an area of the nation where the "outsider" was especially suspect; he was in Birmingham, Alabama, where the "outsider" meant the Northerner, the carpetbagger, the "foreign" element.

King asserts that he is not an "outsider" on three counts: First, because of his organizational ties; second, because of his Christianity; third, because he is an American. At the outset, King makes the point that the Southern Christian Leadership Conference is an organization operating in every Southern state with headquarters in Atlanta, Georgia; further, the organization has eighty-five affiliates all across the South. He reminds his readers that he has come to Birmingham by invitation and that he has come to fulfill a promise. As a Christian he comes to Birmingham to speak and demonstrate because "injustice is here." He compares his situation with that of the early Christian prophets and thus not only argues by analogy, but also enhances his *ethos:* "Just as the eighth-century prophets left their little villages and carried their 'thus saith the Lord' far beyond the boundaries of their home town, and just as the Apostle Paul left his little village of Tarsus and carried the gospel of Jesus Christ to practically every hamlet and city of the Graeco-Roman world, I too am compelled to carry the gospel of freedom beyond my particular town. Like Paul, I must constantly respond to the Macedonian call for aid." Then King asserts that since he is an American he cannot be an outsider:

I cannot sit idly by in Atlanta and not be concerned about what happens in Birmingham. Injustice anywhere is a threat to justice everywhere. We are caught in an inescapable network of mutuality tied in a single garment of destiny. Whatever affects one directly affects all indirectly. Never again can we afford to live with the narrow, provincial, "outside agitator" idea. Anyone who lives inside the United States can never be considered an outsider anywhere in this country.

King's refutation takes into account the criticism by the eight clergymen of the civil rights demonstrations and of King's participation in them. "I would not hesitate to say that it is unfortunate that so-called demonstrations are taking place in Birmingham at this time," writes King, "but I would say in more emphatic terms that it is even more unfortunate that the white power structure of this city left the Negro community with no other alternative." Using a form of refutation known as the Method of Residues, King points out that of the various possible avenues of action which could be used to help solve the problem, the Negro community was deprived of them all, *except* demonstrations. The Negro was left with no alternative except to demonstrate, said King, because (1) the political leaders of the city "consistently refused to engage in good faith negotiations"; (2) leaders of the economic community in Birmingham had made promises, such as removing the humiliating racial signs from the stores, and these promises were never kept; (3) Birmingham was a community which "has constantly refused to negotiate." At the same time he was doing this, King portrayed the dismal Birmingham situation: "Birmingham is probably the most thoroughly segregated city in the United States. Its ugly record of police brutality is known in every section of this country. Its unjust treatment of Negroes in the courts is a notorious reality. There have been more unsolved bombings of Negro homes and churches in Birmingham than any other city in this nation. There are the hard, brutal, and unbelievable facts." The authenticity of these "facts" was not to be challenged by King's audience, for the police brutality, the mockery of justice, and the bombings had been exhibited by various news media for all America to see.

Since the clergymen had claimed in their letter that the Bir-

mingham demonstrations were "unwise and untimely," King
turned to explaining the necessity for nonviolent direct action.
"You may well ask," he writes, "Why direct action? Why
sit-ins, marches, etc.? Isn't negotiation a better path?" He
considers similar questions later in the letter and he thus demonstrates his awareness of what is in the minds of many Americans. Some have asked, he writes, "Why didn't you give the new
[city] administration time to act?" By airing such questions,
King acknowledges his familiarity with the questions that might
be asked by his critics. And by considering these questions,
King demonstrates a certain amount of honesty and fairness. He
asserts again and again his advocacy of negotiation; but the
avenues of negotiation have been closed to the civil rights leaders, he says. Hence the turn to nonviolent direct action. He
tells the eight clergymen: "You are exactly right in your call
for negotiation." As King explains it, "Nonviolent direct action
seeks to create such a crisis and establish such creative tension
that a community that has constantly refused to negotiate is
forced to confront the issue. It seeks so to dramatize the issue
that it can no longer be ignored."

To justify nonviolent direct action King turns to a persuasion
which combines the various means available to the advocate.
All through the letter, of course, he identifies the actions and
principles of the civil rights movement with various men of
renown, philosophers, theologians, and other historical figures;
on the other hand, he identifies his adversaries' cause and
principles with all that is evil. The creative tension which he
hopes to stimulate through nonviolent direct action he compares to Socrates' attempts: "Just as Socrates felt that it was
necessary to create tension in the mind so that individuals could
rise from the bondage of myths and half-truths to the unfet-
tered realm of creative analysis and objective appraisal, we must
see the need of having nonviolent gadflies to create the kind of
tension in society that will help men rise from the dark depths
of prejudice and racism to the majestic heights of understand-

ing and brotherhood." Two paragraphs later, King turns to Reinhold Niebuhr to support the contention that the segregationists and Southern privileged groups are not about to voluntarily give up their privileges. King writes: "Individuals may see the moral light and voluntarily give up their unjust posture; but as Reinhold Niebuhr has reminded us, groups are more immoral than individuals." A few paragraphs later, in a discussion of the differences between just and unjust laws, King turns to St. Thomas Aquinas, Martin Buber, and Paul Tillich to support his position. For those who might not be impressed with the arguments of these Catholic, Jewish, and Protestant theologians, King turns again to the name of Socrates: "To a degree academic freedom is a reality today because Socrates practiced civil disobedience." A clergyman attempting to persuade other clergymen could hardly amass a more formidable and respectable group of philosophers and theologians.

All through his letter King has developed his *ethos* by demonstrating his intelligence, good will, and high purpose. His character is enhanced by his identification with men like Socrates, St. Paul, Niebuhr, Buber, and Tillich. His very familiarity with these great men reflects his intelligence. A feeling of good will pervades the entire letter. It is at times very emotional, yet never does King turn to the use of such emotions as hate, anger, envy, and fear, except in one or two instances. His good will is reflected in the continued call for negotiation and in the reflective, nonbelligerent tone of his entire argument.

Dr. King handles the emotional aspects of the letter just as competently as he does his ethical proof. As he advocates nonviolent direct action and criticizes those people who ask the Negro "to wait," as he reproves those people who denounce the Birmingham demonstrations as "untimely," King reminds them that he has never "yet engaged in a direct action movement that was 'well timed,' according to the timetable of those who have not suffered unduly from the disease of segregation." One of the most emotional passages in the letter comes at that point when King explains why the Negro can no longer "wait." In this passage he piles one upon another the injustices, insults, and indignities suffered by the Negroes:

I guess it is easy for those who have never felt the stinging darts of segregation to say wait. But when you have seen vicious mobs lynch your mothers and fathers at will and drown your sisters and brothers at whim; when you have seen hate-filled policemen curse, kick, brutalize, and even kill your black brothers and sisters with impunity; when you see that vast majority of your twenty million Negro brothers smothering in an air-tight cage of poverty in the midst of an affluent society; when you suddenly find your tongue twisted and your speech stammering as you seek to explain to your six-year-old daughter why she can't go to the public amusement park that has just been advertised on television, and see tears welling up in her little eyes when she is told that Funtown is closed to colored children, and see the depressing clouds of inferiority begin to form in her little mental sky, and see her begin to distort her little personality by unconsciously developing a bitterness toward white people; when you have to concoct an answer for a five-year-old son asking in agonizing pathos: "Daddy, why do white people treat colored people so mean?"; when you take a cross-country drive and find it necessary to sleep night after night in the uncomfortable corners of your automobile because no motel will accept you; when you are humiliated day in and day out by nagging signs reading "white" men and "colored"; when your first name becomes "nigger" and your middle name becomes "boy" (however old you are) and your last name becomes "John," and when your wife and mother are never given the respected title "Mrs."; when you are harried by day and haunted by night by the fact that you are a Negro, living constantly at tip-toe stance never quite knowing what to expect next, and plagued with inner fears and outer resentments; when you are forever fighting a degenerating sense of "nobodiness"—then you will understand why we find it difficult to wait.

King follows this emotional passage with a sentence which carries the emotional impact even further: "There comes a time when the cup of endurance runs over, and men are no longer willing to be plunged into an abyss of injustice where they experience the bleakness of corroding despair." After these highly moving passages, King turns to his critics and says with a smack of irony: "I hope, sirs, you can understand our legitimate and unavoidable impatience."

King handles the emotional passages very well; where other writers might have become saccharine, he maintains balance and dignity. He never permits the highly emotional portions of the letter to run on too long; the moving, specific pictures he creates for the reader are preceded or followed by serious, philosophical thought. On the one hand, we see "tears welling up" in the eyes of the six-year-old girl because she cannot go to the for-whites-only Funland and we can hear the five-year-old son asking "in agonizing pathos: 'Daddy, why do white people treat colored people so mean?' " The innocence of children and the hurt they feel are universal experiences, in the worlds of both black and white. Parents, black and white, know the difficulty of answering such questions posed by the child. On the other hand, King does not dwell long on what might become overly sentimental; he quickly takes the reader back to the philosophical, back to concepts of good and bad laws, back to Socrates, Jesus, Aquinas, Jefferson, Buber, Tillich, and Niebuhr.

King ties the civil rights movement and demonstrations to the American dream, and more than once do the actions of Negroes demonstrating for their rights appear next to the political and social concepts and dreams of the American people. In well chosen language, King pictures the individualism and dignity of the civil rights heroes: "One day the South will recognize its real heroes. They will be the James Merediths, courageously and with a majestic sense of purpose, facing jeering and hostile mobs and the agonizing loneliness that characterizes the life of the pioneer. They will be old, oppressed, battered Negro women, symbolized in a seventy-two-year-old woman of Montgomery, Alabama, who rose up with a sense of dignity and with her people decided not to ride the segregated buses, and responded to one who inquired about her tiredness with ungrammatical profundity: 'My feets is tired, but my soul is rested.' " Here is the pioneering American, the one-time oppressed American struggling for freedom and dignity. As in the rest of the letter, the American is linked to the religious values of the Judeo-Christian heritage: "One day the South will know that when these disinherited children of God sat down at lunch counters they were in reality standing up for the best in the American dream and the most sacred values in our Judeo-Christian heritage, and thus carrying our whole nation back to great wells of democracy which were dug deep by the founding fathers in the formulation of the Constitution and the Declaration of Independence." King makes it clear, again and again, that what happens to the Negro in America is tied directly to the destiny of America: "We will reach the goal of freedom in Birmingham and all over the nation, because the goal of America is freedom. Abused and scorned though we may be, our destiny is tied up with the destiny of America."

In his reasoned, nonbelligerent manner, King goes about the business of answering a question implied in the letter of the eight clergymen, and a question also in the minds of many Americans: "How can you advocate breaking some laws and obeying others?" Recognizing what may appear to some people a contradiction, he devotes a significant portion of his letter to coping with this problem; his willingness to discuss the matter fairly is exemplified in his remarks at the beginning of the section on obeying just laws and disobeying unjust ones: "You express a great deal of anxiety over our willingness to break laws. This is certainly a legitimate concern. Since we do diligently urge people to obey the Supreme Court's decision of 1954 outlawing segregation in the public schools, it is rather strange and paradoxical to find us consciously breaking laws." Here King again draws upon the names of Augustine, Thomas Aquinas, Martin Buber, and Paul Tillich. It is King's contention that one "has not only a legal but a moral responsibility to obey just laws. Conversely, one has a moral responsibility to disobey unjust ones." Like Augustine, King contends that "an unjust law is no law at all." In distinguishing between the just law and the unjust law, King turns to Aquinas for support. "To put it in the terms of Saint Thomas Aquinas, an unjust law is a human law that is not rooted in eternal and natural law. Any law that uplifts human personality is just. Any law that degrades human personality is unjust." King's deductive argument is clearly developed; if one accepts the premises, then one must necessarily accept his conclusion. He argues logically: All laws which degrade human personality are unjust. Segregation distorts the soul and damages the personality (in effect, degrades human personality). Therefore, all segregation statutes are unjust.

Turning from Catholic to Jewish support, King puts the second premise of his deductive argument: "Segregation, to use the terminology of the Jewish philosopher Martin Buber, substitutes an 'I-it' relationship for an 'I-thou' relationship and ends up relegating persons to the status of things. Hence segregation is not only politically, economically, and sociologically unsound, it is sinful." The second premise: Segregation relegates the person to the status of things. Conclusion: Segregation is sinful. Again, King has constructed a logically developed argument.

Using a Protestant theologian as his source for a first premise in the development of another argument, King writes: "Paul Tillich has said that sin is separation." The second premise: Segregation is "an existential expression of man's tragic separation." Therefore, segregation is sin. The validity of King's reasoning here is dependent on the interpretation of the first premise. If "Sin is separation" is to be taken in the "Men are mortal" sense, then the argument is invalid. If, however, "Sin is separation" is to be taken to mean that "Separation is sin," then King's argument is a valid one.

After presenting these arguments and after dealing with the

abstract, King turns to the specific. He distinguishes between the evasion of the law by the civil rights demonstrators and the evasion of the law by the segregationists. The latter evasion he sees as leading to anarchy. But, he argues, "one who breaks an unjust law must do so openly, lovingly, and with a willingness to accept the penalty. I submit that an individual who breaks a law that conscience tells him is unjust and who willingly accepts the penalty of imprisonment in order to arouse the conscience of the community over its injustice is in reality expressing the highest respect for law." Then King demonstrates further *ethos* for his cause by declaring that there "is nothing new about this kind of civil disobedience," which was practiced, he writes, by Shadrach, Meshac, and Abednego in their refusal to obey the laws of Nebuchadnezzar and by the early Christians who "were willing to face hungry lions rather than submit to certain unjust laws of the Roman empire." By piling one example upon another, King demonstrates that the history of civil disobedience goes back many years and that it has been practiced by respected and revered individuals.

King devotes a large part of the letter to his disappointment with the "white moderates" and the Church. Essentially, he is disappointed in both for the same reason. In his consideration of the white moderate who is more devoted to "order" than to justice, King writes: "We will have to repent in this generation not merely for the vitriolic words and actions of the bad people, but for the appalling silence of the good people." Similarly, he says of the Church: "The contemporary Church is so often a weak, ineffectual voice with an uncertain sound. It is so often the arch-supporter of the status quo. Far from being disturbed by the presence of the Church, the power structure of the average community is consoled by the Church's silent and often vocal sanction of things as they are."

In answer to those moderate whites who charge that the civil rights demonstrations, "even though peaceful, must be condemned because they precipitate violence," King again turns to Jesus and Socrates for support. He answers the charge with a series of rhetorical questions which force his audience to indict themselves through their answers: "But can this assertion [that even though peaceful, the demonstrations must be condemned because they lead to violence] be logically made? Isn't this like condemning the robbed man because his possession of money precipitated the evil act of robbery? Isn't this like condemning Socrates because his unswerving commitment to truth and his philosophical delvings precipitated the misguided popular mind to make him drink the hemlock? Isn't this like condemning Jesus because His unique God-consciousness and never-ceasing devotion to His will precipitated the evil act of crucifixion?" King's disappointment in the moderate white is expressed in the bitter realization of a harsh sociological fact; he is at the same time expressing disapproval and an understanding when he states the following: "Maybe I was too optimistic. Maybe I expected too much. I guess I should have realized that few members of a race that has oppressed another race can understand or appreciate the deep groans and passionate yearnings of those that have been oppressed, and still fewer have the vision to see that injustice must be rooted out by strong, persistent, and determined action."

King's disappointment in the Church is no less than his disappointment in the moderate whites and is, in fact, deeper, for he is in "the rather unique position of being the son, the grandson, and the great grandson of preachers." As with his estimate of the moderate white, King confesses the possibility that he has been too optimistic regarding the Church. The questioning of his optimism turns to self-searching: "Maybe I must turn my faith to the inner spiritual church, the church within the Church, as the true *ecclesia* and the hope of the world. But again, I am thankful to God that some noble souls from the ranks of organized religion have broken loose from the paralyzing chains of conformity and joined us as active partners in the struggle for freedom." King sees an inevitability in the goal of freedom and justice for the Negro and he has "no despair for the future," for if the Church fails, King puts his hopes in God and America: "We will win our freedom because the sacred heritage of our nation and the eternal will of God are embodied in our echoing demands." King makes a good case against the Church with its adjustment to the status quo and its clergymen who "have been more cautious than courageous and have remained silent behind the anesthetizing security of stained glass windows." He has amassed enough evidence to warrant his indictment which he phrases, in part, in the following manner: "So here we are moving toward the exit of the twentieth century with a religious community largely adjusted to the status quo standing as a taillight behind other community agencies rather than a headlight leading men to higher levels of justice."

King warns the moderates who see his nonviolent direct action as excessively extremist that his movement has acted as an outlet to the pent-up resentments and latent frustrations experienced by the Negro. So let the Negro march sometimes, says King; "let him have his prayer pilgrimages to the city hall; understand why he must have sit-ins and freedom rides. If his repressed emotions do not come out in these nonviolent ways, they will come out in ominous expressions of violence. This is not a threat; it is a fact of history." And, of course, King is right, as any elementary text on psychology will explain. Those people who reject his nonviolent direct action cannot ignore the ominous threat of reality when he writes: "If this philosophy had not emerged I am convinced that by now many streets of the South would be flowing with floods of blood. And I am further convinced that if our white brothers dismiss us as 'rabble rousers' and 'outside agitators'—those of us who are working through the channels of nonviolent direct action—and refuse to support our nonviolent efforts, millions of Negroes, out of frustration and despair, will seek solace and security in black nationalist ideologies, a development that will lead inevitably to a frightening racial nightmare." King's reference to black

nationalism and the Muslim movement with their racist implications is the closest he ever gets to using the emotion of fear to
persuade his audience. And even here, he asserts that this is
not a threat on his part, "it is a fact of history."

Towards the end of the letter, King turns his attention to the
praise which the eight clergymen had in their letter for the
Birmingham police department. The clergymen had written:
"We commend the community as a whole, and the local news
media and law enforcement officials in particular, on the calm
manner in which these demonstrations have been handled."
King amasses several telling specifics to challenge this evaluation of police conduct by the clergymen. The misconduct of the
police which King described had already been seen by millions
of Americans over television and in the newspapers and magazines; the eight clergymen were obviously in error in their evaluation. With his comments directed to the clergymen, King said:
"I don't believe you would have so warmly commended
the police force if you had seen its angry violent dogs literally
biting six unarmed nonviolent Negroes. I don't believe you
would so quickly commend the policemen if you would observe
their ugly and inhuman treatment of Negroes here in the city
jail; if you would watch them push and curse old Negro women
and young Negro girls; if you would see them slap and kick old
Negro men and young Negro boys; if you will observe them, as
they did on two occasions, refuse to give us food because we
wanted to sing our grace together." Unarmed, nonviolent Negroes being attacked by the police dogs, small groups of unarmed, nonviolent girls and women being beaten by the police,
individual Northern clergymen taking part in the demonstrations being abused—all this was part of the public record, yet
the eight clergymen from Alabama saw fit to denounce the demonstrators and to praise the police. Then with a touch of irony,
King says: "I'm sorry that I can't join you in your praise for the
police department."

"Letter from the Birmingham Jail" ends with a mixture of

irony and conciliation. Although he seems to be speaking directly to the eight clergymen, King concludes his letter with comments relevant to all Americans. He describes the circumstances under which he writes the letter and remarks on the length of the letter: "I'm afraid that it is much too long to take your precious time. I can assure you that it would have been much shorter if I had been writing from a comfortable desk, but what else is there to do when you are alone for days in the dull monotony of a narrow jail cell other than write long letters, think strange thoughts, and pray long prayers?" Of course, King's time is just as precious as the "precious time" of the eight clergymen. It is implied earlier in the letter that the "precious time" of the eight clergymen is being used for nothing more than to maintain the status quo. Further, there is a reprimand, implied criticism in his reference to sitting in the narrow cell while the eight clergymen sit at their "comfortable desks." Although King cannot resist the irony, his letter seemingly ends on a note of conciliation when he asks to be forgiven if he has overstated the truth and when he writes that he hopes "this letter finds you strong in the faith."

At the end of the letter King once more returns to the dichotomy between earthly and divine law when he says: "If I have said anything in this letter that is an overstatement of the truth and is indicative of an unreasonable impatience, I beg you to forgive me. If I have said anything in this letter that is an understatement of the truth and is indicative of my having a patience that makes me patient with anything less than brotherhood, I beg God to forgive me." Once more it is more important to do that which pleases God than man: Understatement would please man, but overstatement of the situation would please God. Under the guise of humility King makes another ironic thrust at the eight clergymen.

Even in his final good wishes to his fellow clergymen, King cannot resist indirectly pleading his cause. For when he says in his final paragraph that he wishes to meet the clergymen not as an integrationist, but as a Christian brother, he is asserting one of the primary aims of his struggle: A true Christian brotherhood of white and Negro.

Considering the time, the place, the audience, the speaker, and the form, "Letter from the Birmingham Jail" can stand side by side with the great public letters of the past. Dr. King has chosen premises, upon which he builds his arguments, that are acceptable to almost all Americans and more particularly to the eight clergymen; he has identified his premises with respected, revered men, from Socrates to Tillich, from Aquinas to Buber. His premises come from laymen and clergymen, Protestant, Jew, and Catholic. There is nothing mean, low, or hateful in his premises. The validity of his arguments stands up to examination. He has amassed more than enough specifics and examples to make his inductive arguments acceptable. King's use of emotional proofs and his style are not only appropriate for his audience but are also consistent with the man, his philosophy, and his movement. He has reasoned with his audience; he has not insulted them by speaking down to them nor has he taken the pose of the intellectual superior. While he has aroused the emotions, he has not turned to exciting anger or hate, fear or envy. Martin Luther King's letter is rhetorically superior to any specific persuasive discourse which his critics and adversaries have produced. He has remained on a high plane; his goal for the brotherhood of man is thus exemplified in the word and in the spirit of his "Letter from the Birmingham Jail."

✪

The Conservative Militant

The phenomenon that is Martin Luther King consists of a number of striking paradoxes. The Nobel Prize winner is accepted by the outside world as *the* leader of the nonviolent direct action movement, but he is criticized by many activists within the movement. He is criticized for what appears, at times, as indecisiveness, and more often denounced for a tendency to accept compromise. Yet in the eyes of most Americans, both black and white, he remains the symbol of militant direct action. So potent is this symbol of King as direct actionist, that a new myth is arising about his historic role. The real credit for developing and projecting the techniques and philosophy of nonviolent direct action in the civil rights arena must be given to the Congress of Racial Equality which was founded in 1942, more than a dozen years before the Montgomery bus boycott projected King into international fame. And the idea of mass action by Negroes themselves to secure redress of their grievances must, in large part, be ascribed to the vision of A. Philip Randolph, architect of the March on Washington Movement during World War II. Yet, as we were told in Montgomery on March 25, 1965,

From "On the Role of Martin Luther King," *New Politics,* Vol. IV (Winter 1965), pp. 52-59. Reprinted by permission of the author.

King and his followers now assert, apparently without serious contradiction, that a new type of civil rights strategy was born at Montgomery in 1955 under King's auspices.

In a movement in which respect is accorded in direct proportion to the number of times one has been arrested, King appears to keep the number of times he goes to jail to a minimum. In a movement in which successful leaders are those who share in the hardships of their followers, in the risks they take, in the beatings they receive, in the length of time they spend in jail, King tends to leave prison for other important engagements, rather than remaining there and suffering with his followers. In a movement in which leadership ordinarily devolves upon persons who mix democratically with their followers, King remains isolated and aloof. In a movement which prides itself on militancy and "no compromise" with racial discrimination or with the white "power structure," King maintains close relationships with, and appears to be influenced by, Democratic Presidents and their emissaries, seems amenable to compromises considered by some half a loaf or less, and often appears willing to postpone or avoid a direct confrontation in the streets.

King's career has been characterized by failures that, in the larger sense, must be accounted triumphs. The buses in Montgomery were desegregated only after lengthy judicial proceedings conducted by the NAACP Legal Defense Fund secured a favorable decision from the U.S. Supreme Court. Nevertheless, the events in Montgomery were a triumph for direct action, and gave this tactic a popularity unknown when identified solely with CORE. King's subsequent major campaigns—in Albany, Georgia; in Danville, Virginia; in Birmingham, Alabama; and in St. Augustine, Florida—ended as failures or with only token accomplishments in those cities. But each of them, chiefly because of his presence, dramatically focused national and international attention on the plight of the Southern Negro, thereby facilitating over-all progress. In Birmingham, in particular, demonstrations which fell short of their local goals were directly responsible for a major Federal Civil Rights Act. Essentially, this pattern of local failure and national victory was recently enacted in Selma, Alabama.

King is ideologically committed to disobeying unjust laws and court orders, in the Gandhian tradition, but generally he follows a policy of not disobeying Federal Court orders. In his recent Montgomery speech, he expressed a crude, neo-Marxist interpretation of history romanticizing the populist movement as a genuine union of black and white common people, ascribing race prejudice to capitalists playing white workers against black. Yet, in practice, he is amenable to compromise with the white bourgeois political and economic Establishment. More important, King enunciates a superficial and eclectic philosophy and by virtue of it he has profoundly awakened the moral conscience of America.

In short, King can be described as a "conservative militant."

In this combination of militancy with conservatism and caution, of righteousness with respectability, lies the secret of King's enormous success.

Certain important civil rights leaders have dismissed King's position as the product of publicity generated by the mass communications media. But this can be said of the success of the civil rights nonviolent action movement generally. Without publicity it is hard to conceive that much progress would have been made. In fact, contrary to the official nonviolent direct action philosophy, demonstrations have secured their results not by changing the hearts of the oppressors through a display of nonviolent love, but through the national and international pressures generated by the publicity arising from mass arrests and incidents of violence. And no one has employed this strategy of securing publicity through mass arrests and precipitating violence from white hoodlums and law enforcement officers more than King himself. King abhors violence; as at Selma, for example, he constantly retreats from situations that might result in the deaths of his followers. But he is precisely most successful when, contrary to his deepest wishes, his demonstrations precipitate violence from Southern whites against Negro and white demonstrators. We need only cite Birmingham and Selma to illustrate this point.

Publicity alone does not explain the durability of King's image, or why he remains for the rank and file, of whites and blacks alike, the symbol of the direct action movement, the nearest thing to a charismatic leader that the civil rights movement has ever had. At the heart of King's continuing influence and popularity are two facts. First, better than anyone else, he articulates the aspirations of Negroes who respond to the cadence of his addresses, his religious phraseology and manner of speaking, and the vision of his dream for them and for America. King has intuitively adopted the style of the old-fashioned Negro Baptist preacher and transformed it into a new art form; he has, indeed, restored oratory to its place among the arts. Second, he communicates Negro aspirations to white America more effectively than anyone else. His religious terminology and manipulation of the Christian symbols of love and nonresistance are partly responsible for his appeal among whites. To talk in terms of Christianity, love, nonviolence is reassuring to the mentality of white America. At the same time, the very superficialities of his philosophy—that rich and eclectic amalgam of Jesus, Hegel, Gandhi, and others as outlined in his *Stride Toward Freedom*—make him appear intellectually profound to the superficially educated middle-class white American. Actually, if he were a truly profound religious thinker, like Tillich or Niebuhr, his influence would of necessity be limited to a select audience. But by uttering moral clichés, the Christian pieties, in a magnificent display of oratory, King becomes enormously effective.

If his success with Negroes is largely due to the style of his utterance, his success with whites is a much more complicated matter. For one thing, he unerringly knows how to exploit to maximum effectiveness their growing feeling of guilt. King, of course, is not unique in attaining fame and popularity among

whites through playing upon their guilt feelings. James Baldwin
is the most conspicuous example of a man who has achieved
success with this formula. The incredible fascination which the
Black Muslims have for white people, and the posthumous
near-sanctification of Malcolm X by many naïve whites (in
addition to many Negroes whose motivations are, of course,
very different), must in large part be attributed to the same
source. But King goes beyond this. With intuitive, but extraordinary skill, he not only castigates whites for their sins but,
in contrast to angry young writers like Baldwin, he explicitly
states his belief in their salvation. Not only will direct action
bring fulfillment of the "American Dream" to Negroes but the
Negroes' use of direct action will help whites to live up to their
Christian and democratic values; it will purify, cleanse, and
heal the sickness in white society. Whites will benefit as well
as Negroes. He has faith that the white man will redeem himself. Negroes must not hate whites, but love them. In this
manner, King first arouses the guilt feelings of whites, and then
relieves them—though always leaving the lingering feeling in
his white listeners that they should support his nonviolent crusade. Like a Greek tragedy, King's performance provides an
extraordinary catharsis for the white listener.

King thus gives white men the feeling that he is their good
friend, that he poses no threat to them. It is interesting to note
that this was the same feeling white men received from Booker
T. Washington, the noted early twentieth-century accommoda-
tor. Both men stressed their faith in the white man; both expressed the belief that the white man could be brought to accord
Negroes their rights. Both stressed the importance of whites
recognizing the rights of Negroes for the moral health and well-
being of white society. Like King, Washington had an extraordinary following among whites. Like King, Washington symbolized
for most whites the whole program of Negro advancement.
While there are important similarities in the functioning of both

men vis-à-vis the community, needless to say, in most respects, their philosophies are in disagreement.

It is not surprising, therefore, to find that King is the recipient of contributions from organizations and individuals who fail to eradicate evidence of prejudice in their own backyards. For example, certain liberal trade union leaders who are philosophically committed to full racial equality, who feel the need to identify their organizations with the cause of militant civil rights, although they are unable to defeat racist elements in their unions, contribute hundreds of thousands of dollars to King's Southern Christian Leadership Conference. One might attribute this phenomenon to the fact that SCLC works in the South rather than the North, but this is true also for SNCC, which does not benefit similarly from union treasuries. And the fact is that ever since the college students started their sit-ins in 1960, it is SNCC which has been the real spearhead of direct action in most of the South and has performed the lion's share of work in local communities, while SCLC has received most of the publicity and most of the money. However, while King provides a verbal catharsis for whites, leaving them feeling purified and comfortable, SNCC's uncompromising militancy makes whites feel less comfortable and less beneficent.

(The above is not to suggest that SNCC and SCLC are responsible for all, or nearly all, the direct action in the South. The NAACP has actively engaged in direct action, especially in Savannah under the leadership of W. W. Law, in South Carolina under I. DeQuincy Newman, and in Clarksdale, Mississippi, under Aaron Henry. The work of CORE—including most of the direct action in Louisiana, much of the nonviolent work in Florida and Mississippi, the famous Freedom Ride of 1961— has been most important. In addition, one should note the work of SCLC affiliates, such as those in Lynchburg, Virginia, led by Rev. Virgil Wood, in Birmingham led by Rev. Fred Shuttlesworth, and in Savannah, by Hosea Williams.

(There are other reasons for SNCC's lesser popularity with whites than King's. These are connected with the great changes that have occurred in SNCC since it was founded in 1960, changes reflected in the half-jocular epigram circulating in SNCC circles that the Student Nonviolent Coordinating Committee has now become the "Nonstudent Violent Noncoordinating Committee." The point is, however, that even when SNCC thrilled the nation in 1960-1961 with the student sit-ins that swept the South, it did not enjoy the popularity and financial support accorded to King.)

King's very tendencies toward compromise and caution, his willingness to negotiate and bargain with White House emissaries, his hesitancy to risk the precipitation of mass violence upon demonstrators, further endear him to whites. He appears to them a "responsible" and "moderate" man. To militant activists, King's failure to march past the state police on that famous Tuesday morning outside Selma indicated either a lack of courage, or a desire to advance himself by currying Presidential favor. But King's shrinking from a possible bloodbath, his accession to the entreaties of the political Establishment, his acceptance of face-saving compromise in this, as in other instances, are fundamental to the particular role he is playing, and essential for achieving and sustaining his image as a leader of heroic moral stature in the eyes of white men. His caution and compromise keep open the channels of communication between the activists and the majority of the white community. In brief: King makes the nonviolent direct action movement respectable.

Of course, many, if not most, activists reject the notion that the movement should be made respectable. Yet American history shows that for any reform movement to succeed, it must attain respectability. It must attract moderates, even conservatives, to its ranks. The March on Washington made direct action respectable; Selma made it fashionable. More than any other force, it is Martin Luther King who impressed the civil rights revolution on the American conscience and is attracting that great middle body of American public opinion to its support. It is this revolution of conscience that will undoubtedly lead fairly soon to the elimination of all violations of Negroes' constitutional rights, thereby creating the conditions for the economic and social changes that are necessary if we are to achieve full racial equality. This is not to deny the dangers to the civil rights movement in becoming respectable. Respectability, for example, encourages the attempts of political machines to capture civil rights organizations. Respectability can also become an end in itself, thereby dulling the cutting edge of its protest activities. Indeed, the history of the labor movement reveals how attaining respectability can produce loss of original purpose and character. These perils, however, do not contradict the importance of achieving respectability—even a degree of modishness—if racial equality is ever to be realized.

There is another side to the picture: King would be neither respected nor respectable if there were not more militant activists on his left, engaged in more radical forms of direct action. Without CORE and, especially, SNCC, King would appear "radical" and "irresponsible" rather than "moderate" and "respectable."

King occupies a position of strategic importance as the "vital center" within the civil rights movement. Though he has lieutenants who are far more militant and "radical" than he is, SCLC acts, in effect, as the most cautious, deliberate, and "conservative" of the direct action groups because of King's leadership. This permits King and the SCLC to function—almost certainly unintentionally—not only as an organ of communication with the Establishment and majority white public opinion, but as something of a bridge between the activist and more traditionalist or "conservative" civil rights groups, as well. For example, it appears unlikely that the Urban League and NAACP, which supplied most of the funds, would have participated in the 1963 March on Washington if King had not done so. Because King agreed

to go along with SNCC and CORE, the NAACP found it manda-
tory to join if it was to maintain its image as a protest organization. King's identification with the March was also essential
for securing the support of large numbers of white clergymen
and their moderate followers. The March was the brainchild of
the civil rights movement's ablest strategist and tactician, Bayard
Rustin, and the call was issued by A. Philip Randolph. But it
would have been a minor episode in the history of the civil rights
movement without King's support.

Yet curiously enough, despite his charisma and international
reputation, King thus far has been more a symbol than a power
in the civil rights movement. Indeed his strength in the movement has derived less from an organizational base than from
his symbolic role. Seven or eight years ago, one might have
expected King to achieve an organizationally dominant position
in the civil rights movement, at least in its direct action wing.
The fact is that in the period after the Montgomery bus boycott,
King developed no program and, it is generally agreed, revealed
himself as an ineffective administrator who failed to capitalize
upon his popularity among Negroes. In 1957, he founded SCLC
to coordinate the work of direct action groups that had sprung
up in Southern cities. Composed of autonomous units, usually
led by Baptist ministers, SCLC does not appear to have developed an over-all sense of direction or a program of real breadth
and scope. Although the leaders of SCLC affiliates became the
race leaders in their communities—displacing the established
local conservative leadership of teachers, old-line ministers,
businessmen—it is hard for an observer (who admittedly has
not been close to SCLC) to perceive exactly what SCLC did
before the 1960's except to advance the image and personality
of King. King appeared not to direct but to float with the tide
of militant direct action. For example, King did not supply the
initiative for the bus boycott in Montgomery, but was pushed
into the leadership by others, as he himself records in *Stride*

Toward Freedom. Similarly, in the late fifties and early sixties, he appeared to let events shape his course. In the last two years, this has changed, but until the Birmingham demonstrations of 1963, King epitomized conservative militancy.

SCLC under King's leadership called the Raleigh Conference of April, 1960, which gave birth to SNCC. Incredibly, within a year, the SNCC youth had lost their faith in the man they now satirically call "De Lawd," and had struck out on their own independent path. By that time, the spring of 1961, King's power in the Southern direct action movement had been further curtailed by CORE's stunning Freedom Ride to Alabama and Mississippi.

The limited extent of King's actual power in the civil rights movement was illustrated by the efforts made to invest King with the qualities of a Messiah during the recent ceremonies at the State Capitol in Montgomery. Reverend Abernathy's constant iteration of the theme that King is "our Leader," the Moses of the race, chosen by God, and King's claim that he originated the nonviolent direct action movement at Montgomery a decade ago, are all assertions that would have been superfluous if King's power in the movement was very substantial. . . .

It is indeed fortunate that King has not obtained a predominance of power in the movement commensurate with his prestige. For today, as in the past, a diversity of approaches is necessary. Needed in the movement are those who view the struggle chiefly as a conflict situation, in which the power of demonstrations, the power of Negroes, will force recognition of the race's humanity and citizenship rights, and the achievement of equality. Equally needed are those who see the movement's strategy to be chiefly one of capitalizing on the basic consensus of values in American society by awakening the conscience of the white man to the contradiction between his professions and the facts of discrimination. And just as necessary to the movement as both of these are those who operate skillfully, recognizing and yet exploiting the deeply held American belief that compromise among competing interest groups is the best *modus operandi* in public life.

King is unique in that he maintains a delicate balance among all three of these basic strategy assumptions. The traditional approaches of the Urban League (conciliation of the white businessmen) and of the NAACP (most pre-eminently appeals to the courts and appeals to the sense of fair play in the American public) basically attempted to exploit the consensus in American values. It would of course be a gross oversimplification to say that the Urban League and NAACP strategies are based simply on attempting to capitalize on the consensus of values, while SNCC and CORE act simply as if the situation were purely a conflict situation. Implicit in the actions of all civil rights organizations are both sets of assumptions—even where people are not conscious of the theoretical assumptions under which, in effect, they operate. The NAACP especially encompasses a broad spectrum of strategies and types of activities, ranging from time-tested court procedures to militant direct action. Sophisticated CORE activists know very well when a judicious compromise is necessary or valuable. But I hold that King is in the middle, acting in effect as if he were basing his strategy upon all three assumptions described above. He maintains a delicate balance between a purely moral appeal and a militant display of power. He talks of the power of the bodies of Negro demonstrators in the streets, but unlike CORE and SNCC activists, he accepts compromises at times that consist of token improvements, and calls them impressive victories. More than any of the other groups, King and SCLC can, up to this point at least, be described as exploiting all three tactical assumptions to an approximately equal degree. King's continued success, I suspect, will depend to a considerable degree upon the difficult feat of maintaining his position at the "vital center" of the civil rights movement.

Viewed from another angle, King's failure to achieve a position of power on a level with his prestige is fortunate because rivalries between personalities and organizations remain an essential ingredient of the dynamics of the movement and a precondition for its success as each current tries to outdo the others in effectiveness and in maintaining a good public image. Without this competitive stimulus, the civil rights revolution would slow down.

I have already noted that one of King's functions is to serve as a bridge between the militant and conservative wings of the movement. In addition, by gathering support for SCLC, he generates wider support for CORE and SNCC as well. The most striking example is the recent series of demonstrations in Selma where SNCC had been operating for nearly two years with only moderate amounts of publicity before King chose that city as his own target. As usual, it was King's presence that focused world attention on Selma. In the course of subsequent events, the rift between King and SNCC assumed the proportions of a serious conflict. Yet people who otherwise would have been hesitant to support SNCC's efforts, even people who had become disillusioned with certain aspects of SNCC's policies during the Mississippi Summer Project of 1964, were drawn to demonstrate in Selma and Montgomery. Moreover, although King received the major share of credit for the demonstrations, it seems likely that in the controversy between King and SNCC, the latter emerged with more power and influence in the civil rights movement than ever before. . . .

Major dailies like *The New York Times* and the *Washington Post,* basically sympathetic to civil rights and racial equality, though more gradualist than the activist organizations, have congratulated the nation upon its good fortune in having a "responsible and moderate" leader like King at the head of the nonviolent action movement (though they overestimate his power and underestimate the symbolic nature of his role). It would be more appropriate to congratulate the civil rights movement for *its* good fortune in having as its symbolic leader a man like King. The fact that he has more prestige than power; the fact that he not only criticizes whites but explicitly believes in their redemption; his ability to arouse creative tension combined with his inclination to shrink from carrying demonstrations to the point where major bloodshed might result; the intellectual simplicity of his philosophy; his tendency to compromise and exert caution, even his seeming indecisiveness on some occasions; the sparing use he makes of going to or staying in jail himself; his friendship with the man in the White House—all are essential to the role he plays, and invaluable for the success of the movement. It is well, of course, that not all civil rights leaders are cut of the same cloth—that King is unique among them. Like Randolph, who functions very differently, King is really an institution. His most important function, I believe, is that of effectively communicating Negro aspirations to white people, of making nonviolent direct action respectable in the eyes of the white majority. In addition, he functions within the movement by occupying a vital center position between its "conservative" and "radical" wings, by symbolizing direct action and attracting people to participate in it without dominating either the civil rights movement or its activist wing. Viewed in this context, traits that many activists criticize in King actually function not as sources of weakness, but as the foundations of his strength.

LOUIS LOMAX

✪

When "Nonviolence" Meets "Black Power"

His close inner circle called him "De Lawd," and wherever Martin Luther King, Jr., was, the *movement* was in the midst of him; for Martin King was the movement.

Along the streets of Montgomery in 1955, one could hear people ask, "Where is the *movement* tonight?"

"At Dexter Avenue," the reply would be. That meant that the nightly meeting in support of the bus boycott would be held at the Dexter Avenue Church. That *movement* rendered bus segregation a thing of the past.

"Honey," a Negro woman in Birmingham said to a neighbor, "the movement is out in the streets with the dogs and fire hoses." . . .

"The white folks have put the whole *movement* in jail!" a Selma woman exclaimed. Indeed a good deal of the *movement,* including Martin King and Ralph Abernathy, was in jail. But in the wake of their suffering and marching the nation got a new and sweeping civil rights bill.

From Louis Lomax, *To Kill a Black Man* (Los Angeles: Holloway House, 1968), pp. 113-122, 159-169, 189-197. Reprinted by permission of Holloway House Publishing Co.

The Southern Christian Leadership Conference was—and is—an umbrella organization. It has a staff of about a dozen people who kept the shop while Martin both answered and generated "Macedonian calls." Martin's early successes inspired many Negro ministers and other professionals in various Southern cities to launch their own *movements* against segregation. Invariably, the local leaders would be scorned and brutalized by their police and then the "Macedonian call" would go out for Martin and his lieutenants to come in and give assistance. Sometimes the local leaders would seek Martin's presence. On other occasions Martin would arrange to be called in. In either case the pattern was almost unchanging: Usually the local leader would have been jailed and released on bond by the time Martin came on the scene. With the local leader at his side Martin would then deliver a series of revivalistic civil rights sermons.

"I got on my marching shoes!" Martin would shout.

"Yes, Lord, me too," the people answered back.

"I woke up this morning with my mind stayed on freedom!"

"Preach, doctor, preach."

"I ain't going to let nobody turn me round!"

"Let's march, brother; we are with you!"

"If the road to freedom leads through the jailhouse—if the road to freedom leads through the jailhouse, then, turnkey, swing wide the gates!"

"Amen; praise the Lord!"

"Some of you are afraid," Martin told them.

"That's right; that's right."

"Some of you are contented."

"Speak, speak, speak," the masses shouted as they eyed the embarrassed black teachers and doctors in the audience.

"But if you won't go," Martin shouted.

"Don't hinder me!" the people joined in as they shared the climax.

At this juncture the organ or the piano struck the first soft notes of "We Shall Overcome."

"We will march nonviolently," Martin continued. "We shall force this nation, this city, this world, to face its own conscience."

"Yes, Lord!"

"We will make the God of love in the white man triumphant over the Satan of segregation that is in him."

"Yes, yes."

"The struggle is not between black and white!"

"No, no," the people confirmed.

"But between good and evil."

"That's it; that's it."

"And whenever good and evil have a confrontation, good will win!"

"Yes, Lord."

"For God is not dead; I know because I can feel him . . ."

"Deep in my soul!" the people shout completing the line from the Negro spiritual.

Then, arm in arm with the local leader, Martin led the people into the streets to face dogs, tear gas, fire hoses, and, frequently, brutality and additional jailing. With a few rare exceptions, the nonviolent ploy worked. The issue was settled either on local terms or through federal action. In his last years Martin's goal was federal legislation that would pre-empt the local issue and set a pattern for the nation as a whole.

This was the *movement* at its best, the leading of thousands of people into the streets to face danger for the sake of a freedom promised and written large in America's founding documents. Ofttimes local white judges would give King an additional weapon: they would enjoin him from marching and thus create a second issue—the right of the people to protest peacefully. This is precisely the path Memphis was traveling when King was assassinated. The garbage collectors, 95 per cent of whom are black, struck against the city for higher wages; weeks of protest passed with no progress, and scorn and recriminations from the white power structure. Then Martin answered a call to come in and give aid; his first march was flecked by violence for reasons I will discuss later. Martin was determined to carry out a peaceful march and received the added impetus he needed when a local judge enjoined him from marching.

"I do not believe the injunction is constitutional," Martin told a cheering crowd. "And I will not obey an illegal court order."

The pattern was the classic one and it was clear that Martin was preparing the people, and himself, for jail. The creative tension was building; it was just a matter of time before officials, either in Memphis or in Washington, would have to resolve the issue and restore calm.

As seen on television, the *movement* was an exciting and probing maneuver. The behind-the-scenes control of the demonstrations was yet a different matter.

Local leaders had created the issue long before Martin arrived in town. Inevitably, Martin became the focal point of national attention, ofttimes creating envy and jealousy. Black leadership is heady business and there is something about the prospect of appearing on "Meet the Press," and then making the "Liberal" circuit as a banquet speaker, that causes some men to do unusual things. Then there was the organizational question. Martin's staff was better educated and more experienced than the lieutenants of the local organizations they moved in to assist. Invariably, as the United States did to the government in Saigon, Martin's people would move in and assume the full direction of the *movement*. Many local leaders resented this; some of them withdrew and refused to participate further.

Money always breeds trouble. Once Martin King moved into a city and began demonstrations, thousands of people from around the world would send money, ofttimes loose cash, to finance the effort. To whom—what organization, that is—did this money really belong? The local movements were always penniless and the leaders felt the money should go into their coffers; Martin's earlier lieutenants felt they should manage the funds and pay only those local expenses they had authorized. In his last years, Martin's staff developed a method of avoiding this conflict; criticism based on the handling of money died out.

The Albany Movement of 1961, one of Martin King's true failures, provides an excellent insight into the strains and conflicts that inevitably accrued to the kind of organization Martin structured. The NAACP Youth Council of Albany elected to integrate bus terminal facilities in that Georgia city. They had a ready-made cause and plenty of marching bodies. A Negro state college was located there and the black servicemen stationed at the army base in Albany had been complaining about local segregated services for fifteen years. Following the NAACP tactic, the students made a quiet test; they sought service at the bus station and were refused. Once the issue was joined, the youths took the matter to court and settled back to what would have been a two- or three-year wait for a Supreme Court decision.

The Albany situation came to the attention of the Student Nonviolent Coordinating Committee in Atlanta, a student-oriented civil rights group that had been midwifed and financed by King's organization. SNCC launched "freedom rides" into Albany and mobilized local Negroes in support of the freedom riders. This put SNCC—and, tangently, Martin King—in direct odds with the NAACP. Hundreds of students, black and white, were jailed for violating state and local segregation laws. As the jailings and beatings mounted in Albany, blacks of all classes began to demonstrate in the streets; they were solidly behind the students. To avoid further conflict the Albany Movement was created; this allowed all of the groups to work together and receive equal acclaim. Dr. G. T. Anderson, a local physician and black leader, was named head of the movement. Another Montgomery was in the making and the nation's eyes began to focus on Albany.

At this juncture Martin King and Wyatt Walker, then his principal aide, flew in to Albany to give "aid and assistance." Martin's presence as an inspirational leader coupled with his willingness to endure jail was most welcome. But Walker had the power, the green power; SNCC was simply the conduit through which King's organization had financed the Albany Movement. The conflict was overshadowed, however, when world opinion condemned the jailing of Martin and Dr. Anderson. Tension mounted as both King and Anderson announced that they would stay in jail "until a change came." The secondary leadership carried out daily negotiations with the town fathers and always came away empty-handed. The city verged on a race riot and some definitive action would have occurred had Martin remained in jail as he promised. To everyone's dismay King elected to accept bond and walk out of jail. The chain that kept the creative tension was thus snapped and the bus station facilities were not integrated. . . .

This was King's most difficult hour; he was loudly criticized in every black community and people vowed never to follow him again. . . .

There were several key black leaders in Albany. The evidence suggests that one of them became mentally ill as a result of the days of danger and stress. During the march that led to King's jailing, this particular leader began to view himself as a holy man, perhaps Jesus; as he marched along with King he began making gestures which indicated that in his own mind he was sprinkling holy water on the black crowds that lined the sidewalk and cheered. Once in jail this leader's illusions of holy grandeur expanded to the point that, again in his own mind, he began to walk on water and feed a multitude of five thousand with the slice of bread the jailer brought him for supper. Martin and others of those jailed conferred and agreed that it would be disastrous for the movement if the white jailer discovered and informed the world that one of the key local black leaders was mentally ill. During jail visits, Martin's associates all agreed and every effort was made to persuade the man to accept bond. The local leader was adamant; he refused to quit jail as long as Martin remained in confinement. Martin had invited religious leaders from all over America to come to Albany and spend Christmas in jail with him. Scores were preparing to do just that.

Then one night the jailer noticed the black leader's peculiar behavior.

"That nigger acts like he done gone crazy!" the jailer observed within Martin's hearing. The following day Martin came out on bond and brought the ill leader with him. The leader in question soon left Albany and, after several months in a rest home, is completely recovered.

"A Major Defeat for Martin Luther King" the *New York Tribune* headline said of Albany. Perhaps it was, but Martin went on to march again in Birmingham. And in Birmingham the pattern of organizational conflict continued as King upstaged the Reverend Fred Shuttlesworth, the local black leader. But the two men had been friends for years and the problems never became personal or abrasive. More significantly, the Birmingham demonstrations were a major factor in bringing about federal legislation outlawing segregation in interstate commerce. Finally, then, the bus station facilities in Albany were integrated.

Like most inspirational and creative men, Martin King was not an effective administrator. He was apt to announce programs on the spur of the moment, and without careful planning, whenever "the spirit moved" him. In his early days he had several such men as his top aides, and the combination led to serious organizational problems. The Southern Christian Leadership Conference's annual convention of 1961 in Nashville is a case in point. During a press conference there, King had his aide, at that time the Reverend James Lawson, at his side.

"What is the program of your organization for the next year?" a reporter asked.

King deferred to Lawson who was program director of SCLC and Lawson replied, "We plan to send a nonviolent army through the South next year!"

The white reporter swallowed hard and then asked, "How many will be in your army?"

"Oh," Lawson answered, "I would say about a quarter of a million Negroes."

This was the first—and last—anybody but Lawson, including Martin Luther King, had ever heard about the nonviolent army of a quarter of a million blacks that would march through the South.

Perhaps the spirit of the times was such that these two traits, poor planning and the tendency to enter movements others already have underway, would one day produce Martin's gravest difficulties. After James Meredith was shot during his 1966 March through Mississippi, Martin and other black leaders decided to take up the march at the spot where the not too seriously wounded Meredith fell. Along with Martin on the march was Stokely Carmichael . . . King, the head of SCLC, Carmichael, the leader of SNCC, and Floyd McKissick, the director of CORE, formed a coalition to complete Meredith's march. The creative tension they induced along the highway was second only to the tension that was developing among the triumvirate itself. McKissick and Carmichael objected to the presence of white sympathizers who wanted to join the march; Martin, of course, insisted upon an integrated march. But this was not the gut issue; as they marched deeper into Mississippi the three men became absorbed in a debilitating argument over the basic philosophy that would undermine the civil rights movement from that point forward. The group marched into Greenwood, Mississippi, where hundreds had gathered in a local park for a rally. And it was there that Carmichael mounted the platform and issued his now famous and rasping call for "black power!"

Later Carmichael was to confess that he raised the issue during the march to get national attention; then he added, "Martin, I deliberately raised the issue here to force you to take a stand for black power."

Martin smiled dryly and then commented, "I have been used before; one more time will not hurt."

Perhaps it did not hurt, but Martin Luther King was to spend the remainder of his life and all of his energies attempting to combat the forces unleashed by Carmichael's strident call for "black power." To counteract these rioting forces, Martin determined to lead a "poor people's" march on Washington during the spring and early summer of 1968. Such skilled civil rights organizers as Bayard Rustin, the person who manned the March on Washington, strongly advised King against the effort; their argument was that black people are now too volatile for such a march to be staged and that, as presented to a Miami planning conference, the march was poorly organized. Martin insisted and Rustin lapsed into silent opposition.

. . . it seems clear that [King] viewed Memphis as an opportunity to aid the garbage workers as well as a training ground for the march he was to carry out in Washington. As Martin himself admitted, the first Memphis march was not properly organized. He promised both God and the people he would do better the next time around.

It was his ability to inspire people, not his organizational genius, that caused millions to give Martin Luther King, Jr., their total love and loyalty. In the beginning many suspected him of pursuing personal grandeur; but after he had climbed every mountain and then went on to die fighting for garbage men, history can only assess him as a man of total conviction.

His close associates knew this about him from the onset. This is why they called him "De Lawd."

．　．　．　．　．

The scene was a Miami Beach hotel early February, 1968. Some one hundred clergymen from across the nation had gathered there to assist Martin Luther King in his efforts to organize a poor people's march on Washington, D.C. With the lone exception of a white clergyman who pastors a church in the black ghetto of St. Louis, all of the ministers in attendance were black. King himself wore a button that read "Black Is Beautiful." The Martin King of this meeting was a totally different man from the flaming integrationist who had worked miracles in Montgomery, Birmingham, and Selma with scores of white Protestant, Catholic, and Jewish clergymen at his side. The times had forced Martin to embrace a modified form of black power.

The turning point had come during the summer and fall of 1964, in Selma, Alabama. King had mounted his Selma campaign with the aid of white liberals and young students from the Student Nonviolent Coordinating Committee. The black students marched with King but their hearts were not in the protest; some of them were jailed with Martin but—for them, that is—it was an empty gesture. They had seen too much, mourned the violent death of too many of their comrades, to any longer believe that King's brand of nonviolent demonstration would produce meaningful results.

The students' attitude toward Martin was that of any child who becomes convinced that his father is senile. They were kind, loving, and—for the most part—obedient; but they seized every opportunity to let Martin know they felt he was wrong. The divisive issue, of course, was Martin's insistence that the conscience of white America could be moved to action by nonviolent protest. Not only did the black students doubt the good faith of white America but they were hostile toward the white liberals who came into the South as civil rights volunteers as well.

The Selma march incurred the wrath of Sheriff Jim Clarke who ordered his men to tear-gas the marchers. As the marchers scattered in search of pure air many were chased by police and beaten to the ground; scores were injured and even more, including Martin King, were jailed. The entire episode was shown on national television and the nation recoiled in disbelief. As Martin languished in jail his lieutenants sent out the call for his black and white supporters from across the nation to converge on Selma for a march to the state capital, Montgomery, Alabama.

Each night King's lieutenants held a rally in a local church to drum up physical, financial, and psychological support for the march. The clue to what the young students involved were thinking lies in the fact that two SNCC members quietly invited Malcolm X, who had just returned from Africa, to speak. . . .

The police brutality at Selma had confirmed the students' dire prophecies. And the sight of scores of black men and women falling to the ground, curling up fetus-like, as white policemen beat them with clubs caused many people to wonder if this type of nonviolence was not itself immoral. "There is something morally wrong about allowing a man to beat you when you are in the right," a Los Angeles minister remarked to me at the time. "The good man must strike back and chastise the evil-doers (the police)."

Martin's followers did not strike back. The people rose from the ground, Martin emerged from jail, and together they led some fifty thousand blacks and whites on the sixty-mile trek to Montgomery. More, the Selma police brutality caused the Congress to pass the comprehensive voting rights bill of 1965. As a technical and legal matter all American Negroes finally had the franchise. But, significantly enough, the Selma-Montgomery march marked the end of the nonviolent civil rights era that began in Montgomery ten years earlier and catapulted Martin Luther King, Jr., into national prominence.

Two things had happened: Negroes had grown weary of being beaten and jailed for attempting to exert their constitutional rights; and the unprecedented civil rights gains that were recorded failed to sift down to the black masses, particularly in the Northern ghetto.

It was no accident, then, that Martin Luther King shifted both his target and his goals. He elected to improve the economic plight of the ghetto masses and Chicago was selected as the target city. By the time Martin made the decision to move against Chicago it was abundantly clear that the ghetto was the new center of racial concern. Watts had exploded into what was then the worst racial rampage in the nation's history; at least two score other cities also belched flames during the fiery and bloody summer of 1965.

Garbed in blue denims to reflect his oneness with the poor, Martin King moved into a Chicago apartment and began hanging out on the street corners with the oppressed and disillusioned black men whose fury imploded into violence. That was a new Martin—the man who played pool and drank beer with the hustlers. For the first time he understood that integrated bathrooms and restaurants were totally irrelevant to the lives of blacks trapped in the gateless poverty of the Northern ghetto. He also finally understood why nonviolence was becoming increasingly unacceptable. . . .

To make good his identity with the black ghetto dwellers of Chicago, Martin packed up his family and moved into a run-down Chicago apartment building. After a month there Martin noticed a chilling change in his children; they became sullen and hostile; they would not obey. His son became outright defiant. With no place to play, being constantly surrounded by hope-lessness and despair, the King child absorbed the syndrome of the ghetto. It was only a matter of time before they too would begin throwing bricks and fashioning Molotov cocktails. The children were shipped back home to the fresh air of black middle-class America.

The King children had the money to get out of the ghetto; they had a safe and secure home of grandparents as a refuge. The real ghetto dweller had no such escape; he was there with the core of the problem. In an unusual personal statement Martin wrote about his long nights of debate with those who felt that violence was the only solution for the ghetto dweller:

Over cups of coffee in my apartment in Chicago, I have often talked late at night and over into the small hours of the morning with pro-ponents of Black Power who argued passionately about the validity of violence and riots. They don't quote Gandhi or Tolstoy. Their Bible is Frantz Fanon's *The Wretched of the Earth.* This black psychiatrist from Martinique, who went to Algeria to work with the National Liberation Front in its fight against the French, argues in his book—a well-written book, incidentally, with many penetrating insights—that violence is a psychologically healthy and tactically sound method for the oppressed. And so, realizing that they are a part of that vast company of the "wretched of the earth," these young American Negroes, who are predominantly involved in the Black Power movement, often quote Fanon's belief that violence is the only thing that will bring about liberation. As they say, "Sing us no songs of nonviolence, sing us no songs of progress, for nonviolence and progress belong to middle-class Negroes and whites and we are not interested in you."

Nor was that all; black power advocates chose the Chicago campaign as an opportunity to openly attack their father-mentor. It was as if one's only begotten son had plunged the dagger in his father's back. I can feel the tears in Martin's soul as he described what transpired:

Unfortunately, when hope diminishes, the hate is often turned most bitterly toward those who originally built up the hope. In all the speaking that I have done in the United States before varied audiences, including some hostile whites, the only time that I have been booed was one night in a Chicago mass meeting by some young members of the Black Power movement. I went home that night with an ugly feeling. Selfishly I thought of my sufferings and sacrifices over the last twelve years. Why would they boo one so close to them? But as I lay awake thinking, I finally came to myself, and I could not for the life of me have less than patience and understanding for those young people. For twelve years I, and others like me, had held out radiant promises of progress. I had preached to them about my dream. I had lectured to them about the not too distant day when they would have freedom, "all, here and now." I had urged them to have faith in America and in white society. Their hopes had soared. They were now booing because they felt that we were unable to deliver on our promises. They were booing because we had urged them to have faith in people who had too often proved to be unfaithful. They were now hostile because they were watching the dream that they had so readily accepted turn into a frustrating nightmare.

. . . But King persisted and encountered yet another reality of Northern ghetto life—the open opposition of entrenched black middle-class politicians who were inseparably allied with the white power structure.

Black Chicago is the political plantation of veteran Congressman William L. Dawson, who is "H.N.I.C. (Head Nigger In Charge)" for Mayor Richard Daley. Dawson cracked the whip and a bevy of black clergymen raced on television to demand that Martin King get out of town. . . . By making a national public issue of the plight of Chicago's Negroes, Martin was on the verge of exposing not only a corrupt political system but the influence of the underworld in ghetto economic life as well. . . . In Chicago, Martin Luther King found himself fighting *The System,* that powerful combination of exploitative merchants, corrupt politicians, and amoral gangsters. These were the men who controlled ghetto life. They still do. . . .

Taking on Bull Connor in Birmingham and Jim Clarke in Selma was one thing; taking on *The System* in Chicago was quite another. Poor Martin; no longer was his adversary a white bigot; rather it was that amalgam of unprincipled greed and political corruption that resulted in the indictment of Newark Police Commissioner Dominick Spina and the public exposé of Senator Edward Long and Congressman Cornelius E. Gallagher. *Life* magazine exposed Senator Long's connection with the mob and just this year the people turned him out of office. Spina was indicted for his link to those who control gambling in riot-torn Newark. And as for Gallagher, not only does *Life* lay bare his alleged trafficking in an illegal cancer drug, but the magazine goes on to show why the New Jersey Congressman (from the suburbs of Newark) was of immense value to the mob:

"Among Gallagher's considerable attributes, so far as the

mob was concerned, was his seat on the prestigious House Foreign Affairs Committee."

These disclosures may have been as much of a shock to the readers of *Life* as they were to Martin Luther King. But they are common knowledge to the man in the black ghetto. Mobsterism, death, as well as corruption in high places are his daily fare.

King's Chicago campaign, then, was doomed from the onset. He made some modest gains through "Operation Breadbasket" which forced some companies to hire blacks, some merchants to lower their prices, and a few landlords to make necessary repairs. King's march into Cicero, the suburban gangland of Chicago, was a total disaster that erupted into almost unprecedented white violence.

Chicago was Martin's first, and last, campaign outside the South. It was his big effort to stave off the black violence then spreading across the Republic; it was his final stand against black power. Chicago was a failure, not for Martin himself, but for his Christian, nonviolent attack upon complex socio-economic problems. Chicago was final evidence that *The System* that controls the ghetto would not yield power to the nonviolent and the civilized. Only those who were willing to burn and loot had the power to get things done.

Back home in Atlanta, Martin closeted with his staff and brooded. They realized that Oswald Spengler's prediction that the American race problem would dissolve into a class problem had come true. Thus it was that Martin announced that he would lead a poor people's march on Washington.

The seed money for Martin Luther King's march on Washington came from white people, but such were the times that Martin could not afford to have his white followers in on the planning. He would have lost his Negro followers had whites been allowed to participate. More, Martin was under incredible pressure from both blacks and whites who argued that it was no longer possible to stage a nonviolent march in America.

Martin was determined to stage the Washington march. He assembled the black clergy from across the nation in Miami in the full faith that they not only would support his march but that, in the process, they would inherit the power in the ghetto and thus displace the black power militants who openly advocated burning the community down.

Martin Luther King was a dreamer. His assumption that black clergymen could take power in the ghettos was, by far, the most ethereal dream he ever entertained. Black power militants reserve their most passionate hate for the black Christian church. But in a blatant compromise with reality Martin King went "black." He dressed in the overalls of the poor, he proudly displayed his "Black Is Beautiful" button, and he wrote a book in which he adopted a modified form of black power.

The black clergy assembled in Miami, voted to support Martin although even they pondered the wisdom of congregating so many black and poor people in the nation's capital. By then Martin's innards were twisted in a double knot; his faith in Christians had been deeply shaken by the behavior of the white Protestants and Catholics in Chicago; now Martin's closest black supporters and fellow clergymen were doubting that an assemblage of black protesters ever again could remain nonviolent.

Martin Luther King needed a proving ground, an arena in which he could stage a successful nonviolent march and at the same time assume a modified black power stance that would reclaim the black militants who had defected after marching with Martin dozens of times only to drink the bitter water of white brutality.

Then came a Macedonian call from Memphis, Tennessee. The garbage workers, 95 per cent of whom were black, were in trouble and on strike. Memphis was the proving ground Martin needed to revalidate his credentials to march on Washington. He answered the call to come to Memphis. He would not leave that Southern town alive.

.   .   .   .   .

Black violence was a bitter thought for Martin Luther King, Jr., to entertain. Yet it was real, present, and uncompromising. What had started out as an incredible attempt to bring about major social change through nonviolent methods was transmuted into violence, burnings, looting, and riots in every major American city. Not that King's forces turned toward violence—far from it. Rather those black masses who reaped so little of King's civil rights harvest lost faith in both King and the American Republic. It was a bitter and difficult moment for a man who had built a movement upon the firm faith that white America had a conscience, that this conscience could be changed through nonviolent struggle and suffering.

As magnificent as his dream was, Martin Luther King's philosophy was fundamentally flawed from the onset. Power, as Lord Acton remarked, yields only to power, and even then not without a struggle. History simply does not support King's faith in the ultimate goodness of men, black or white. Rather, history, without a single exception, teaches that freedom belongs to those who have the power to take it. King understood this; but he translated "power" as "redemptive love and suffering"—a super-Christian concept which meant everything to the ethical philosopher, but nothing to the white bigot. Indeed the men King came up against viewed the brutality they visited upon him and his followers as not only a civic responsibility but the will of God as well.

The amazing thing is that King's tactic worked as well as it did. By marching, singing, praying, and suffering, Martin Luther King let America out of the prison of legal segregation. Only after the prison walls fell was it fully laid bare that the inmates of segregation had been maimed for life. Their tortured souls could be heard groaning in agony and despair from Mississippi to Cleveland's Hough, from Georgia to Watts, from Alabama to Harlem. King—admittedly with much help—had opened the door but the newly freed men were too crippled by experience to walk in. The black masses were but a disturbing statistic.

Comparatively speaking, their plight was worse at the time of his death than it was when he first entered the civil rights arena. The entire American economic wagon had rumbled forward but the gap between the front and back wheels—the whites and the blacks—had grown wider, not narrowed.

The long hot summers had rendered it all but impossible for large numbers of blacks to gather, except for religious and middle-class affairs, without the real possibility of violence and rioting. More painful to Martin Luther King was the undeniable fact that violence paid off. As killings, burning, and looting spread from city to city, the white power structure responded with reforms King never could have gotten through nonviolent supplication. In the wake of Martin's death Congress passed the national open housing law, the very goal King sought during his violence-scarred march through Cicero, Illinois.

The Martin who marched on Memphis was a driven man. More than any other black American he bypassed several excellent opportunities to quit the forefront of the civil rights movement, to go in another direction. A hundred pulpits were his for the asking; there was not a single major university that did not have a vacant chair waiting for Martin Luther King to take occupancy. No one would have blamed him for accepting one of those offers; he did not have to die by an assassin's bullet. But he elected to risk death in Memphis.

King's determination to stage a poor people's march on Washington cost him the support of some of his best allies and most brilliant tacticians—notably Bayard Rustin who had choreographed the magnificent March on Washington in 1963. Rustin took to the floor of the Miami meeting called by King and bluntly told the black clergymen assembled that Martin no longer had the power to lead such a prolonged nonviolent protest. Rustin flatly refused to direct the protest march and then called a press conference to tell all the world that he was not associated with the project.

Little was said about it publicly but King had depleted his political capital in Washington. Most of his splendid victories had come when Washington—in the Eisenhower, Kennedy, and Johnson administrations—intervened to stop white brutality and enact legislation. But King's strong opposition to the Vietnam war had alienated him from the Johnson administration. Many of the black clergy in attendance hesitated; they had different thoughts about Vietnam and feared that by following King, the leader of the poor, they would be interpreted as following King, the "dove" on Vietnam. When the final vote was taken they all agreed to march with King as he led the poor—ragged, tattered, and on mules—to the seat of power.

Lurking in the foreground were the shadows of Stokely Carmichael and H. Rap Brown. Beginning in 1966, these two leaders of SNCC unleashed a black power doctrine which said, in essence, if it takes violence to change America, then there will be violence. During his last year Martin's stance was that of a tolerated "Uncle Tom" as he talked about the goodness of the Lord and the moral sensitivity of the American white man. The word was out that Carmichael and Brown were already laying plans to infiltrate the poor people's march and turn it into violence.

"We must not refrain from doing good," Martin intoned, "simply because outsiders might infiltrate our ranks and do evil." Yet no one knew better than Martin that if the Washington march erupted into violence the blame would be laid at his feet regardless of who set off the violence.

The world watched and America grew tense, then, as Martin moved into Memphis during the first of April, 1968, to march and champion the cause of the long-suffering blacks of Memphis. The protest movement started out as a strike by Memphis garbage workers, almost all of whom are Negroes. But as the strike dragged on it involved the entire black community and the issues fissioned to include the problems of the black ghetto as a whole. Reflecting unprecedented organizing ability, the Memphis movement enlisted some six thousand supporters to march in King's nonviolent march. But days before the march began there were unmistakable signs of trouble. Members of the gang known as the Invaders actually maneuvered their way onto the planning committee and openly proposed that the march be deliberately turned into a violent demonstration.

"Man," one of the Invaders preached, "you know, we want to get something done. I mean, all this stuff about marching downtown, all these bourgeoisie wanting to march downtown and get their pictures on national television doing their civil rights thing, man, that's nothing. That ain't digging. That ain't going to help my brothers."

The Invaders mustered enough brass to ask a Memphis black clergyman to allow them to run off the formula for Molotov cocktails on the church mimeograph machine. The minister refused but the Invaders found an ally and the Molotov cocktail formulas were distributed.

At this point King's advance men arrived in town and pleaded their case for nonviolence before the Invaders' tribunal.

"Man," snapped one of the tribunal, "if you expect honkies to get the message you got to break some windows."

Even so the moderates seemed to have carried the day and the indication was that the Invaders would either remain non-violent or boycott the march. What actually happened on the day of the march is . . . under deep dispute. A secret federal government report . . . suggests that the Memphis police incited the violence—that they actually imported highway patrolmen from the neighboring state of Arkansas to deliberately foment trouble.

As the public record now stands, this is what occurred:

First off, black students at Hamilton High School raced out of the building to join the march. Riot-ready white police attempted to force the youngsters back into the school building. The students filled the air with rocks and bottles; the police responded with their billy clubs. When the turmoil settled, one

Negro girl lay seriously injured. The Invaders passed the word that the girl had been killed by the police.

Meanwhile marchers were gathering at Clayborn Temple Methodist Church, the staging ground for the march. Middle-class black women moved through the marchers asking individuals if they were "with the old folks or the young?" If they were with the "young," then they were for violence and were asked to quit the staging area. The Invaders left the march but they did not quit the area. When Martin Luther King and his lieutenants arrived at the staging area, the Invaders and other hostile black youth were gathered in a knot of anger and hostility on the periphery of the marching column.

King and his lieutenants, arm in arm, had led the marchers only a few yards when King was shoved from behind by a group of jeering youths. Other black militants raced ahead of the marchers and began smashing store windows; picket signs turned into weapons; looters began racing into alleys laden with clothes and liquor. As police moved in with tear gas and flailing billy clubs, King's aides hustled him into a white Pontiac and sped him to the safety of his eighth-floor suite at the white-owned Holiday Inn. The riot lasted three hours. The statistics: sixty injured; two hundred and eighty arrested; one dead.

Another casualty was the already weak hope that Martin Luther King—or anybody else, for that matter—could ever lead a nonviolent black protest march again. President Johnson took to television three times that day to speak of "mindless violence," and the nation turned an even more anxious eye toward King's projected march of the poor on Washington.

But as the nation grew increasingly apprehensive about Martin's ability to lead a nonviolent march, King became totally adamant. All of the fervor and dedication he had once invested in desegregating a Mississippi restroom was now committed to demonstrating that black Americans *en masse* could protest nonviolently.

A lesser man would have written off Memphis as the wrong march in the wrong city for the wrong reason. Not Martin.

"Nonviolence is on trial in Memphis," King lectured one of his staff workers. "It's either nonviolence or nonexistence." King was not just addressing himself to black Americans; the winner of the Nobel Peace Prize was talking to the world. *He who lives by the sword, shall die by the sword. Either man brings an end to war or war will bring an end to man. . . .*

And Martin did go back to Memphis. This time he assigned his advance men to mediate the turbulence, to make an amalgam of the black militants and the middle-class Negroes who wanted progress without violence. Martin's genius was his ability to work a miracle while dancing in the fire of certain defeat. He was on the verge of doing precisely that. All of the blacks, militants and moderates, sat quietly in the Mason Street Temple as Martin King's supporters set the scene for the new march that was to come, the nonviolent march that was to vindicate King's career-long philosophy.

"It is important that nothing happens to Dr. King," one minister shouted.

"Amen," the people answered.

"But for Dr. King," the clergyman continued, "Memphis would be smoking right now!"

"Yes, Lord."

"King is the man, O Lord, that has been sent to lead us out of the land of Egypt."

"Amen," the people answered.

Then, as loud applause and screaming "Amens" resounded through the hall, Martin Luther King moved to the lectern. He was tired, worried. Those who were standing closest to him recall that his eyes were faintly liquid. The opening line was a familiar one; then he went on to be more prophetic than even he knew:

"It is no longer a question of violence or nonviolence: it is a question of nonviolence or nonexistence."

By then the rain was tapping out a staccato tune on the tin roof of Mason Temple.

"There was a bomb threat on my plane from Atlanta," King told the shocked audience of several hundred. "But it doesn't matter to me now. I've been to the mountaintop; I've looked over and I have seen the promised land. So I'm happy tonight. I'm not worried about anything. I'm not fearing any man. Mine eyes have seen the glory of the coming of the Lord."

The meeting was adjourned with the understanding that they would all meet again the next night. This meeting was but the first of a series of such pep rallies designed to bring about total black unity for a nonviolent demonstration. King and his aides huddled late into the night in room 306 of the Lorraine Hotel, a Negro-owned establishment to which King had moved after militant blacks complained that he was "living downtown with the white folks."

As it always was with the *movement,* meetings began all over again the next morning, Thursday.

"Dr. King really preached us a sermon," Hosea Williams, one of King's aides, recalled later. "He sensed that some of us had doubts about nonviolence. He said that the only hope of redeeming the soul of this nation was through nonviolence. He talked about the lives of Jesus and Gandhi, and he told us 'I have conquered the fear of death.' "

Martin Luther King had a dinner date to keep but he lingered over the balcony rail to talk with another staffer, Jessie Jackson, who was in the courtyard below.

"Doc," Jackson shouted up to King. "This is Ben Branch, the musician who is going to play for our rally tonight."

"Yes, yes," King answered back. "Branch is my man. Be sure to play 'Precious Lord,' Brother Branch. Be sure to play it pretty."

"It's chilly tonight, Dr. King," yet another aide standing behind Martin said. "You had better take along your coat."

"You are right," Martin said as he straightened up from the

balcony rail. The cool Tennessee air was shattered by a shot from a high-powered rifle.

Martin Luther King, Jr., had crossed over the mountaintop and away from this life.

VINCENT HARDING

⭐

The Crisis of Powerless Morality

In his most recent work, *Where Do We Go from Here?* [Martin Luther] King attempts an assessment of black power that is significant and revealing, not for its originality or its challenge, but for the basic weakness of his response to the realities evoked and addressed by the ideology. There is in one chapter a favorable interpretation of the "positive" aspects of black power as a psychological healing force. Then as King attempts to define the elements which will bring the "necessary" power to the black community, he refers to power as "the strength required to bring about social, political, or economic changes," and identifies this power in many of the same ways as the churchmen and the leading black power advocates. When the words come from Martin Luther King, however, they bear somewhat more powerful implications. He writes:

There is nothing essentially wrong with power. The problem is that in America power is unequally distributed. This has led Negro Americans in the past to seek their goals through love and moral suasion devoid of power and white Americans to seek their goals through power devoid of love and conscience. . . . It is precisely

From "The Religion of Black Power," in *The Religious Situation, 1968*, edited by Donald R. Cutler (Boston: Beacon Press, 1968), pp. 32-37. Reprinted by permission of the Beacon Press, copyright © 1968 by Beacon Press.

181

this collision of immoral power with powerless morality which constitutes the major crisis of our times.

In religious (as well as political) terms, King's words constitute something of a crisis in themselves and raise many difficult issues. They tempt us, most importantly, to ask whether Martin Luther King was describing his own movement when he spoke of Negroes in the past who sought goals "through love and moral suasion" because no other way was available to them. If this identification is precise, then one must surely question the nature of such love and the motives of the moral suasion. And if the love was "powerless," why were so many past references made to "the power of love and nonviolence"—references found even in King's current work?

Surely the talk of love and suasion that was a kind of last resort is not in keeping with the insights of the great teachers of nonviolence, who set out this way for men who were not cowards, who had other weapons available, but who chose to put them aside for the sake of a better way. King's statements cause one to ask if there was really a nonviolent movement at any point. Was "too much love" really the problem? Could it be that nonviolence was simply impossible for a people who had never had an opportunity to affirm their manhood or to choose violence as a way of response on a widespread scale? Perhaps the late, lamented nonviolent movement can really come only after the Malcolms, Stokelys, and Raps have offered another real choice to millions of black folk.

Even more significant for the present discussion is King's failure to deal clearly and precisely with the central black radical conviction concerning America. Its advocates believe (and they have a growing company of fellow believers) that this nation will not allow black men the freedom, opportunity, and restitution needful for meaningful lives without a total, violent disruption of the society. Like revolutionaries before them, they believe that the national fabric must be rent before white people will believe in the validity of black demands for life. Here is the price of three centuries of racism, they say. King does not really respond to this assumption. He warns against cynicism, but fails to set out in clarity his response to a situation in which even massive, disciplined nonviolent resistance will continue to meet increasingly violent (and/or sophisticated) repression.

Somehow the night of that terror seems too dark for King to enter. His only real attempt at an answer to the black power conviction is a vague statement of faith, but the object of the faith also remains vague. King writes:

Our most fruitful course is to stand firm, move forward nonviolently, accept disappointments, and cling to hope. Our determined refusal not to be stopped will eventually open the door to fulfillment. By recognizing the necessity of suffering in a righteous cause, we may achieve our humanity's full stature. To guard ourselves from bitterness, we need the vision to see in this generation's ordeals the opportunity to transfigure both ourselves and American society.

There are missing links and false notes apparent in any religiously focused examination of this central statement. Nowhere is there any explanation of why King believes that the door "will eventually open." Is it faith in American goodness, in the power of a nonviolent movement that he hardly discusses, or faith in an abstract justice in the universe? (King's God often seems no less dead than anyone else's—at least if one judges life by appearance in the printed pages.) Without such clarification, his call could be dismissed as a Pollyanna voice attempting to challenge the whirlwind.

Even more important is his failure to discuss the possible reasons for an amorphous, variously motivated group of black people to suffer without retaliation the continued scorn and injury of people they consider at least fools and at most devils. When King referred to "powerless morality" and identified authentic power for black people with economic and political power, he was then likely obligated to ask who would be willing to live without such power once it became possible either to kill for it or to kill to protest its denial.

It would appear that, unless King is ready to face black men with the need to suffer without retaliation and also to live without the power he considered "necessary," much of his argument against violence falls apart. For the violence of revolutionaries comes not from "hatred," as he says, but from the insistence of the oppressed that they must have at least a proportionate share of the power which the oppressor insists upon keeping and defending by violent means. Leaders like Karenga say such power is absolutely necessary for black men. So does King. Black power leaders are convinced that the country will not make such power available without armed struggle of one kind or another. What does a believer in religious nonviolence have to say to such a situation? Is it enough not to face it squarely? And if he does, must King eventually choose between armed struggle and a powerless future for black people in the United States?

In a sense this dilemma is a reminder of how much the present black situation—especially in its religious dimensions—is a microcosmic expression of the main lines of the development of American Christian ethics in this century. Within the microcosm King stands for the liberal tradition, continuing to maintain faith in American goodness, in reason, in the ordered nature of the world. Such a stance seems to require his refusing to look directly into chaos, seems to demand that he fail to trace the deepest lineaments of the nation's racist core. In a sense King appears to hope that dark "principalities and powers" in massive array are only figments of overexercised religious imagination. In their place he substitutes an eloquent dream.

On the other hand stand the proponents of black power, like some dark blossoms of "realism" gone beyond control. They look with cynical but not dishonest eyes at the forces of evil in the society, at their depth and their extent. They see without flinching the possibility that power will not be shared voluntarily, that atonement cannot come without the shedding of blood, and they are determined that as little of the blood as possible will flow from them. They see the night and prepare men for its terror. They refuse to dream. But like much of the realist position, they also fail to acknowledge sufficiently (perhaps because of insensitivity on certain levels of their being) the reality of creative, healing forces in the situation. Somehow the power of resurrection is totally irrelevant to the struggles they outline, except in the most personal applications to individual "dead" black men.

Moved out of the metaphorical microcosm, these two perspectives are badly in need of each other for the mutual sharing and the possible mutual growth which may well be the nation's only visible hope in the racial crisis. The necessary, relentless determination of black power to look fully on the evil of American life must be informed by some hope even more solid than King's, some expectation of creative possibilities (even of Messiahs), some determination not to succumb to the enemy's disease. Even more soberly put, it may be that all who speak with any seriousness about addressing the profound social and psychological distortions wrought by American racism must be prepared to experiment with totally new weapons, and be ready (how hard the words!) for complete defeat—at least as it is commonly counted.

For if racism rages as deep into American life as it appears and if violence is its closest brother, then a black revolution will no more solve the problem than a civil war did (even if Rap Brown gets his atomic bomb). So it may be most responsible to ask if it is more than despair to speak of a long, grueling battle with no victory—and no illusions—this side of the grave? Has it been important and necessary simply to learn that there are no large citizen armies of white deliverers? Was it not absolutely necessary that all trust in courts and troops and presidents be shattered? Is this part of a black coming of age, a coming which will eventually reveal that even the black God of the ghetto is dead?

Perhaps, though, he is not dead. Perhaps this new God has not lived long enough to die. Perhaps there is still a Beloved

Community ahead. But if it is, it must be seen as the Kingdom whose realization does not depend upon whether whites (or anyone else around) really want it or not. If it comes, it may come only for those who seek it for its own sake and for the sake of its Lord, recognizing that even if He is black, the final glory is not the glory of blackness, but a setting straight of all the broken men and communities of the earth. In some strange ways black power may be headed in that way, but it probably needs some new and stripped-down coming of Martin King's most fervent hopes to accompany its path.

On the other hand, if the night is already too dark for the way to be found, or if society should make it impossible for these two black tendencies to live and find each other, then there seems little to expect that is not apocalyptic. This has always been a religious implication of life, especially black life. It is certainly one of the deepest implications of a wishful liberalism and an inescapable possibility for a black power that finally accepts not only America's weapons but also its ultimate definitions of manhood, power, majesty, and might.

Was it for this that we have come so painfully far together—and yet apart—in this strange land? Was it only for this? Is there no saving message from the drums of our homeland, or did all gods die at once?

✪

When "Civil Rights" and "Peace" Join Forces

He is perhaps the best speaker in America of this generation, but his speech before the huge crowd in the U.N. Plaza on that afternoon in mid-April was bad; his words were flat, the drama and that special cadence, rooted in his Georgia past and handed down generation by generation in his family, were missing. It was as if he were reading someone else's speech. There was no extemporizing; and he is at his best extemporaneously, and at his worst when he reads. There were no verbal mistakes, no surprise passions. (An organizer of the peace march said afterwards, "He wrote it with a slide rule.") When he finished his speech, and was embraced by a black brother, it seemed an unwanted embrace, and he looked uncomfortable. He left the U.N. Plaza as soon as he could.

On that cold day of a cold spring Martin Luther King, Jr., made a sharp departure from his own past. He did it reluctantly; if he was not embittered over the loss of some old allies, he was clearly uneasy about some of his new ones. Yet join the peace

movement he did. One part of his life was behind him, and a
different and obviously more difficult one lay ahead. He had
walked, marched, picketed, protested against legal segregation in America—in jails and out of jails, always in the spotlight.
Where he went, the action went too. He had won a striking place
of honor in the American society: if he was attacked as a radical,
it was by men whose days were past. If his name was on men's
room walls throughout the South, he was celebrated also as a
Nobel Prize-winner, the youngest one in history; he was our
beloved, *Time* magazine's man of the year; his view of Christianity was accepted by many Americans who could never have
accepted the Christianity of Billy Graham. In the decade of
1956 to 1966 he was a radical America felt comfortable to have
spawned.

But all that seemed long ago. In the year 1967, the vital
issue of the time was not civil rights, but Vietnam. And in civil
rights we were slowly learning some of the terrible truths about
the ghettos of the North. Standing on the platform at the U.N.
Plaza, he was not taking on George Wallace, or Bull Connor,
or Jim Clarke; he was taking on the President of the United States,
challenging what is deemed national security, linking by his very
presence much of the civil rights movement with the peace
movement. Before the war would be ended, before the President and King spoke as one on the American ghettos—if they
ever would—his new radicalism might take him very far.

On both these issues there had been considerable controversy
and debate within the King organization, especially among those
people who care most deeply for King, and see him as the posses-
sor of a certain amount of moral power. On the peace issue none
of King's associates really questioned how he felt; rather they
questioned the wisdom of taking a stand. Would it hurt the civil
rights movement? Would it deprive the Negroes of King's desperately needed time and resources? And some of these peace
people, were they really the kind of people King wanted to play
with? On the ghettos there were similar problems.

No one is really going to accomplish anything in the ghettos, goes the argument, until the federal government comes in with massive programs. In the meantime King can only hurt and smear his own reputation; he will get dirt on his hands like the other ward heelers if he starts playing with practical day-by-day politics in the North. In the North, in addition to the white opponents, there are all the small-time Negro operators who will be out to make a reputation by bucking Martin King. Yet the ghettos exist, and to shun them is to lose moral status.

After the New York peace rally I traveled with King for ten days on the new paths he had chosen. It was a time when the Negro seemed more than ever rebellious and disenchanted with the white; and when the white middle class—decent, upright— seemed near to saturation with the Negro's new rebellion. The Negro in the cities seemed nearer to riots than ever; the white, seeing the riots on TV, wanted to move further away from the Negro than ever before. A terrible cycle was developing. At press conference after press conference he said no, he didn't think his stand on Vietnam was hurting the civil rights movement or damaging the Negro cause with the President; no, he didn't think Stokely Carmichael's cry of black power had hurt the Negroes; no, he didn't plan to run for the Presidency. It was a week which began in New York with an announcement that King would go to the Holy Land in the fall on a pilgrimage.

Then came the first question: "And do you relate this to Vietnam?" No, King said, there were no political implications.

A Negro reporter who had been out to St. Alban's Hospital in Queens and had talked to the soldiers there said, "The war doesn't bother them. The soldiers are for it."

Later, on the way to the airport (most of King's life is spent going to airports, and it is the only time to talk to him), King's top assistant, Andy Young, commented on the fact that the Vietnam question had come from a Negro reporter. "It always does," he said. "Every time we get the dumb question, the patriot question, it's a Negro reporter." A New York minister said it was the Negro middle class wanting respectability and playing it close on Vietnam. "They're very nervous on Vietnam, afraid they're going to lose everything else." King added, "Yes, they're hoping the war will win them their spurs. That's not the way you win spurs." The ghettos, he said, were better on the war issue than the middle class.

The most important stop on King's trip would be Cleveland, where he was thinking of making a major summer effort to break down some of the ghetto barriers. It is a strange thing the way a city can rise to national and international fame over racial problems. Sometimes it is predictable. The word was always out in the South, for instance, that Birmingham was a tough city with a tough police force and Bull Connor; Negroes in Georgia and Mississippi knew about Bull Connor fifteen years before. Little Rock, which we once heard so much about, was an accident, its crisis deriving from its own succession laws and Orval Faubus' ambition.

Now there are cities imprinted on our memories that we barely know about, cities which we have forgotten, but in the Negro world, and in that part of the white world which is trying to cope with the coming fire, the word is out: Cleveland, where four people died in riots last summer, is likely to be a very tough place with all the worst aspects of the ghetto, and almost none of the safety valves. Unlike New York, where Mayor John Lindsay at least visits the slums, Mayor Ralph Locher seems to have written off the Negro vote, and to depend on the Italians, the Poles, and other white minorities. The Negro ministers there are interested in King's coming in for the summer action program, and though this is early May, a chilly day, and King is asking someone to find him a topcoat, there is a feeling that we will hear a good deal more about Cleveland before the summer is over, probably more than we want to.

King is edgy because the Negro community is divided. He does not want to get caught in a cross fire, and he is sensitive to what happened with his ill-fated organizing effort in Chicago last year.

Yet there are advantages in Cleveland. It is smaller than Chicago, better laid out geographically, and the Mayor is not so smart as Daley. His Chicago machine has enough Negro support to keep the Negro community divided; Locher's indifference to the Negroes in Cleveland may eventually force them to unite. But they must be brought together by someone from the outside. Here, then, is one of the ironies: for years the crisis was in the South, and Northern Negroes sent money and support there. In the process the most skilled leadership rose up in the South, fashioned out of the crises faced there, while in general the Northern leadership, so far lacking such direct and dramatic crises, lacks prestige; it must summon help from the South.

King is met at the airport by one of the older Negro ministers who is representing the Negro Ministers' Association. The preacher is about sixty, very pleased to be meeting King. As soon as we are in the car he starts talking about an earlier King speech and how much he liked it. Everyone else smiles politely, and there is a murmur of approval from King, which dies as the preacher continues, "I mean the way you got up there, Doctor King, and you told those Negroes they got to improve themselves, they got to help themselves more, isn't anyone else going to help them, and they got to clean up themselves, clean up their houses, clean up the filth in the streets, stop livin' like pigs, they've got to wash up. They can't just wait for someone to come to their doors with a welfare check, they got to help themselves."

There is silence in the car as he continues, his voice gaining in enthusiasm as he carries on, for he is preaching now, and driving a little faster too.

King says nothing, but from the back of the car, quite softly, the Reverend Bernard Lee, a King assistant, says, "You got to have something worth cleaning up, Reverend," almost as an apology.

The tension rises a little in the car; King is silent, and Bernard Lee speaks again. "It's easier said than done, Reverend. You've got six generations just trying to make do, and they've given up fighting."

But the Cleveland Reverend keeps on; the Negroes have got to clean it up; they've lost these homes.

This time it is Andy Young: "You ain't lost it, Reverend. They lost it for you. You never had it."

In all this King has said nothing, letting Lee and Young do the talking. (Later I am to find that this is his standard technique, holding back, letting others talk themselves out, allowing his men to guide the conversation to the point where it can be finally summed up by him.) "Well, Reverend," King finally says, "these communities have become slums not just because the Negroes don't keep clean and don't care, but because the whole system makes it that way. I call it slummism—a bad house is not just a bad house, it's a bad school and a bad job, and it's been that way for three generations, a bad house for three generations, and a bad school for three generations."

Then Andy Young starts telling of a home-owning community in Atlanta. Recently somewhat lower-class white, it was now turning quickly black, and somewhat middle-class black: "And so, of course, as soon as they've moved they all get together and have a big meeting about how to keep the neighborhood clean . . . and they want that garbage picked up, you know all that, and in the middle of the meeting, a man stands up at the back of the room and he tells them they're kidding themselves. 'Forget it,' he says, 'just forget it, because you're not going to get these services. I work for the sanitation department and I want you to know that they've just transferred twenty men out of this area, so you can just forget it all.' "

"Same old story," Bernard Lee says. "Negroes buy houses and immediately the services stop, and these aren't Negroes on relief, Reverend."

King, to ease the tension, asks about the Negro community of

Cleveland, and the preacher becomes so eloquent on the subject of the division within the Negro church community that Andy Young finally says, "Reverend, go back all the way to the New Testament. Even Peter and Paul couldn't get together."

"But *they* got it. They already got theirs, and we're trying to get our share," the preacher says.

King then asks, Is the Mayor a racist? No, says the preacher, it's not racism, "it's just ignorance. He doesn't know the pulse of the new Negro. The wrong kind of people are advising him, telling him handle the Negro this way, give him just a very little bit of this and a very little bit of that; give him a pacifier, not a cure, a sugar tit, that's what we used to call it in the South, a sugar tit, just enough to take away the appetite but doesn't fill you up . . . feed one man, give one man a job, and you've taken care of the Negroes." As he finishes, one can sense the relaxation in the car. The preacher has rehabilitated himself, he's not as much of a Tom as you think.

Then King starts talking about the cities. So very few of the mayors have the imagination to deal with the complexity of the problems, and the handful who do can't really handle it because they lack the resources. The problems are so great that they must go to the federal government, but most of them don't even know the problems in their own cities. It is almost as if they are afraid to try to understand, afraid where that trip would lead them. "Why, this Mayor Locher here in Cleveland," he says, "he's damning me now and calling me an extremist, and three years ago he gave me the key to the city and said I was the greatest man of the century. That was as long as I was safe from him down in the South. It's about the same with Daley and Yorty too; they used to tell me what a great man I was."

That was a simpler time. He had exuded love and Christian understanding during the nation's dramatic assault on legal segregation. In retrospect it was not so much Martin Luther King who made the movement go, it was Bull Connor; each

time a bomb went off, a head smashed open, the contributions
would mount at King's headquarters. They bombed King's own
house, an angry black mob gathered ready to do violence, and
King came out and said, "We want to love our enemies. I want
you to love our enemies. Be good to them and let them know
you love them. What we are doing is right and God is with us."
And, of course, it was a time of television, we could tune in for
a few minutes and see the cream of Negro youth, the slack-
jawed whites answering their love with illiterate threats and violence, shouting what they were going to do to the niggers, and
reveling in this, spelling their own doom.

King was well prepared for his part in that war; the weapon
would be the white man's Christianity. He knew his people, and
he could bring to the old cadences of the Southern Negro
preacher the new vision of the social gospel which demanded
change in America. He was using these rhythms to articulate
the new contemporary subjects they were ready to hear
("America, you've strayed away. You've trampled over nineteen million of your brethren. All men are created equal. Not
some men. Not white men. All men. America, rise up and
come home"). Before Birmingham, the Montgomery bus
strike was a success, and other victories followed. Grouped
around King were able young ministers, the new breed, better
educated; in a changing South he became the single most important symbol of the fight against segregation, culminating in
his great speech before the crowd which had marched to Washington in 1963. Those were heady years, and if not all the battles
were won, the final impression was of a great televised morality
play, white hats and black hats; lift up the black hat and there
would be the white face of Bull Connor; lift up the white hat
and there would be the solemn black face of Martin King, shouting love.

But in Cleveland in 1967 the Negro ministers are in trouble.
They are poorly educated products of another time when a call

to preach, a sense of passion, was judged more important than what was being said. Their great strength is organization; they try to hold their own separate congregations together. They get their people out of jail and they get them on welfare, and if that is not very much, there is nothing else.

But now they are divided—by age, by denomination, by style, by petty jealousies. They have not yet found the unifying enemy which bound their contemporaries together in the South, and they are unable to deal with the new young alienated Negroes, for whom their talk about damnation and salvation is at best camp; in the ghettos they cannot help those who need aid most. They are frightened by the Nationalists and Muslims, the anger spawned in the streets, the harshness and bitterness of these new voices, the disrespect to elders, the riots. In the South in the fifties all the preachers were on the outside looking in, but here in the North there is sometimes the illusion that they have made it and opened the door to the Establishment. So there is double alienation, not just black from white but black from black middle class.

When King arrives in Cleveland, he is immediately hustled off to a meeting of the ministers. The meeting lasts more than three hours, and there is a general agreement that King should come into Cleveland to organize; there is some doubt expressed because of what happened to his Chicago program, doubts which some of the ministers counter by listing otherwise unknown accomplishments and blaming the white press.[1]

---

[1] But many white reporters sympathetic to King, who thought the most important thing that could happen in America last year was for King to succeed in Chicago, consider his Chicago program a failure and a great tragedy. The problems had just been too great, the divisions within the Negro community too sharp, and the Daley machine too clever for him. The Daley machine was like nothing he had ever been up against before, with its roots in the Negro community. To this day there is no love by King for Daley, but there is considerable respect for Daley as a political operator. King sees Daley as a man for whom the machine is an end in itself, a man with little social vision, but with a sense of how social uses can be tailored to the perpetuation of the machine.

Afterwards, King has dinner in a Negro restaurant with eight key preachers, some of them old friends. At least one went to Stockholm with him to get the Nobel Prize, and he is letting people know about that. There is something here of a self-consciously jovial atmosphere, curiously reminiscent of white Rotary clubs in the South. . . .

Everyone tells King how glad they are to learn what a success the Chicago program was, and that they should have known that the distortions were the fault of the white press. The white press is soundly castigated. "Even here in Cleveland," one of the ministers says, "why, some white reporter asks Martin a question about the Mayor and Martin makes the answer that he thinks the Mayor is apathetic, and the next day the headline says, 'King attacks Mayor.' They got to sell newspapers that way." [2]

The dinner is pleasant, a discussion of the problems of Cleveland ("the middle-class Negroes are our problem, they've all gone to Shaker Heights and don't give a damn about being Negro anymore"); King says yes, it's the same all over. Finally there is some mild joking and one of the preachers, very dark in skin, points to another and says how much darker the other is. There is almost a reproach in King's remark: "It's a new age," he says, "a new time. Black is beautiful."

Just as they are about to break up one old friend, the one who went to Stockholm, starts talking about what a great man Martin Luther King is, how he is sent to them from Above. Then the preacher tells about the Nobel Prize ceremonies in Stock-

[2] Yet there is an increasing difficulty in covering racial news. Two years ago if a white reporter even hinted that there was division in the movement, he was accused of trying to create that very division. As the divisions became more obvious, each time you were with an established leader like Roy Wilkins, he would complain how the press *invented* radical leaders, created by the white press because of its guilt feelings. The next day you might be in Harlem talking with one of the more radical Negroes, and he would give a bitter discourse on how the white press played up only Whitney Young and Roy Wilkins; the white press was out to make the Negroes think that this mild leadership was all they had.

holm and Martin King, Senior. "There was to be a huge party afterwards," he explains, "and the champagne was all ready to be popped, and Daddy King stopped them. He's a complete teetotaler, and he said, 'Wait a minute before you start all your toasts to each other. We better not forget to toast the man who brought us here, and here's a toast to God.' And then he said, 'I always wanted to make a contribution, and all you got to do if you want to contribute, you got to ask the Lord, and let Him know, and the Lord heard me and in some kind of way I don't even know He came down through Georgia and He laid His hand on me and my wife and He gave us Martin Luther King and our prayers were answered and when my head is cold and my bones are bleached the King family will go down not only in American history but in world history as well because Martin King is a Nobel Prize-winner.' When he finished everyone was so moved, why the champagne just stayed there, and they made the toast to God and the champagne just stayed there afterwards. No one drank any, not even Bayard Rustin."

There was a moment of silence, and then one of the other ministers said, "Yes, sir, the Negro preacher is something. He sure is. God has use for him even when the Negro preacher didn't know what he was saying himself." . . .

In Cleveland King was to meet with both the preachers and the Black Nationalists, who have the support of the alienated young people.

The leader of the Nationalists is a tall mystic young man named Ahmed, who has a particular cult of his own combining racism and astrology—the darkness of the white man and the darkness of the skies. Earlier in the year he predicted that May 9 would be the *terrible day* when the black ghetto erupted. He made this prediction partly because there was to be an eclipse of the sun that day. Everyone laughed, old Ahmed, that crazy astrologer, but the police picked up him and a group of his followers that day just in case. Ahmed is mocked not only by the whites, but by the preachers as well. To them he represents nothing, has no job, all he does is talk.

King's people, however, believe Ahmed has a considerable, if somewhat fluid, influence. At first Ahmed and his men put out the word they were not interested in meeting with King; they were down on preachers, and he was a sort of Superpreacher. "He's really a Tom, you know," one of them told a King aide, "and one thing we don't need, that's more lectures from more Toms."

King went out to meet with them, however; he talked with them, but more important he listened to them, and it went surprisingly well. While he spoke nonviolence to them he did tell them to be proud of their black color, that no emancipation proclamation, no act of Lyndon Johnson, could set them free unless they were sure in their own minds they liked being black. And of course he talked with them on Vietnam, and they liked that also. The most important thing, however, was the simple act of paying attention to them. In Cleveland, King's people believe, the Nationalists are extremely important. Cleveland has particularly restless youths, up from Mississippi, either born there, or the first-generation children of parents born there. They are ill prepared for the cities. They come to these compact places like Hough, so that finally the inner ghetto is filled with the completely hopeless, floating, and rootless. It is estimated that one-third of the people in the inner ghetto change residence every year.

"There's a little power in these street gangs," one Negro says, "but power that doesn't go beyond a few blocks. Within those few blocks a man can be pretty big, you know he can shout, 'This is wrong, this is wrong, this is wrong.' But it doesn't go much beyond that. Past Fifty-fifth Street (the ghetto line), they're nothing, so they speak for the poor, but only to the poor."

That night the meeting was stormy. There had been some

talk that Ahmed and his people might walk out, but they remained inside and, indeed, dominated the meeting. "The preachers were afraid of them, but they weren't afraid of the preachers," said one of King's aides. Outside one of Ahmed's followers had decided to lecture to other younger Negroes: "Do you think ol' whitey, he's going to come by and say, 'Why there's Chuck Hill. He's a good black man. I'm going to spare that good black Chuck Hill.' No, whitey's not going to do that. He's going to shoot you down like all the others. Whitey doesn't care about any black man."

Inside the meeting, one of the more conservative ones said something about good things coming and the need for only a little more patience, and Ahmed jumped up angrily and said, "How can you trust a man that would kidnap a little child, bring him to a country he raped, put him down on stolen property, and then say, 'Just you wait a few days, I'm going to give you your freedom and lots of other good things'?"

A few minutes later there was a heated debate between Ahmed and a middle-class Negro. Ahmed had been talking, giving his program, when the man rose and shouted:

"Have you got a job? Have you got a job? Have you got a job?"

Ahmed answered, "My job is to free the minds of my people."

"No no no!" the man shouted. "Do you have an eight-hour job? Do you have an eight-hour job?"

"My job is a twenty-four-hour job," Ahmed replied, "and as a matter of fact, it's got just as much risk and danger as your job. Anytime you want to switch I'd be delighted."

The next day King's people were delighted with Ahmed. "He was so warm, so beautiful last night," one of them said, and in the middle of the press conference the next day announcing that King planned to come to Cleveland to organize for better housing and jobs, a King aide suggested to a Negro reporter that he ask Ahmed, sitting next to King, what he thought of King. Ahmed answered that King was a black brother; there was a happy sigh of relief from King's people.

One wonders whether King's alliance with the Nationalists can last. King is hot and they are cool; he overstates and they understate; he is a preacher and their God is dead. They are of the ghetto the way Malcolm X was, and like Malcolm they are flawed by it; that was his great strength. King is not of the ghetto, he is not flawed (*he never went around fighting with himself like we all did*), he is of the South. The people he touches most deeply are the people they left behind.

When one raises this question with Andy Young, he talks about the church being a force with young people, but one senses that he shares some of the doubts. He tells of when they went to Rochester, during the riots there. The Negro youths refused to talk with them until they beat them at basketball, beat them at shooting craps, proved they weren't squares. He tells of how the tough kids in Chicago didn't want to meet King. They finally did, and they were impressed with him, with the sheer power of his moral presence, but when he left they slipped right back into the gangs.

"We see the ghettos now as a form of domestic colonialism," Andy Young says. "The preachers are like the civil servants in Ghana, doing the white man's work for them." King has decided to represent the ghettos; he will work in them and speak for them. But their voice is harsh and alienated. If King is to speak for them truly, then his voice must reflect theirs, it too must be alienated, and it is likely to be increasingly at odds with the rest of American society.

His great strength in the old fight was his ability to dramatize the immorality he opposed. The new immorality of the ghettos will not be so easy to dramatize, for it is often an immorality with invisible sources. The slum lords are evil enough, but they will not be there by their homes waiting for King and the TV crews to show up, ready to split black heads open. The schools are terrible, but there is no one man making them bad by his own ill will, likely to wait there in the schoolyard with a cattle prod. The jobs are bad, but the reasons Negroes aren't ready for decent jobs are complicated; there won't be one sinister hillbilly waiting outside the employment agency grinding cigarettes into the necks of King and his followers.

King admits he is becoming a more radical critic of the society, and that the idea of "domestic colonialism" represents his view of the North. I suggest that he sounded like a nonviolent Malcolm; he says no, he could never go along with black separatism. For better or worse we are all on this particular land together at the same time, and we have to work it out together.

Nevertheless, he and his people are closer to Malcolm than anyone would have predicted five years ago—and much farther from their more traditional allies like Whitney Young and Roy Wilkins. King's people are privately very critical of both men; they realize that both work through the white Establishment to get things for Negroes, that they often have to tolerate things they privately consider intolerable because they feel in the long run this has to be done. The white man is there, he owns 90 per cent of it, and the only course is to work through his Establishment. King's people privately feel that this is fine, but that the trouble is the white Establishment has become corrupt, and in modeling yourself after it and working with it and through it, you pick up the same corruptions.

There are some very basic differences at issue here, much deeper than the war in Vietnam (though King's people see Vietnam as an example of the difference, for they believe that some high-level Negro acceptance of Vietnam is effected not because of agreement with the Johnson administration's position, but as a price to pay in order to get other things from the administration). In the split it is King who is changing, not Young or Wilkins. "For years," King says, "I labored with the idea of reforming the existing institutions of the society, a little change here, a little change there. Now I feel quite differently. I think you've got to have a reconstruction of the entire society, a revolution of values."

This means, he says, the possible nationalization of certain industries, a guaranteed annual income, a vast review of foreign investments, an attempt to bring new life into the cities. His view of whites has also changed deeply in the last year; previously he believed that most of America was committed to the cause of racial justice, "that we were touching the conscience of white America," that only parts of the white South and a few Northern bigots were blocking it. But after Chicago he decided that only a small part of white America was truly committed to the Negro cause, mostly kids on the campuses. "Most Americans," he would say, "are unconscious racists."

King is a frustrating man. Ten years ago *Time* found him humble, but few would find him that way today, though the average reporter coming into contact with him is not exactly sure why; he suspects King's vanity. One senses that he is a shy and sensitive man thrown into a prominence which he did not seek but which he has come to accept, rather likes, and intends to perpetuate. Colleagues find him occasionally pretentious; and the student leaders have often called him De Lawd, a title both mocking, and at the same time a sign of respect.

Being with him is a little like being with a Presidential candidate after a long campaign; he has been through it all, there has been too much exposure, the questions have all been asked before; the reporters all look alike, as do the endless succession of airport press conferences. King on the inside seems the same as King on the outside—always solemn, always confident, convinced that there is a right way and that he is following it; always those dark, interchangeable suits; the serious shirt and responsible tie.

He has finally come to believe his myth, just as the people

in the Pentagon believe theirs and the man in the White House believes his; he sticks to the morality of his life and of his decisions, until there becomes something of a mystic quality to him. His friend, Reverend Wyatt Tee Walker, who is not a mystic, and indeed something of a swinger and finds King almost too serious says, "I am not a mystic but I am absolutely convinced that God is doing something with Martin King that He is not doing with anyone else in this country." And Martin Luther King, Senior, believes his son is "a prophet. That's what he is, a prophet. A lot of people don't understand what he's doing and don't like it, and I tell them he *has* to do these things, things that aren't popular. Prophets are like that, they have special roles. Martin is just a twentieth-century prophet."

Friends believe King has become decreasingly concerned with worldly things, and has no interest in money. There are many fine Negro homes in Atlanta, but King's is not one of them; he lives in a small house right near one of the ghettos. He takes little money from his church and tends to return a good deal to it; despite this attitude his children are protected because Harry Belafonte, a friend of King's, has set up an educational trust fund for each one.

From Cleveland we flew to Berkeley for a major speech. Berkeley is now the center for the new radicalism in America, and King was likely to get a very warm response there; Berkeley would make him forget about the ghettos. Thousands of cheering young people would be there, applauding him. They would be there not because he led the March on Washington, for those days are easily forgotten (to some of them the March smacks of Tomism now), but because he is saying what they want to hear on Vietnam.

It was Vietnam, of course, which linked him with the new radicalism. His dissent was coming; that had been obvious for some time. Last winter when the peace groups and the New Left planned a major peace demonstration for the spring, the head of it was the Reverend James Bevel, a top King deputy who had organized for King in both Birmingham and Chicago. Bevel is the radical wing of the Southern Christian Leadership Conference, deeply Biblical and mystic, weaving in the new politics with the Old Testament. He is also something of a link between King and SNCC.

Bevel is an intense, fiery man, and these days the words genocide and race war come quickly to his lips, and he is obsessed with Vietnam: *"The war in Vietnam,"* he has said, *"will not end until Jesus Christ rises up in the Mekong Delta; the Lord can't hear our prayers here in America, because of all the cries and moans of His children in the Mekong Delta, and that is all He can hear as long as the war continues, so forget your prayers until the war is over, America."*

King's Southern Christian Leadership Conference is a rather loosely knit organization, and at Atlanta headquarters, there is a certain fear of what are now called Bevelisms. Recently there was a sharp kickback when Bevel spoke of a Catholic college and apparently made some remarks slurring the Virgin Mary. A young Jesuit questioned him sharply, and Bevel said, yes, he was interested in Mary, "but which Mary, all the thousands of Marys walking the streets of the ghettos, the thousands of peasant Marys being killed in the Mekong Delta, or some chick who lived thousands of years ago?"

The far-left groups who organized the peace march went for Bevel because they wanted King. King had seemed interested himself, but very slightly so. They contacted Bevel and they found he was interested, and ended up coming to their meetings. "Then the question was," one of them said, "could he deliver King? He said he could and he promised, but weeks went by and no King. We began to wonder. Then finally he came through."

They wanted King because they wanted a mass basis; they already had the automatics, the pacifists, their very own, but they wanted a broader constituency. As one peace organizer said, "There were a lot of people we felt wanted to come in on this, you know, good-hearted Americans for whom someone like King would make it easier, be a good umbrella. We could then call some of these unions and church groups and just middle-aged people who were nervous about coming in, who wanted to come in a little bit, but didn't like the whole looks of it, and we could say, Look here, we've got King, and it makes them all breathe easier. They think, Why it's King, it's all right, it's safe."

King repeats over and over again that he does not take stands because of what Stokely Carmichael says. Nonetheless, someone like Carmichael creates pressures to which King must inevitably react in order to retain his position. King would have reacted to the pressures of the ghettos and of Vietnam anyway, but without pressure and the alternative voices of a Stokely or a Floyd McKissick, he might have done it more at his choosing in his own good time. Stokely's outspoken stand on Vietnam made King's silence all the more noticeable. For King is a moralist, a fairly pragmatic one, and he does not intend to lose his position with young, militant, educated Negroes.

What was decisive in Bevel's role was that a trusted lieutenant in the most important of King's projects wanted out so he could join the peace movement. *That* moved King. Here was one more sign that a bright and passionate friend judged Vietnam more important than civil rights. It was symbolic of what King saw the war doing, taking all the time, money, energy, and resources of America away from its ghetto problems and focusing them thousands of miles away on a war the wisdom of which he doubted in the first place.

There are friends who feel that other factors affected him profoundly too, one of these being the right of a *Negro* to speak out. This had come to a point in early March at a fund-raising evening in Great Neck. King, Whitney Young, and John Morsell of the NAACP had appeared for an evening of speeches, questions, and answers. The subject of Vietnam came up, and King was asked how he felt. He answered with a relatively mild criticism of the war, the morality of it, and what it was doing to America.

Young was asked the same question and he dissented. There was the other war here in the ghettos, and that was the war the Urban League was fighting; he as an individual couldn't speak for the Urban League, but then he made his personal stand clear: communism had to be stopped just as Hitler should have been stopped in World War II. As the evening was breaking up, Young and King got into a brief but very heated argument. Young told King that his position was unwise since it would alienate the President, and they wouldn't get anything from him. King angrily told him, "Whitney, what you're saying may get you a foundation grant, but it won't get you into the kingdom of truth." Young quite angrily told King that he was interested in the ghettos, and King was not. "You're eating well," Young said.

King told Young that was precisely why he opposed the war, because of what it was doing to the ghettos. The argument, with a number of people still standing around, was so heated that King's lawyer quickly broke it up. Afterwards King felt badly about having spoken so angrily in public, and telephoned Young to apologize. They talked for more than an hour, failing of course to resolve their very basic differences.

This had happened to him once before. In 1965, when he was fresh from the Nobel Prize, King had briefly opposed the war and called for negotiations. There was a violent reaction. President Johnson got in touch with him and persuaded him to talk with that wooer-of-the-strayed, Arthur Goldberg. Goldberg assured him that peace was in the air. Similarly, King admits he was stunned by the extent of the pressure and reaction to him. "They told me I wasn't an expert in foreign affairs, and they were all experts," he said. "I knew only civil rights and I should stick to that." So he backed down, feeling a little guilty and suspecting he had been told that it wasn't a Negro's place to speak on Vietnam. This continued to rankle him, and after the Great Neck meeting he felt that if he had *backed* the war he would have been welcomed aboard, but that if he didn't back the war it was his place to remain silent.

Though King says he could never live under communism, he does not see the chief division in the world as between the communist and capitalist. His is a more U Thantian view, with the division being between the rich and the poor, and thus to a large degree the white and nonwhite (the East European nations would become Have nations, to the surprise of many of their citizens). His views of violence in Vietnam and violence in Angola are quite different. Yet he is also terribly American, more American than he knows; his church is Western, his education is Western, and he thinks as a Westerner, though an increasingly alienated one.

He does not particularly think of the war in Vietnam as a racial one (although the phrase "killing little brown children in Vietnam" slips in); rather he sees the American dilemma there as one of face-saving, of an inability to end a miscalculation and a tendency to enhance it with newer and bigger miscalculations. Because there is a good deal of conservatism in King, there was a lively debate among his advisers as to whether he could go into the Spring Mobilization. The Call to the march had the whole works, genocide and race war; and a number of King allies, traditional liberal, advised him against it. The old ladies in Iowa wouldn't buy it.

But after much negotiating, which King's people clearly enjoyed, it was finally decided he should go in without signing the Call. "I went in because I thought I could serve as a bridge between the old liberals and the New Left," he says. He is still somewhat wary of much of the peace movement, however; he does not know all the people as he does in civil rights, and he lacks a sure touch for the vocabulary of peace. He is also angry about having been ambushed by the New Politics people who leaked to the press in Boston recently that King was considering running for President; he was not yet considering it, and he felt they were trying to push him faster than he wanted to go; he remains wary of some of the peace people, and he realizes they are all out to exploit his name for their own purposes.

His stand on Vietnam is not necessarily the most popular one he has ever taken. It is popular on the campuses, of course, but it has hurt him with the editorial writers (Vietnam and civil rights don't mix), gladdened George Wallace, hurt him in the suburbs, and it has made the ghettos a little uneasy.

Peace is not a sure issue in the ghettos. There have been wars in which the Midwest provided many of the boys, and the small towns rallied around them. There are no picket fences in the ghettos and the American Legion posts are weaker there, but right now *our boys* are coming from the ghettos, and so it is a very delicate issue. One radical Negro leader thought Vietnam would be an easy whipping boy until he began to hang around Harlem bars, where he found you don't knock the war (black faces under green berets) and so he toned down his attacks. But some of King's best friends fear that Roy Wilkins may be wiser than King about how Negroes in the ghetto feel about Vietnam.

But Berkeley is another country. We went there one sunny day, and they were ready for him. They came to pick him up early in the afternoon, a young Negro dean and some bright young students, and they predicted a great reception for him —a demonstration for a King-Spock ticket.

We rode out together and I relaxed while a young student editor interviewed King; she had her questions all written down (Declining U.S. moral status in the world? Answer, yes. Doing this because of Stokely? Answer, no). The ride was pleasant, and the students were talking about the dove feeling on the campus, and King said, "I guess it's not too popular to be a hawk at Berkeley," and someone asked if he's for their right of dissent. "I'm too deeply committed to the First Amendment to deny the right of dissent, even to hawks," he said.

On the campus there are a lot of young men wearing pins which say simply, "October 16." That is their day, they explain, when all over the country they plan to go down to recruiting centers and turn in their draft cards. On the campus there are numerous signs saying "King-Spock."

His speech there is an attack on American values; it cites Berkeley as the conscience of the academic community and the center for new values ("we have flown the air like birds, and swum the sea like fishes but we have not learned the simple act of walking the earth like brothers"). It is looser and more natural than the peace-march one, and the biggest ovation of the day comes when King denies that he and Berkeley are against our boys in Vietnam:

"We're for our boys. We're their best friends back home, because we want them to come home. It's time to come home. They've been away too long."

A few minutes later, after answering questions (no, he will not run for President, though he is touched by their support; indeed he says they must be careful who runs against Johnson, perhaps it will be "Mr. Nixon, or your good Governor") he heads for a meeting of the Afro-American students.

Suddenly a white graduate student steps out and blocks his way. "Dr. King," the student says, "I understand your reservations about running for President, but you're a world figure, you're the most important man we've got, you're the only one who can head a third-party ticket. And so when you make your decision, remember that there are many of us who are going to have to go to jail for many years, give up our citizenship, perhaps. This is a very serious thing."

King is stunned; this requires more than a half minute, and the student presses on: "This is the most serious thing in our lives. Politically you're the only meaningful person. Spock isn't enough. So please weigh our jail sentences in the balance when you make your decision."

I have watched King with dozens of people as he nods and half-listens, and this is the first time I have ever seen anyone get to him. He waits for a moment, for the student to say more, and then realizes there is nothing more to say, and he finally says, "Well, you make a very moving and persuasive statement."

That meeting had shaken King a little, and on the way back to San Francisco we talked about the sense of alienation of the students. At the meeting one of the students claimed that the white man was planning to exterminate all American Negroes, every last one, that the war in Vietnam was being used solely for that purpose as a testing ground for weapons. "He really believed that," King said, "really believed that." Another student was deeply committed to separatism—move away from the white community completely, forget all the whites. "What's your program?" King had asked. "What are you offering?" But all he had was more radical rhetoric. Another student had advocated more violence, but King had answered "We don't need to talk mean, we need to act mean."

In the car King mused that the trouble with the people who talk mean is that they're always gone when the trouble finally strikes. "They lead you there and then they leave." Then he mentioned a confrontation with Charles Evers, the very able head of the NAACP in Mississippi. He said Charles had really whipped a crowd up one night, putting it to them on violence and the need for it, and King had finally said, "Look here, Charles, I don't appreciate your talking like that. If you're that violent, why you just go up the highway to Greenwood and kill the man who killed your own brother." And they applauded.

The students, King said, were disenchanted with white society, there had been too few victories, and they were losing faith in nonviolence—this and a sense of guilt over their own privileged status. Some of this is good, the fact that they identify with the ghettos much more than they did ten years ago, but there is also the danger of paranoia. One of the white students had mentioned how influential the autobiography of Malcolm X is with the students, both black and white, and added, "You won't believe this, but my conservative old Republican grandmother has just read it and she thinks it's marvelous, a book of love."

"That is what we call the power to become," King said, "the ability to go on in spite of. It was tragic that Malcolm was killed, he was really coming around, moving away from racism. He had such a sweet spirit. You know, right before he was killed he came down to Selma and said some pretty passionate things against me, and that surprised me because after all it was my own territory down there. But afterwards he took my wife aside, and said he thought he could help me more by attacking me than praising me. He thought it would make it easier for me in the long run."

The car finally reached the hotel. He had covered three thousand miles in the last few days, and now he was ready to recross the country, five stops on the way. The people, the faces, the audiences, the speeches were already blending into each other; even the cities were becoming interchangeable. Only the terrible constancy of the pressures remained. One sensed him struggling to speak to and for the alienated while still speaking to the mass of America, of trying to remain true to his own, while not becoming a known, identified, predictable, push-button radical, forgotten because he was no longer in the mainstream. The tug on him was already great, and there is no reason to believe that in the days ahead it would become any less excruciating.

✪

The Consequences of Decision

On a crisp, clear evening last April 4 [1967], the Reverend Martin
Luther King stood in New York City's Riverside Church and delivered the most scathing denunciation of U.S. involvement in
Vietnam ever made by so prominent an American. He labeled
the United States "the greatest purveyor of violence in the world
today" and accused it of "cruel manipulation of the poor." He
said that the people of Vietnam "watch as we poison their
water, as we kill a million acres of their crops."

He stated that U.S. troops "may have killed a million South
Vietnamese civilians—mostly children." He said that American
soldiers "test out our latest weapons" on the peasants of South
Vietnam "just as the Germans tested out new medicine and
new tortures in the concentration camps of Europe." He accused President Johnson of lying about peace overtures from
Hanoi and urged Americans to become "conscientious ob-
jectors."

Reaction across the nation and around the world was immediate and explosive. Radios Moscow and Peking picked up
King's words and spread them to distant capitals. In the White

Reprinted with permission from the September 1967 *Reader's Digest*.
Copyright 1967 by The Reader's Digest Assn., Inc. Originally published
under the title "Martin Luther King's Tragic Decision."

House, a Presidential aide shouted, "My God, King has given a speech on Vietnam that goes right down the commie line!" President Johnson, reading the wire-service reports, flushed with anger.

Civil rights leaders wrung their hands and began to plan steps to take the already splintered movement for Negro equality out from under the onus of King's broadside. Such prominent Negroes as Roy Wilkins, executive director of the National Association for the Advancement of Colored People, Ralph Bunche, Nobel Prize-winning United Nations undersecretary, and Senator Edward Brooke disagreed publicly with King. The directors of Freedom House called the program that King advocated "demagogic and irresponsible in its attack on our government." The *Washington Post,* long a supporter of King, said, "Dr. King has done a grave injury to the great struggle to remove ancient abuses from our public life. He has diminished his usefulness to his cause, to his country, and to his people."

What sort of person is this man who has been awarded a Nobel Peace Prize and denounced as a knave, all within three years? What do Martin Luther King and his recent actions mean to the nation and to the searing disputes that now rend the civil rights movement? . . .

How did King rise to the pinnacle? He had charisma—a down-to-earth sincerity, an ability to wear the mantle of the church in such a way as to suggest a special closeness to God. He won the grudging admiration of white Americans and the support of millions of foreigners through his dignity, his willingness to take verbal abuse, to go to jail quietly—and to turn the other cheek in the process—in order to achieve his goals. He seemed impervious to provocation. He earned the reputation of a selfless leader whose devotion and wisdom were larger than life.

When a group of badgered, beaten Negroes in Gadsden, Alabama, were on the verge of violence, King asked them to put down their arms. "Get the weapon of nonviolence, the breastplate of righteousness, the armor of truth, and just keep marching," he pleaded. They did. And when the young minister said to whites, "We will match your capacity to inflict suffering with our capacity to endure suffering. We will not hate you, but we cannot in all good conscience obey your unjust laws," he disarmed many who held latent hostility toward the Negro.

"There is no arrogance about him, no intellectual posturing," reported *The New York Times* in 1961. "He voices no bitterness against the whites who have handled him roughly." If he became involved in crisis after crisis—the restaurant sit-in in Atlanta in 1960; demonstrations in Albany, Georgia, in 1961; the explosive Birmingham protests of 1963; the Selma, Alabama, march of 1964—it was because, as one of his aides said, "You've got to have a crisis to bargain with. To take a moderate approach, hoping to get white help, doesn't work."

But, inexplicably, something began to happen after a while. King seemed to develop an exaggerated appraisal of how much he and his crisis techniques were responsible for the race-relations progress that had been made.

He could, indeed, make a pretty convincing argument that it was the crisis he and his followers precipitated in Birmingham in 1963 that capped the Negro's revolution and won the support necessary for the passage of the civil rights laws of 1964 and 1965. But other Negro leaders, while not belittling demonstrations, argued that the Negro could never forgo a reliance on the law. They pointed out that Negroes might still be walking instead of riding buses in Montgomery had the lawyers not won their case in the Supreme Court. They said that the Negro had to continue to seek strong legislation and just court decisions. They argued that the cause required a shrewd, sometimes sophisticated wooing of public opinion.

Negroes had, in fact, begun to grow uneasy about King. He no longer seemed to be the selfless leader of the 1950's. There was grumbling that his trips to jail looked like publicity stunts.

When arrested in Albany, Georgia, in 1961, he had declared dramatically that he would stay behind bars until the city desegregated public facilities. Two days later, he was out on bail. In St. Augustine, Florida, after getting Negroes fired up for massive demonstrations, he went to jail amid great fanfare. But two days later he was bailed out again, so he could receive an honorary degree at Yale University.

King really gave both critics and admirers serious cause for concern in 1965, when he began to talk about foreign policy. In July of that year, he told a Los Angeles group that the issues of racial injustice, poverty, and war are "inextricably bound together." When advisers expressed doubts about the wisdom of linking the three, he retorted: "One cannot be just concerned with civil rights. It is very nice to drink milk at an unsegregated lunch counter—but not when there is strontium 90 in it."

A month later, he announced that he intended to write President Ho Chi Minh of North Vietnam, and the leaders of South Vietnam, Russia, and the United States in an effort to move the war to the conference table.

Then, in September, 1965, he called on Arthur Goldberg, chief U.S. delegate to the United Nations, and urged the United States to press for a U.N. seat for Communist China. Also, he asked for a halt in American air strikes on North Vietnam, and he recommended negotiations with the Vietcong. At this point, even some of his strongest supporters began to demur.

The *New York Herald Tribune* said: "Dr. King is already committed to a massive, unfinished task in an area in which he has great influence. He can only dissipate that influence by venturing into fields that are strange to him." In a harsher comment, liberal columnist Max Freedman asked, "Is he casting about for a role in Vietnam because the civil rights struggle is no longer adequate to his own estimate of his talents?" NAACP leader Roy Wilkins, Whitney Young, executive director of the Urban League, Socialist leader Norman Thomas, and Bayard

Rustin, a chief planner of the great civil rights march on Washington in 1963 and himself a pacifist, all pleaded in vain with King not to wade into the Vietnam controversy.

Why did King reject the advice of his old civil rights colleagues? Some say it was a matter of ego—that he was convinced that since he was the most influential Negro in the United States, President Johnson would *have* to listen to *him* and alter U.S. policy in Vietnam. Others revived a more sinister speculation that had been whispered around Capitol Hill and in the nation's newsrooms for more than two years—talk of communists influencing the actions and words of the young minister. This talk disturbed other civil rights leaders more than anything else.

I report this not to endorse what King and many others will consider a "guilt by association" smear, but because of the threat that these allegations represent to the civil rights movement. When King was simply challenging Jim Crow, murmurings that he was associating with, or influenced by, "enemies of the United States" had only limited impact. Most Congressmen and editors knew that American Negroes did not need a communist to tell them that they disliked being herded into the rear of buses, the balconies of theaters, the back doors of restaurants, or a ramshackle school across the briar patch. But now that King has become deeply involved in a conflict where the United States is in direct combat with communists, the murmurings are likely to produce powerfully hostile reactions. They cannot help but imperil chances of passage of the civil rights bill that would protect civil rights workers in the South and make housing discrimination illegal.

King answered his critics. He had become convinced, he said in his April 4 speech at New York's Riverside Church, that America would never invest the necessary funds or energies in rehabilitation of its poor "so long as adventures like Vietnam continue to draw men and skills and money like some demonic destructive suction tube." He told the Riverside audience that "we are taking black young men who have been crippled by our society and sending them eight thousand miles away to guarantee liberties in Southeast Asia which they have not found in southwest Georgia and East Harlem."

The latter is an old cry that some Negroes have uttered in every American war. But in no conflict has a Negro with King's prestige urged Negroes to shun battle because they have nothing to fight for. King must have assumed that the "new Negro," full of frustration as he is, would be sympathetic to this argument. But a recent Harris survey showed that almost one of every two Negroes believes that King is wrong—and another 27 per cent reserved judgment.

I find this opposition to King remarkable, considering the amount of emotion and anger involved in the Negro revolution. It suggests that most Negroes are proud of the integrated performance of colored GIs in Vietnam; that most Negroes still think of America as *their* country and do not want to seem unpatriotic.

Beyond doubt, King's speech at Riverside Church and his subsequent remarks have put a new strain and new burdens on the civil rights movement. He has become *persona non grata* to Lyndon Johnson, a fact that he may consider of no consequence. It is also likely that his former friends in Congress will never again listen to or be moved by him the way they were in the past. This, too, may not bother King. But it can make the difference between poverty and well-being for millions of Negroes who cannot break the vicious circle of poverty and unpreparedness that imprisons them unless the President provides leadership and Congress provides the circle-breaking programs and laws.

Martin Luther King has alienated many of the Negro's friends and armed the Negro's foes, in both parties, by creating the impression that the Negro is disloyal. By urging Negroes not to respond to the draft or to fight in Vietnam, he has taken a tack that many Americans of all races consider utterly irresponsible.

It is a tragic irony that there should be any doubt about the Negro's loyalty to his country—especially doubt created by Martin Luther King, who has helped as much as any one man to make America truly the Negro's country, too.

★

Our Lives Were Filled with the Action

Martin,

I miss you and it has been just a few days. I thought I would write you a short letter. It is probably more for my good than it is for yours. I hope it will not be too long before you read it. In Heaven I know you have so much to do, so many people to see. And I know many of them have already been looking and waiting for you. It wouldn't be a surprise to me, Martin, if God didn't have a special affair just to introduce his special activist black son to so many others like you that have gone on ahead. I know you wouldn't believe that could happen but then you did not always understand how wonderful you are.

But look up these black friends and talk to the ones you and I have talked about; and the ones that you and I led; and the ones who so gallantly followed your leadership. Say thanks to those prophets we quoted all over America and everywhere else that they asked for us. Give a special word from me to Peter, the man who was once sand, but Jesus made him a rock. Give my warmest felicitations to my favorite apostle, John, who loved my Master so much until he stood with his mother at the foot of the Cross. Pass my greetings on to Isaiah, who had the prophetic vision to see the coming of a Saviour whose name

From "My Last Letter to Martin," *Ebony* (July 1968), pp. 58-61.

would be Wonderful, a Mighty Counselor, an Everlasting Father, and a Prince of Peace. Stop by and chat with Hosea. And
find Mahatma K. Gandhi, the man who inspired us so much in
our struggle to free black people through the philosophy and
techniques of nonviolence. And in the midst of your conversa-
tions, Martin, mention me. Look up Bartholomew. For some
strange reason I always liked him.

But, above all, I want you to see Jesus. Go to the throne and
tell how thankful we are. Yes, go see Jesus, and tell Him about
us down here, all of us, and all of our families, and how we have
sustained ourselves in the many battles all through our lives.
Tell Him how much we love Him. Tell Him how His name is
music in our ears. Tell Him how at His name our knees will
forever bow and our tongues will always confess. Tell Him
that we follow not only His words but we follow His life, for
His footprints lead to Bethany, for that's where He stayed;
but they lead to Gethsemane, for it was there He prayed.
They lead to Calvary where salvation was complete. There
we were saved by His grace.

Then, Martin, go from the throne and find the Reverend
George Lee, that stalwart hero who could barely read and write,
who was shot down on the streets of Belzoni, Mississippi, simply because he wanted to vote. Check with Medgar Evers, who
was shot down by mean and cruel white men, who thought they
could turn us around by taking the life of this young man. Check
with William Moore, another casualty in Alabama. And then
Jimmy Lee Jackson, who died on the battlefield of Alabama.
Oh, I wish you would look up Mrs. Viola Liuzzo, a white woman
who was killed, you remember, on Highway 80; and then check
with Jonathan Daniels, a young theological Catholic student
who died in Haynesville, Alabama, down in Lowndes County,
standing up for the rights of black people. James Reeb should
be seen also, Martin. For James Reeb, a Unitarian minister,
was beaten to death when he came to march for us in Selma.
And don't forget Michael Schwerner and Andrew Goodman

and James Chaney. You remember those three freedom fighters
that they killed in Mississippi and buried their bodies beneath
an earthen dam. Express our thanks to them. And then, Martin,
don't forget the four little innocent girls who died in a Sunday
School class in the Sixteenth Street Baptist Church in Birmingham. They've been waiting to hear from us. Give them a good
and complete report. And tell them that you left your people
on your way. And we're determined that we ain't gonna let nobody turn us around.

And then, Martin, find Frederick Douglass, that great and
marvelous human personality who lived in even more difficult
times than we live today. Check with Nat Turner, and Marcus
Garvey, for they, too, are heroes in our crusade. And oh, I wish
that you would pause long enough at the mansion that is occu-
pied by Abraham Lincoln, the man who freed us from physical bondage here in this country. Then, Martin, we owe a
great debt of gratitude to John Fitzgerald Kennedy who less than
five years ago, young as you were, brilliant as you were, filled
with new ideas as you were, was shot down and killed as you
were in cold blood by a mean, vicious, and angry society. And
don't forget Malcolm X. Look for Malcolm X, Martin. Remember
our God is a loving God and He understands things we don't
think that He understands. Malcolm may not have believed
what we believe and he may not have preached but he was a
child of God and he was concerned about the welfare of his
people. And then, Martin, please do not forget about all of those
who died across Alabama, Mississippi, Louisiana, Chicago, and
New York, and all other places where men have died for the
liberty and justice of other men. Martin, it may seem like a big
order, but if you find one of them, he will know where the rest
are. And he will take you to them. I know that they have
founded the grand international company of freedom fighters,
and can't wait to introduce you to take over the final hours.

A man on Hunter Street said, "I envy the way that he died. He
will be with so many who have died like he did."

I know that you have a lot to talk about and you will have a wonderful time, but, remember, your brother, Ralph, will be coming along one day. One thing, we won't have any critics up there, Martin. I don't think they will make it, that they will be there. Every day will be Sunday. None but the righteous will see God.

The day after I last saw you in Memphis, I remembered you from the first time I saw you. It was in Montgomery, Alabama. This was a very jovial memory. In fact I first saw you in church. You were still a student at Crozer Theological Seminary. You were preaching at the Ebenezer Baptist Church. Even then you moved me. You remember that you were preaching that Sunday on the subject of *The Christian and Faith*. Afterwards when everybody was shaking hands with you, I shook your hand, also. And I remembered your handshake. It was warm and strong. It was soft and tender. I liked you even then.

Strangely enough, Martin, the second time I saw you was at Spelman's Sisters Chapel. You were well dressed and you were giving your attention to a very pretty lady. You escorted her there in the prime of your life. I need not remind you that it wasn't Coretta, for this was long before she came into your life. You were young, then. You were a student and you were just playing the field. How different now, dear friend. You had come there to see others. Now others are coming to see you. I know you can hardly believe it as you look down on us and see those long silent lines of people waiting in the cool evening, the early mornings, the springtime noon, and even in the weary midnight hours, passing under the budding green trees past your silent bier. Well, Martin, if you ever had any moments of doubt about whether people loved you, now in the time of death, you no longer have to doubt. You kept the faith with them, and you brought us through the dark and difficult days and nights of our movement. Now they keep it with you throughout the night, around the clock. Today so much is happening in Sisters Chapel, the second place where I saw you.

And even more will happen in the Ebenezer Baptist Church and the Morehouse Quadrangle and all across the world in the days and the years to come.

It was after that third time, Martin, that I met you when we really became fast friends. You will remember this meeting. It was in my home, the parsonage of the First Baptist Church in Montgomery. We were never separated until the other day, as you know. I was right behind you there as I have always been. I don't know why they got you and left me. I can't help but talk about it. I ran to you as quickly as I could and I said, "It's me, Ralph." You rolled your eyes around in your head, and, even with your jaw shot out and your vocal cords gone, you still tried to talk to me. Those were some of the last thoughts. You who had been our spokesman couldn't speak any more. But don't worry, Martin, for they're playing your words all around the world and this will continue for a few days. But you may be assured that we won't ever let your words die. Like the words of our Master, Jesus Christ, they will live in our minds and our hearts and in the souls of black men and white men, brown men and yellow men as long as time shall last.

Let me go back to our third meeting. It was so different in that third meeting. You had arrived to become the new pastor of the Dexter Avenue Baptist Church in Montgomery. I left the parsonage and came over to greet you. You remember you had picked up that great preacher, Vernon Johns, by accident, and brought him back to preach at the First Baptist Church. He had preceded you at Dexter and everyone was happy to see you two together. The great old preacher, Vernon Johns, with his quick wit and pervading wisdom, served as a softening force to our personal thoughts and feelings. We became real friends and true companions that afternoon. Thank God we have remained so through the years. That was the beginning. Our families spent many nights and days together. We were at one house and then the other house, discussing the great issues and ideals, simply because there were no restaurants or motels or hotels that we could go in on a nondiscriminatory basis. Those were fighting times for thought and for planning. We got to know each other very well and we got to know the souls of each other in those moments. As I write, I realize that God made us good friends so that He could later make us a working team. As a man in the movement says, God knows what He is doing. That stays on my mind these days. But I wish so very much that it were the other way. Looking back, things seem clearer now than ever before. Dates come to me. How people looked is clearer, and the meaning of some events that have come to me with greater emphasis.

It was early in the morning on December 2 when I received a telephone call from E. D. Nixon, a Pullman porter, who told me how Mrs. (Rosa) Parks had been jailed, fingerprinted, and mugged like a common criminal. He said to me that something ought to be done because this woman only wanted to sit down on the bus. And she refused to give her seat to a white man. But, before doing anything, I checked with you, Martin. Upon your suggestion, I went into action, began organizing the ministers, calling meetings. And from that day until now, our lives have been in action together. I remember how we talked together about who should be the leader of the new movement. You had not been in Montgomery very long. You were just out of the seminary and some people wanted me because they knew me. And I was president of many organizations in Montgomery. And I could have forced myself to be the leader. But I never, as you know, Martin, wanted to be the leader. I only wanted to stand with you, as Caleb stood with Moses.

From the grand action of the Montgomery movement, our lives were filled with the action of doing God's will in village, hamlet, and city. We used to talk theology and then we learned to do theology. It was great. It has been great, Martin. Remember Gee's Bend down in Wilcox County, Alabama? Remember that day we stopped at a little filling station and bought jars of pickled pig's feet and some skins in Mississippi because they would not serve us at a restaurant. Remember, Martin, they wouldn't let us eat downtown? But our staff in that little crowded black man's country store had a fellowship, a *kononia,* together. We had a purpose and we had a universal sense of love that they did not have downtown. Some of my experiences with you will never be forgotten. You will recall how we went to Greensboro, North Carolina, when the sit-ins broke out, and how we sat in, in order that black men might stand up all over the world. You remember the Freedom Rides and how we were incarcerated and how we were forced to spend the night in the First Baptist Church in Montgomery with thousands of our followers while angry mobs stood on the outside. You remember the Albany movement and how Police Chief [Laurie] Pritchett and his forces tried to turn us around, and a divided Negro community became disgusted and despondent? You said to me, "Ralph, we must go on, anyhow." You remember Bull Connor brought out his vicious dogs, his fire engines, and his water hoses and tried to stop us in Birmingham. But it was you, Martin, who said to me, "Ralph, don't worry about the water, because we've started a fire in Birmingham that water can't put out."

You will recall Savannah, Georgia, and how we went there to the aid and rescue of Hosea Williams. Hosea is still with me and he has promised to be to me, Martin, what I tried to be to you. You remember the March on Washington, when more than 250,000 Americans and people from all over the world came to hear you talk about "I Have a Dream"? You remember Danville, Virginia, and how they put us in jail? You remember St. Augustine, Florida, and Hoss Manuci when he said that he did not have any evil vices whatever? He did not drink liquor, he did not chase after women, he did not smoke. His only hobby was beating and killing niggers. But we knew how to deal with Hoss and we changed him from a Hoss into a mule. You remember how we worked on Bull Connor and changed him from a bull into a steer? You remember how we marched across Edmund Pettis Bridge in Selma and the state troopers lined across upon the orders of Governor George Wallace and said that we could not pass. But we kept on marching. And when we got there, it opened up, like the Red Sea opened up for Moses and his army. You remember how Mayor [Richard] Daley tried to stop us in Chicago. But we would not let him turn us around.

My dear friend, Martin, now that you have gone, there are some special thoughts that come to me during this Lenten season. There are so many parallels. You were our leader and we were your disciples. Those who killed you did not know that you loved them and that you worked for them as well. For, so often, you said to us: "Love your enemies. Bless them that curse you and pray for them that despitefully use you." They did not know, Martin, that you were a good man, that you hated nobody. But you loved everybody. They did not know that you loved them with a love that would not let you go. They thought that they could kill our movement by killing you, Martin.

But Martin, I want you to know that black people loved you. Some people say that they were just burning and looting in the cities of the nation at this time. But you and I know that just folk, poor people, have had a hard time during these difficult days in which we have lived on this earth. And, in spite of the burning, I think they are saying: "He died for us." It may seem that they are denying our nonviolence for they are acting out their frustrations. And even a man of good, as you were, was killed in such an evil world as we live in today. And they are merely seeking to express their frustrations. They do not see a way out.

But I want you to know, Martin, that we're going to point to them a way. That was the frustration of Jerusalem during this same season nearly two thousand years ago. But we know, Martin, because we love people, that, after the venting of frustration, there will be the need for reconciliation. There you will be invisible but real. Black and white will need you to take them from their shame and reconcile them unto you and unto our Master, Jesus Christ. Your words of love are there and we will be there to follow your leadership. There has been a crucifixion in our nation, but here in this spring season as we see the blossoms and smell the fresh air we know that the resurrection will shortly appear. When the Master left the disciples, they felt gloom at first. Then they gathered themselves together in a fellowship. They must . . . Many grew up overnight. They were covered with their ancient words and with despair. We promise you, Martin, just as the disciples tarried in that upper room, that we're going to wait until the power comes from on high. We're going to wait until the Holy Ghost speaks and when the Holy Ghost comes and when the Holy Ghost speaks, we're going to speak as Peter spoke. And others will be converted and added to the movement and God's kingdom will come. We promise you, Martin, that we will tighten our fellowship and cover our word. Don't worry, my friend. We will pull our load. We will do our best. With the help of our friends and above all with the help of God. The Poor People's March will be our first attempt to properly do your will for the poor people of this nation. Just a few lines from your friend and your fellow freedom fighter.

Sincerely,
RALPH

Bibliography

Books

Ahmann, Mathew H., ed. *The New Negro* (Notre Dame, Ind.: Fides, 1961).

Bennett, Lerone, Jr. *What Manner of Man: A Biography of Martin Luther King, Jr.* (Chicago: Johnson Publishing Co., 1964; 1968).

Clark, Kenneth B., ed. *The Negro Protest* (Boston: Beacon, 1963).

Hamilton, Michael P., ed. *The Vietnam War: Christian Perspectives* (Grand Rapids: Eerdmans, 1967).

Harcourt, Melville, ed. *Thirteen for Christ* (New York: Sheed and Ward, 1963).

King, Martin Luther, Jr. *The Measure of a Man* (Philadelphia: United Church Press, 1958).

——— *Strength to Love* (New York: Harper and Row, 1963).

——— *Stride Toward Freedom: The Montgomery Story* (New York: Harper and Row, 1958).

——— *The Trumpet of Conscience* (New York: Harper and Row, 1968).

——— *Where Do We Go from Here: Chaos or Community?* (New York: Harper and Row, 1967).

——— *Why We Can't Wait* (New York: Harper and Row, 1964).

Lomax, Louis E. *To Kill a Blackman* (Los Angeles: Holloway House, 1968).

Miller, William Robert. *Martin Luther King, Jr.: His Life, Martyrdom and Meaning for the World* (New York: Weybright and Talley, 1968).

Reddick, Lawrence D. *Crusader Without Violence: A Biography of Martin Luther King, Jr.* (New York: Harper and Row, 1959).

Articles

Abernathy, Ralph D. "My Last Letter to Martin," *Ebony* (July 1968).

Baldwin, James. "The Dangerous Road before Martin Luther King," *Harper's* (February 1961).

Bennett, John C. "Martin Luther King, Jr., 1929–1968," *Christianity and Crisis* (April 15, 1968).

Bosmajian, Haig A. "Rhetoric of Martin Luther King's Letter from Birmingham Jail," *Midwest Quarterly,* Vol. VIII (January 1967).

Cleaver, Eldridge. "Requiem for Nonviolence," *Ramparts* (May 1968).

Cleghorn, Reese. "Martin Luther King, Jr., Apostle of Crisis," *Saturday Evening Post* (June 15, 1963).

Cook, Bruce. "King in Chicago," *Commonweal* (April 29, 1966).

Cowan, Wayne H. "Selma at First Hand," *Christianity and Crisis* (April 5, 1965).

229

Galphin, Bruce M. "Political Future of Dr. King," *The Nation* (September 23, 1961).

Garland, Phyl. "I've Been to the Mountaintop," *Ebony* (May 1968).

Halberstam, David. "The Second Coming of Martin Luther King," *Harper's* (August 1967).

Harding, Vincent. "The Religion of Black Power," *The Religious Situation, 1968,* ed. Donald R. Cutler (Boston: Beacon Press, 1968).

King, Coretta. "How Many Men Must Die?" *Life* (April 19, 1968).

King, Martin Luther, Jr. "Dreams of Brighter Tomorrows," *Ebony* (March 1965).

Lincoln, C. Eric. "Weep for the Living Dead," *The Christian Century* (May 1, 1968).

Maguire, John David. "Martin Luther King and Vietnam," *Christianity and Crisis* (May 1, 1967).

———— "Martin Luther King, Jr., 1929–1968," *Christianity and Crisis* (April 15, 1968).

Meier, August. "On the Role of Martin Luther King," *New Politics,* Vol. IV (Winter 1965).

Meyer, Frank S. "Principles and Heresies," *National Review* (April 20, 1965).

Miller, Perry. "The Mind and Faith of Martin Luther King," *The Reporter* (October 30, 1958).

Parks, Gordon. Untitled article, *Life* (April 19, 1968).

Pitcher, Alvin. "Martin Luther King Memorial," *Criterion,* Vol. VII, No. 2 (Winter 1968).

Rose, Stephen C. "Epitaph for an Era," *Christianity and Crisis* (June 10, 1963).

Rowan, Carl T. "Martin Luther King's Tragic Decision," *Reader's Digest* (September 1967).

Sharma, Mohan Lal. "Martin Luther King: Modern America's Greatest Theologian of Social Action," *Journal of Negro History,* Vol. LIII (July 1968).

Tallmer, Jerry. "Martin Luther King, Jr., His Life and Times," *New York Post,* April 8, 1968.

Unsigned Articles

"Dr. King and the Paris Press," *America* (November 13, 1965).

"Dr. King's Disservice to His Cause," *Life* (April 21, 1967).

"The Execution of Dr. King," *Ramparts* (May 1968).

"Georgia Imprisons Martin Luther King, Jr.," *Christian Century* (November 9, 1960).

"King Acts for Peace," *Christian Century* (September 29, 1965).

"King Speaks for Peace," *Christian Century* (April 19, 1967).

"Man of the Year," *Time* (January 3, 1964).

"Martin Luther King," *Reporter* (April 18, 1968).

"Memo to Martin Luther King," *National Review* (December 12, 1967).

Contributors

RALPH DAVID ABERNATHY, president of the Southern Christian Leadership Conference, was a very close friend of Martin Luther King, Jr. Mr. Abernathy was one of the organizers of the Montgomery Improvement Association and the Southern Christian Leadership Conference. He is a leader of the Poor People's Campaign and a Baptist minister.

JAMES BALDWIN, a native of Harlem, is a well-known writer and lecturer. Among his novels, essays, and plays are *Giovanni's Room* (1956), *Noboody Knows My Name* (1961), *The Fire Next Time* (1963), *Blues for Mr. Charlie* (1964), *Going to Meet the Man* (1965), and *Tell Me How Long the Train's Been Gone* (1968).

LERONE BENNETT, JR., is senior editor of *Ebony* magazine. He is author of *Before the Mayflower: A History of Black America* (1962; 1969), *What Manner of Man: A Biography of Martin Luther King, Jr.* (1964; 1968), *The Negro Mood and Other Essays* (1964), *Confrontation: Black and White* (1965), and *Black Power U.S.A.: The Human Side of Reconstruction, 1867–1877* (1967).

HAIG A. BOSMAJIAN, Associate Professor of Speech at the University of Washington, is a contributor to many journals. He is the author of *Readings in Speech* (1965), *Rhetoric of the Speaker: Speeches and Criticism* (1967), and editor of *Readings in Parliamentary Procedure* (1968).

REESE CLEGHORN, writer-in-residence with the Southern Regional Council in Atlanta, is co-author (with Pat Watters) of *Climbing Jacob's Ladder* (Harcourt, Brace & World, 1967), a book on the civil rights movement and the South.

DAVID HALBERSTAM is a contributing editor at *Harper's* magazine. He was the recipient of the Pulitzer Prize for international reporting in 1964 and served as *The New York Times* correspondent in Vietnam and Warsaw, Poland. He is author of *The Noblest Roman* (1961), *The Making of a Quagmire* (1965), and *The Unfinished Odyssey of Robert Kennedy* (1969).

VINCENT HARDING, director of the Library Project of the Martin Luther King Memorial Center, is chairman of the History Department at Spelman College. Dr. Harding is editor-at-large for *The*

Christian Century and has written articles for many journals. He is author of *Must Walls Divide?* (1965).

LOUIS E. LOMAX is visiting professor of the Humanities and Social Sciences at Hofstra University. Formerly a reporter and newscaster, Mr. Lomax is author of *The Reluctant African* (1962), *The Negro Revolt* (1962), *When the Word Is Given: A Report on Elijah Muhammad, Malcolm X, and the Black Muslim World* (1963), and *Thailand: The War That Is, the War That Will Be* (1967).

AUGUST MEIER is Professor of History at Kent State University. Dr. Meier is author of *Negro Thought in America 1880–1915* (1963); co-author (with Elliott M. Rudwick) of *From Plantation to Ghetto: An Interpretive History of American Negroes* (1966; 1970) and (with Milton Meltzer) of *Time of Trial, Time of Hope: The Negro in America 1919–1941* (1966); and co-editor of *Negro Protest Thought in the Twentieth Century* (1966) and *The Making of Black America* (2 vols.; 1968; 1969).

WILLIAM ROBERT MILLER is the author of *Martin Luther King, Jr.: His Life, Martyrdom and Meaning for the World* (1968). As managing editor of *Fellowship,* he published Martin Luther King's first article, "Walk for Freedom." Mr. Miller also wrote "How to Practice Nonviolence," a leaflet widely distributed in the South before and during the era of the sit-ins. Currently, he is on the editorial board of *Africa Today.*

LAWRENCE D. REDDICK, professor at Coppin State Teachers College, Baltimore, was a close friend of Martin Luther King's and accompanied the Kings on their trip to India. His published work includes *Crusader Without Violence* (1959) and "The Negro as Southerner and American" in C. G. Sellers, ed., *The Southerner as American* (1961).

CARL T. ROWAN, a columnist for the Chicago Daily News Publishers Newspaper Syndicate, received the 1954 Sigma Delta Chi award for the best general reporting on segregation cases pending before the U. S. Supreme Court, and the 1964 National Brotherhood Award of the National Conference of Christians and Jews. He is author of *South of Freedom* (1952), *The Pitiful and the Proud* (1956), *Go South to Sorrow* (1957), and *Wait Till Next Year: The Life Story of Jackie Robinson* (with Jackie Robinson) (1960). He is former U. S. Ambassador to Norway and the former Director of the U.S. Office of Information.

JERRY TALLMER is a reporter and drama critic for the *New York Post,* and has contributed many articles to various publications. He served on the staff of the *Nation* and was associate editor, drama critic, and one of the founders of the *Village Voice.*

C. ERIC LINCOLN was born in Athens, Alabama, in 1924. He graduated from LeMoyne College in Memphis in 1947 and holds an M.A. from Fisk University, a B.D. from the University of Chicago, and a Ph.D. from Boston University. He is currently Professor of Sociology and Religion at Union Theological Seminary, Adjunct Professor of Religion at Columbia University, and Adjunct Professor of Sociology at Vassar College. He is founding president of the *Black* Academy of Arts and Letters and the author of *The Black Muslims in America, The Negro Pilgrimage in America,* and other books on black Americans.

✪

AÏDA DIPACE DONALD is a graduate of Barnard and received an M.A. from Columbia and a Ph.D. from the University of Rochester. A former member of the History Department at Columbia, Mrs. Donald has been a Fulbright Fellow at Oxford and an A.A.U.W. Fellow. She has published *John F. Kennedy and the New Frontier* and *Diary of Charles Francis Adams.*